NO REGARD FOR MONEY

NO REGARD FOR MONEY

The Memoirs of a Racing Man

CHARLES BENSON

Quartet Books
London   New York

First published in Great Britain by Quartet Books Limited 1988
A member of the Namara Group
27/29 Goodge Street
London W1P 1FD

Copyright © by Charles Benson 1988

British Library Cataloguing in Publication Data

Benson, Charles
    No regard for money: the memoirs of a
    racing man.
    1. Racehorses. Racing. Reporting. Benson, Charles
    I. Title
    070.4'497984'00924

    ISBN 0 7043 2662 0

Typeset by Reprotype Limited, Peterborough, Cambs
Printed and bound in Great Britain by
Camelot Press Plc, Southampton

To my wife Carolyn who never believed I would write this book

Acknowledgements

I wish to record my thanks to Conan Nicholas whose editorial skills helped to improve my text, to Alexandra Miller for the long hours she spent typing it, and to Anita Petersham for her invaluable help in searching for and providing the pictures of Lady Camilla Bingham and herself and that of Dominick Elwes painting the Earl of Suffolk. I am also grateful to Greville Howard and Melissa Wyndham for letting me use pictures from their private albums.

Contents

Early Years

MOST small boys pass through a phase when they want to be an engine-driver or a pilot, or go in for some such macho profession. Later the emphasis falls on something more skilful, a surgeon perhaps. I may have passed through these phases but, from the age of about 15, I wanted to be a racing correspondent. Not any racing correspondent but the 'Scout' of the *Daily Express,* the title then held by my hero Clive Graham.

It is a matter of record, now, that I did indeed join the *Daily Express* against considerable odds and ended up, on the regrettable death of Clive in August 1974, as the 'Scout', a position I held for about twelve years until my resignation in April 1986.

There was nothing in my pedigree, background or education to suggest that I was particularly suited to a career as a writer about horse-racing. My parents were, admittedly, both quite interested in racing and had been known to enjoy a bet, though my father did not have a lot of time or money to indulge in any aspect of the sport particularly in the later stages of his life.

My father, a barrister, married my mother in 1934. She was a widow, her first husband, Edwin Cawston, having died of TB. She already had two sons, Dick and Derrick, by her late husband. They were about twelve and ten years old when I was born on 23 October 1935. I was born just a few yards from where I live now in Trevor Square, just a stone's throw from Harrods on one side and Hyde Park on the other, and thus in the very centre of residential London.

Later my mother gave birth to a fourth and final son, my brother Jonathan, born on 14 February 1939.

My mother was born a Hawkins, a descendant of the famous seaman

1

of that name, whose portrait decorated the wall of her wealthy father's drawing-room. Her father, known as Chas, was a wiry little man, teased for being tight with his money, but who always seemed quite generous to my brother and me. He lived into his nineties and nothing gave him greater pleasure than to beat me at billiards, snooker or golf. He owned a major share in Addington golf club, living near by. I remember playing against him there when he was in his eighties and could not hit the ball very far. He was a cunning old devil, though, and had used his influence to have special patches cleared in the rough, often away from the obvious line to the hole, which he could reach in comfort and thus negotiate his own unique passage to the green.

Money has played as important a part in my life as it probably has in the next man's, but I have never had much regard for it, either my own or anyone else's. This is probably because I started with none, my family was always struggling, and I will probably end with none. Yet the paradox is that I have always been lucky enough to live in comfort, eat and drink well, and generally want for nothing except ludicrously expensive and basically needless possessions, whether they by toys when young or cars and boats and hi-fis when older.

The whole thing has not been done by mirrors but it is still not easy to explain.

My half-brothers became very successful in their chosen professions, Dick pioneering documentary film-making techniques, now widely emulated, when he worked for the BBC and Derrick becoming one of the youngest ever directors of J Walter Thompson, the world-wide advertising agency. Dick became head of BBC documentaries and also made all the royal films for the BBC, including the Queen's annual Christmas day broadcast until he died in 1986.

My full brother Jonathan has enjoyed a successful career as a film-maker and writer, his most notable credit being the Oscar-winning *Chariots of Fire*, on which he was assistant director and had a piece of the action.

My father was a relic of a bygone age, a man so honest and decent that he was almost too good to be true. He may well have had more flaws when he was younger and my brother Jonathan, three-and-a-half years younger than me and a deeper thinker, never quite held the same idealistic view of our father that I did.

Stephen Benson, born in Shropshire in 1896, was a barrister and ended up, when he died in November 1961, as recorder of Abingdon and deputy recorder of Oxford. This meant that he was a judge at

Abingdon assizes and deputy judge at Oxford, and, in his former capacity, senior Recorder of England. But although this all sounds very grand – one minute he was sending down criminals for five years, the next defending a man accused of stealing a million pounds and gaining an acquittal – there was no money in it. He received no expenses to speak of and would not have known what an expenses-paid lunch was. He would trot off each day from our house in Cliveden Place to the underground in Sloane Square, his little red sack containing his briefs over his shoulder, and catch the train to Temple station, close to his chambers in Middle Temple. All the great advocates, and the lesser ones too, had their chambers in the Temple, just across the Strand from the Law Courts and down the road from the great criminal courts at the Old Bailey.

Ironically, too, it was within walking distance of my own office in the *Daily Express* in Fleet Street. So in the last five years of his life, while I, a very junior racing writer on the *Daily Express* would travel to the track on a first-class rail voucher supplied by the firm, my father would be sitting in a third-class compartment with his red sack in the luggage rack on his way to sit in judgment and perhaps alter the lives of scores of alleged criminals, or else defend or prosecute other alleged offenders in courts mostly to the west of London. But I anticipate.

More than half of his work was done at his chambers in London and the Law Courts but the rest took place on the Oxford circuit and, of course, at Abingdon and Oxford.

He was something of a legend among his colleagues and received a long and touching obituary in *The Times* when he died. Even to this day, more than twenty-six years after his death, I run into distinguished legal men, most of them highly ranked QCs and judges who say that they knew him and admired or loved him. Most of them have some anecdote about him. One of my favourites, appropriate to my chosen profession, was when some small-time bookmaker came up in front of him at Abingdon.

After the jury had pronounced their verdict of guilty, my father looked down at the man in the dock. 'I see you are a racing man. I shall be lenient with you and sentence you to six months. If you behave yourself you will observe that, with your two months' remission, you will be free for the start of the flat-racing season.'

I used to love going down to the Law Courts and listening to my father in action. There was, and still is, an indefinable but almost tangible and unique atmosphere both in the courts and in his chambers

3

across the road. Maybe Dickensian in flavour, yet, at the risk of sounding xenophobic, I still believe that British justice is the best in the world. I certainly know few of my many American friends who would disagree with this. I would gladly have chosen the law for my profession but for twenty years I had observed my father's financial struggles, and at that stage of my life I favoured a more immediately rewarding, less arduous, and possibly more entertaining profession – hence racing journalism.

My father's inherited talents, which to some extent he passed on to me, were an acute musical ear, the ability to play games – an eye for a ball if you like – and a sense of humour. You can certainly make a conventional success of life, earn plenty of money, and command respect without any of these three attributes but they help, particularly if money is in short supply. But while my father continually had to struggle for money to feed, house, and educate my brother and me, we ourselves never felt constrained by this. We received the benefit of the best possible education and, although I do not make a habit of referring back to my time at Eton, the greatest and most famous school in the world, neither do I deny the benefit of that education, which has helped me on numerous occasions all over the world.

My extended five years at Eton gave my father great pleasure despite the fact that it created a major financial burden for him. His pleasure was compounded by the fact that all his forebears, as far back as, and possibly before, 1750 had been there, but he himself had lasted only half a term, or 'half' as a term is called at Eton, before he was stricken with rheumatic fever from which he nearly died and which restricted him to his bed for six months. When he recovered, medical opinion decreed that Eton, being right on the river Thames adjoining Windsor and Windsor Castle, was too damp for him and he was accordingly switched to Charterhouse, a perfectly good and well-known public school but healthily positioned up in the hills outside Godalming in Surrey.

Most Old Carthusians are proud of their time at Charterhouse but not my father, desperately disappointed at missing out on Eton and having to listen to his brothers' stories of glory. He referred to his adopted college as 'the worst school in England' for the rest of his life.

He had many stories of his own disobedience and taste for practical jokes both at school and in the army during the First World War. The best school anecdote concerned a particularly weak-looking young master, tall and bespectacled, whom he held in total contempt. He and his neighbouring friend had been behaving particularly badly in class and were summoned by the young master to explain themselves. 'I will give you a choice of punishment. You can either do 500 lines or take a beating,' decreed the master. Grinning at each other, they readily opted for the beating, eyeing the master's limp and lanky frame. It was the friend's turn first. My father waited confidently outside the door until he heard the first thwack of the cane followed simultaneously by a high-pitched shout. The shouts turned to screams as the cane drove home six times and his friend came out in floods of tears, half doubled in pain. Much chastened, my father went in for his turn and quickly said 'I've changed my mind, Sir. I'll take the lines.' 'Too late,' came the curt reply and my father still remembered the pain of the punishment to his dying day.

The master's name was Mallory and some years later, he may well have been the first man to climb Mount Everest. He was last seen on the final assault when he disappeared from view. His body was never found but professional opinion in mountaineering circles has often favoured the theory that he made it before dying. Moral – never judge a man or woman by his or her appearance. I have occasionally benefited from this mistake by those who have eyed my overweight figure before issuing a tennis challenge.

The effects of the rheumatic fever were believed to have mangled my father's heart, a fact that was finally confirmed at the autopsy after his death. In the event, therefore, he did well to reach the age of sixty-five and one month before dropping dead of a heart attack in mid-joke in the offices of the Chelsea Building Society in which he was paying off the last instalment of his mortgage on the house in Cliveden Place. It was an appropriate way to go and, incredibly, the autopsy showed that, while he undoubtedly died of a heart attack, it was a coronary completely unrelated to the mangled, but apparently effective state of his heart.

In view of his medical history, it seems extraordinary that the authorities allowed him to join up and fight in the First World War, but they did. He reached the rank of captain in the Kent Regiment, the Buffs, being quite severely wounded in the back of his head by part of a cannon-shell in the Middle East.

His favourite practical joke in Palestine involved his observation that senior officers retired to the primitive lavatories after breakfast each morning. The facilities involved holes in the ground over which the officers dangled their bottoms while modesty was preserved by a strip of canvas around this open-air latrine screening the upper parts of the body, including the head and therefore the rank of the practitioner. It was therefore his habit from time to time to slip up behind the row of heaving, senior bottoms and go down the line administering a hefty whack with his cane on each one. Despite the angry shouts and cries of the victims he was never caught because he quickly mingled into the crowds of soldiers near by and the high-ranking officers were much too embarrassed to explain the reasons for their discomfort.

Later in life, when I was around, his honesty and decency were a byword in the family, but my brother and two older half-brothers by my mother's first husband who had died of tuberculosis, and even my mother, who was honest and decent herself, all felt that he rather overdid it on occasions. When we walked down the street, particularly in Frinton, where we had a modest holiday home, we would greet every one in sight, particularly working men, road-sweepers, dustmen, and the like, with the words 'Good morning, guv', or 'Good afternoon, guv', according to the time of day. And for two pins he would then engage them in conversation if given encouragement. This was, of course, basically an attractive characteristic but when one is young one is terribly embarrassed about that sort of thing and, to be frank, most working men don't really want to talk to a middle-aged toff, usually wearing a cap at a jaunty angle and accompanied by two scowling small boys.

During the war the family took unfair advantage of this decent and honourable soul though luckily he never knew about it until many years later. The family was evacuated from London in 1940 for the duration of the war to a house overlooking the sea at Bude in North Cornwall, well away from the attention of the Germans. Behind our house were endless stretches of undulating downland alongside the Cornish cliffs and it was there that the army, both British and American, had shooting- and bombing-ranges galore. I suppose there must have been a reasonably effective safety screening when shooting or bombing areas were actually in use, but we would roam freely around the area, avidly collecting spent cartridge-cases, shells, and bullet-heads. Sometimes we were lucky enough to find a live bullet or shell, a particular prize. But the day that my father was put to the sword came in 1944 when he was making one of his rare visits. He was still based in or around London throughout the war, continuing his practice for crime did not cease during the hostilities, and Bude, more than 200 miles from London, was a long way to travel in those days.

Somewhere off the coast of Cornwall an American supply ship and a tanker either collided or were sunk by enemy action. The first we knew

6

of this was when somebody noticed first one, then two, then three and eventually scores of packing-cases bobbing and pitching in the surf towards the sand. We all rushed down to the beach and so, more or less simultaneously, did the entire population of Bude and, as each packing-case drifted or was dragged ashore, it was torn open by a forest of hands and everyone grabbed what they could. It was just like a film-set and incredible scenes of greed and sometimes foolhardy courage ensued.

Being of slightly above average intelligence, my family quickly worked out the that the smart thing to do was to move ourselves down the coast to the remote areas. A certain amount of stealth was needed since the average local tended to follow like sheep those they believed to have officer qualities even if such qualities were shown by eight- and five-year-olds.

Basically, up to that moment the trophies had consisted of incredibly exciting and, to us, unobtainable items like boxes of Hershey chocolate bars, even more delicious chocolate-coated nut bars called Pecan Petes, cans of peanuts, and all brands of American cigarettes including Philip Morris, Camels and, my mother's own favourite, Chesterfields. We were constantly filling our hands with trophies and cradling huge loads in our arms back to the house before we moved on to the more remote beaches.

It was there that Derrick, the younger of my two half-brothers swam far out through the surf to grab the bobbing packing-cases well before they reached the shore and the grasp of others. He very nearly drowned himself but, by chance, he did gain the greatest prize of all. It was a cask of Watermans' fountain-pens, prized loot by any standards in those days. Once we had opened even our own cases, it still became a free-for-all, but we had first run on the fountain-pens and this time even my mother went berserk, grabbing fistful after fistful, despite the shouts of complaint from the outsiders. 'They're for my boys, my soldiers. Try thinking of others for a change,' she shouted angrily as the locals tries to barge past her. The gentlest and kindest of women, she was formidable that day and between us we salvaged more than a hundred pens. She was of course telling the truth. She was a member of the Church Army, a woman's voluntary body that would fill a van with whatever goods were available plus urns of tea, and tour the outlying army bases and outposts in the area. Her boys, as she called them, were always asking for things, most unobtainable, and one of them was fountain-pens. In those days ball-points were unheard of in England. So the following week my mother was the hero of the troops as she handed out free

7

fountain-pens to all while stocks lasted. Everything from the Church Army was free, or very cheap, of course.

By this time the American military authorities and the British Customs were beginning to take a more intrusive interest in proceedings and the Customs men, particularly, were taking a keen interest in cigarette collectors. Before a general announcement was broadcast that all goods collected must be declared, my father, Mr Honesty himself, had already worked out that this must be the case and he announced to the fury of the rest of the family that he would personally go out and find a Customs official to inspect our collection. This was where the family took advantage of his absence. We were damned if we should have risked in one case life and in all cases limbs, since we were covered in scratches and bruises, for the benefit of HM Customs. So, at the instigation of my half-brothers, we rushed around the house while my father was away, hiding carton after carton of cigarettes, particularly in the drawers in our bedrooms underneath our clothes. Goodness knows how many Chesterfields nestled under my mother's knickers in her room for even she had swallowed her moral standards at my father's scrupulous honesty.

We still paraded around substantial piles of loot, sensibly mixed in the vast hallway of the house and awaited the arrival of the enemy. Needless to say, my father and the Customs man were on the best of terms by the time they came through the door and there was a lot of 'guvs' to be heard and mutterings from my father of 'in my position you can't be too careful', and such. He was telling the complete truth of course so, not surprisingly, the Customs Officer was completely duped. After examining the loot he announced, 'since you have all been so honest, it is a pleasure to deal with Mr Benson and his family. I therefore propose to split all these items with you.' We held our breath, all had a quick drink with him, and helped him fill sacks with his 50 per cent. We heaved a collective sigh of relief when he left but nobody said a word to my father, knowing full well that he would have grassed on us, his own family, and called back the Customs.

Before you make a final judgement on our morality, and particularly my mother's, I should add that she gathered up a huge amount of loot and distributed it among the British troops, her boys. Much of this she did despite our protests as we saw our zealously acquired chocolate, nuts and cigarettes disappearing. Jonathan and I could hardly bear to watch as she handed out our goodies, for we often accompanied her on her rounds, crouched on the back of the van beneath the dripping tea urn. I think we both occasionally wiped away a tear stain as well as a tea stain from our cheek. We were too young to appreciate the needs of the soldiers or their gratitude.

However, I think my mother showed a measure of pragmatism by dishing out Camel and Philip Morris cigarettes and we were still finishing the carefully rationed chocolates and nuts when we finally left Bude at the end of the war in Europe.

On 23 April 1945, when I was exactly nine and a half (I kept track of such things in those days), I left the bosom of my family for the first time for any duration to go to prep school in Sussex. Sending off young boys and girls to boarding-school is a pretty barbaric British custom, but, for the most part, we soon get used to it.

I found myself at Windlesham House, nestled beneath the Downs at Washington and Findon, not far inland from Worthing and Brighton.

The talk of my first term had been of the discovery of a vast arms cache by a slightly older boy, Gerry Albertini, heir to the Reynolds railroad fortune from America until some unpleasant family litigation, plus his own spending and gambling habits, removed most of it.

Gerry had been probing the adjoining woods when he came across the hidden treasure – mortar bombs, hand-grenades, rifle-bullets, and other live shells bigger and probably more dangerous. Instead of reporting his find, he let a few friends into the secret and piled a selection of the most explosive items in his tuck-box. Thus, the school train to Victoria could have been blown up at any minute by Albertini's tuck-box, a concept which scared the living daylights out of the school and military authorities when the story was uncovered.

Gerry's mother and stepfather lived at White Lodge in Richmond Park in those days. His stepfather, Lt-Col James Reynolds Veitch, was Commandant POW camps, Ascot area, on the American military staff and it was he who discovered Gerry's hoard. He was horrified and contacted both the authorities and the school. His state of mind was further disturbed by the recognition that these were American arms, left behind by US troops who had, until a short time before, occupied the school.

In the end, it was decided to hush the whole thing up and for Gerry to receive the most comprehensive beating ever from the headmaster – or principal as he called himself – the normally mild-mannered Christopher Scott-Malden.

Gerry has remained a friend and the only comparable beating he ever

9

received in later life was a financial one when he was sold a racehorse, Solarium, by the wily Earl of Carnarvon. The price was £20,000, a great deal in the 1950s, and all the more when Solarium developed various physical problems and was virtually useless thereafter. Ironically, Gerry was offered the choice of another two-year-old at the same time by his trainer Sam Armstrong – a French horse, Phil Drake, who won the Derby the following year.

Perhaps in gratitude for the discreet manner in which the arms scandal was despatched, Gerry's mother and stepfather would entertain us at White Lodge to tea after our annual visit to one of the England rugby football internationals at nearby Twickenham. With their money and American connections the Veitches were able to lay on an annual feast far beyond anything else obtainable in those days and the extent of their largesse can be gauged from the fact that we consisted of the entire first rugger fifteen, plus assorted Maldens and masters, a party of about twenty.

I had been at the school for only just over a fortnight when on 8 May 1945 the Germans surrendered, and we were given a day's holiday in celebration. However, I celebrated in painful fashion, crushing my right little finger-nail in a makeshift seesaw and, to this day, that finger-nail is larger than its counterpart on my left hand.

I was a total sports freak by then but extremely naïve in other respects. By the time I finished my stint and had passed my Common Entrance exam into Eton in July 1948, I had become captain of cricket and soccer and vice-captain of rugger. A big fish in a very small pool! My vice-captain in cricket and soccer and captain in rugger was a boy called Chris Ridsdell-Smith. We were great friends and he went on to further sporting distinctions in his public school career, but once he nearly killed me. I was pushing and he was pulling by the spring handle a fairly heavy roller up and down the cricket-pitch. As a joke, he let go of the handle, the junction of which hit me on the top of the head, making a hole from which spurted blood and knocking me over. I was probably concussed and was taken to the sanatorium. I still have a small lump there to this day. This was probably the first of a series of concussions that I sustained in my school-days which led to an epileptic condition from which I suffered for a while in the 1960s.

As an example of the insensitive lack of concern for the future health of small schoolboys in those days, I recall my experience when playing an away rugger match at a rival school in the Brighton area. I played full back and I recall hurling myself head first at the feet of the attacking hoard of opposing players near our goal-line and being kicked echoingly on the head. I was obviously knocked out and concussed since my next recollection was of coming to lying by our goal-posts, and seeing play going on down the other end of the field. No one had taken a blind bit of notice of me and I discovered that the other side had actually scored a try during my unconsciousness, converted it, and play had recommenced.

This negligence was bad enough but worse was to follow. In the bus returning home, I was suffering from blurred vision and vomited some eight times. Far from receiving any sympathy or attention, I was treated as a complete pain in the neck by the master or masters in charge and naturally by the other boys, who wouldn't have known any better.

I was also a confirmed sleep-walker and again this inadvertent habit was treated with severity. Anyone who suffers or who has suffered from this often frightening habit will know that one does strange, inexplicable things which bear no relation to one's conscious inclinations. At prep school, while sharing a room in a sanatorium with another boy, I poured a glass of milk over his head while fast asleep, and on another occasion I walked from my dormitory into the bathroom and basin area where the undermatron was taking her bath. She screamed and yelled at me and I woke up in fright and disarray. Both times I was treated like a criminal.

I put the way I was treated down to ignorance rather than callousness, from the need to instil manliness which was the prevailing attitude in most schools in those days. Basically the authorities were kind and administered a benign regime.

Like most of my schoolmates there, I was very naïve and ignorant of the facts of life. My parents had an old-fashioned attitude towards sex, never even mentioning it. So I was mystified at being treated like a master criminal when I was caught one night in the dormitory performing some childish and oafish ballet dance with another boy, both of us stark naked. There was no contact and there is nothing very evil in the minds of ten- or eleven-year-old boys when performing such pranks.

So it was in a state of keen anticipation that I went to the headmaster's study, in company with a number of other boys who were departing for their public schools, to receive our leaving lecture. Secrecy had always prevailed about the contents of this talk among earlier generations of leavers, all of whom were sworn to silence. I, too, observed the same tight-lipped attitude towards my friends once I had been let in on the secret, though I had another reason, apart from the pledge of silence, for having little to say about the lecture: the fact was

11

that I didn't really understand it! We all leaned forward with that earnest expression on our faces to show keenness and interest, every now and again interjecting, 'Yes, of course', or 'I thought as much'. The trouble was that the principal was a devout Christian and probably didn't know a grand amount about the joys of sex himself. His ability to reproduce was not in doubt since he had a large and quite good-looking son and daughter by his equally large but not so attractive and extremely austere wife. So sex in the life of this kindly man had probably been as strictly rationed as had chocolate and ice-cream to us war-time kids.

The religious flavour set the tone for the talk and he referred to our reproductive organs by pointing down towards his groin and describing them as 'God's own part'. This was indeed a revelation to us since we had never discovered any hint of dick worship in our prayer book! However, we got the drift of the general activities of 'God's own part' and its destructive power. Later in life, with more information beneath my belt both literally and metaphorically I was to discover all too often the pleasure, and occasionally the problems, that God and his wretched part would cause me.

Eton

AT the age of twelve years and ten months, I ventured forth into the heady world of Eton, a world of privilege and responsibility way above anything I had hitherto experienced.

By coincidence, the housemaster with whom I had been registered since birth, an Eton necessity, had employed for his own son the nanny who had subsequently and until fairly recently looked after my brother and myself. The nanny, Hilda King, had then gone on for the rest of her life to the Soames family, guiding the destinies for five of Sir Winston Churchill's grandchildren before becoming doyen of the nanny corps.

As a result of this connection, my parents had kept in touch with the housemaster, Brian Whitfield, and his massive wife, Edna. So the first thing my parents and I did on leaving prep school was to go down to Eton and take lunch with the Whitfields. There was one other boy there, John Leon, with his mother and stepfather, Kay Hammond and John Clements, both well known on stage and screen.

John, who later inherited a baronetcy from his father, was subsequently in the same regiment as me during National Service. He changed his name to John Standing for professional purposes and became a successful actor himself, being particularly adept in light comedy following the Noël Coward tradition. We are still good friends and he lives in Los Angeles now.

Before lunch I had gone to Denman and Goddard, one of the approved tailors in Eton High Street, to be measured for my tail-coat and striped trousers, the unique school uniform. If you were below a certain height, 5 ft. 2 in., you were meant to start off in a considerably less dignified school uniform, a short black jacket, known as a 'bum freezer', and a large, stiff white collar. For a variety of reasons, this

13

uniform was universally disliked. It marked you down as a squirt, a midget to be mocked and teased. The bottom was accentuated below the jacket, making it a natural target for missiles and weapons. And flicking ink at the back of the collar was a traditional pastime in class for those in tails and therefore not subject to reprisal. Once you were condemned to wear a jacket, you were not allowed to graduate to tails until reaching 5 ft. 4 in., which could take as much as two years or more. There were even a few unfortunate boys who failed to reach even this modest height while achieving academic seniority and they occasionally received special dispensation to avoid continuous derision.

My height on the day of measurement was 5 ft. 1½ in., half an inch below the required height. But luckily I was being attended by a wise and compassionate tailor and he said 'Close enough, I think don't you?' to me and my parents and so I was fitted up for the coveted tails.

In view of my family's permanent lack of funds, we purchased one second-hand set of tails, in regular supply, and ordered only one new set. War-time restrictions had meant that the mandatory wearing of a black silk top hat had now become voluntary and we only bought one of these for the Fourth of June, the school's annual speech day celebrating the birthday of King George III, St Andrew's day, and one or two other big occasions.

The important thing to remember with the topper was to hide it since the most popular pastime among junior boys and bullies was to discover top hats and sit on them, a destructive habit which effectively ruined them for life. Many a boy could be seen in the playing-fields or on the High Street wearing on his head something resembling a black concertina.

When I arrived at Eton for the first time that September, I was still a clear month short of my thirteenth birthday. I had taken Middle Fourth in my Common Entrance exam, right in the middle of the qualifiers and an ideal rating for a lazy boy of below average age. I was thus able to cruise through my extended five years' education there with the minimum of effort since I was neither under the pressure accorded to the brighter boys nor the similar pressure upon more stupid boys above average age. It was necessary to pass one's exams, known as 'trials', at the end of each 'half' and move up a division.

The twenty-eight or so houses were known by the initials of the housemaster, or 'tutor' as he was known. My tutor's initials were BGW and we were one of the élite houses, particularly strong on the sports field, which was as intended by BGW himself. Although he was a great

14

classical scholar, he was also a sports fanatic, particularly as far as cricket was concerned, and he had deliberately built up the sporting strength of his house.

When I arrived, he only had two years to go since housemasters have to relinquish their post after fifteen years. This was a pity for me since we had a good relationship. He had a somewhat austere demeanour and a thin, squeaky voice, a result of being gassed in the First World War. But he had a tremendous sense of humour and we all worshipped him. He made a tour of all the boys' rooms – we had one each, no dormitories – every evening and one of his favourite opening gambits to juniors was, after an exaggerated sniff, 'nasty smell of lower boy breath in here'.

I was in the first Lower Boy cricket game my first summer, 1949, and played for the under-fourteen-and-a-half first eleven. So the next summer, still at the age of fourteen, I just managed to scrape into my house first eleven and we were able to give BGW the send-off he deserved by winning the final against the house of his great rival, Nigel Wykes. This was quite an achievement in its small way since the Wykes eleven contained no less than five members of the school first eleven, while we had three, a very good percentage bearing in mind that there were 28 houses in the school

I batted eleventh and the last in our first innings and was proud to help put on a valuable 25 runs for the last wicket with our finest player, Colin Ingleby-Mackenzie, who became a close, life-long friend and godfather to my elder son. I should add in the interests of historical accuracy that, of those 25 runs I scored 1. But, in cricket parlance, I had kept my end up. Colin scored about 170 runs and I did not have to bat again in the second innings. For once, I can safely say that, for all schoolboy selfishness and vainglory, the whole team was happier for Whitfield on virtually his final day than for ourselves. It was a 'Goodbye Mr Chips' situation.

Our athletic prowess was surprising in view of the atrocious food. We lunched and dined in our own houses and were therefore in the hands of the tutor. Much as we all loved B. G. Whitfield, it did seem highly probable that he was saving a little retirement money out of his catering allocation. With rationing still in force, as well, this was easily the worst feature of my schooldays. Meat was particularly scarce on our menus and sometime in the summer of 1950, my patience snapped. We had been given fish for something like six or seven consecutive meals and nauseating stuff it was too, nothing like sole or shellfish.

I suppose that I was developing some slight leadership over my

15

contemporaries and was sitting, facing another boy, at the top of the second long table. There was no one at either end. I got hold of every one at the table, which went down to pretty junior boys, though the youngest of all were deployed at side-tables, and said, 'If we get fish again tonight, we will walk out. I and the boy opposite me will stand up first and leave the room and every one else should follow in pairs at ten-second intervals.' Every one agreed.

We sat down and in came the inevitable fish – cold, white-and-grey smelly fish salad. I waited until everyone had been served, then nodded to the boy opposite and we stood up and left the room. I was not sure that everyone would follow but they did, though some of the younger boys hesitated since the heat was much more on them that it was on me. When the other boy and I left hardly anyone at the top table noticed. It was only when the third and fourth couple walked out that some sort of uproar began and the tenth couple or so were under the eyes and scrutiny of the senior boys and the tutor, who were beginning to shout. Of course there was an inquiry though, theoretically, we hadn't broken any major rule except the custom to wait until the tutor left.

I had to admit to being the ringleader on this occasion and was suspended from the debating society, a semi-privileged body with no authority. I was also made to apologize to the Dame and assure her that the protest had nothing to do with her or the food! I was reinstated to the debating society a few weeks later but the food did not improve.

The house was taken over by David Graham-Campbell, initials DJG-C, and such was the sporting excellence of the house built by Whitfield that we immediately won the house football cup in DJG-C's very first half – the unique Eton field game which rated higher than soccer or rugger in those day – and then, at the end of his first year, won the cricket again, this time by a staggering innings and 304 runs in the final, an amazing margin.

This time, my fifteen-year-old ego was well boosted when I went in to join our most senior boy, Jerry Carr, a member of the first eleven who looked and may well have been about 25 years old. We put on 70 runs of which I scored a rapid 46, including thumping the opposition's feared fast bowler, Chucker Howard, for three boundaries in one over. One remembers these things. Colin, incidentally, scored 164 runs in this final and it was small wonder that he went on to be captain of Hampshire, leading them to the Championship for the first ever time in 1961. He finished No.3 sportsman of the year in a poll including all the footballers, jockeys, athletes, tennis-players, and swimmers as well

16

as cricketers, and was widely recommended to captain England, though he never quite made that.

That summer, I was forced to make what seemed then an agonizing decision between my future major summer sport at Eton, cricket, or tennis. Cricket then was the game and tennis very much a less regarded sport. We played cricket either on a house, junior, or senior league basis, or in school groups according to age and ability with such exotic names as Upper Sixpenny, Upper Club, and the like, and, of course, school matches against other sides at different ages and levels of ability.

However, although I was in the top school game of my age-group Upper Sixpenny, I formed the view that I would probably just fail to make the coveted first eleven and would end up in the XXII, the school second eleven. Meanwhile I had been spotted by the tennis master playing a friendly game and he invited me up for a trial in front of the captain of tennis, or 'keeper' as he was known. The keeper happened to be a boy in my house, Francis Black, but I don't think it was favouritism which caused him to offer me a place in the school team. Hence my dilemma. I would have to give up cricket on a regular basis, though I would still be able to play in house matches, and abandon any hope of a final place in the school eleven which was my father's particular ambition for me.

But a place in the school six was a heady incentive to dangle in front of me. I would be in the third pair, and so I succumbed to the glamour of playing in school matches with the additional lure of away fixtures. I think my father was slightly disappointed by my choice but I never made a better decision in my life. I have always enjoyed cricket and still play in my own annual match. I particularly enjoy watching and have made many friendships with well-known players, particularly Australians. But, socially speaking, tennis is streets ahead and, apart from achieving a certain amount of success in tournaments and competitions, the game has given me enormous and continuous pleasure.

Even now, almost my most favourite day of the year is the middle Sunday of Wimbledon when John Aspinall sponsors his annual pro-am on the grass courts at Queen's Club in London. I have always played with an Australian partner, usually John Alexander, Australia's former number one, or Kim Warwick, who won the French Open doubles as recently as 1985, and, of course, it is a particular pleasure to play against such legendary figures as Ken Rosewall, my boyhood hero. Wimbledon fortnight is an almost shut-down for me as far as other activities are concerned since I go practically every day and tend to mix with the

17

players in the evenings to the irritation of my wife, who may be a sport but is certainly not a sportswoman.

So, back as school in the summer of 1951, I was the proud wearer of the school tennis cap, fawn with white crossed racquets.

The following year I was up to first pair with the captain, Martin French, and in 1953 I was keeper myself and the crossed racquets turned to gold to mark this distinction. By this time I was very full of myself, captain of tennis, about to be captain of my house, and cruising without effort or much achievement through my studies. Unfortunately, this conviction that I was on top of the world nearly led to my expulsion from Eton.

We were to play an away match against a school called UCS up in the Hampstead area of London. The tennis master, whose name was Lefevre, was to meet us at UCS at 2.15, first matches at 2.30 sharp. I and my team were a cocky and sophisticated little group, and I decreed that we might as well take the opportunity to enjoy a decent lunch in London before the match. We split into two groups of three with myself and my partner, Ewen Bowater, son of the Lord Mayor of London, to lunch with a third member of the team, Colin Clive, at his parents' flat overlooking the Hurlingham Club, while the other three elected to feed themselves at Les Ambassadeurs, then probably London's most famous and expensive lunch- and dining-club and one of my regular holiday haunts, too.

With some inner forewarning of problems to come, I was, by my own relaxed standards, fairly stern with the Ambassadeurs trio. 'Don't let me down,' I instructed, '2.15 sharp, and don't forget taxi-drivers may not know UCS too well. It's in Frognall, around Hampstead, I think,' I added lamely, having only been there once before two years earlier when we had travelled direct from school in the conventional manner.

We enjoyed our lunch and it was after 2 o'clock when we set off to cross from south-west to north-west London, taking much longer than we had anticipated. It was well after 2.30 when we arrived to be confronted by a seething, red-faced Lefevre, and some pretty irritated opposition. That was bad enough but my heart sank even further when I realized that there was no sign at all of the other three.

When they arrived at about 3.25, there was talk of the match being called off and indeed relations between the schools severed. To make matters even worse the Les A. three sauntered in in the worst Etonian manner, with silly grins on their faces and probably the worse for drink. It all looked very bad for me and I did the only thing I could to save

18

myself, playing my best tennis of the year, spurred by sheer funk. I did not want to be expelled and thus disgrace my family, worse than that, disappoint my father.

My final match was against their first pair whose names I remember to this day, Hatton and Stuart. These two were easily the best public school pair in the country and probably the best pair in England. Ewen also played his heart out and we got as near as dammit to beating them before going under 7–5 in the final set.

We were rather subdued on the way back and even the team was embarrassed knowing that I would carry the can. Lefevre had muttered angrily as we parted that I would be hearing more about it. To make matters worse, it being Saturday, there was the whole of Sunday to sweat through before my inevitable summons to appear before the headmaster on Monday morning. Thankfully, the head man, Dr Robert Birley, saw fit to let me off with a severe caution and I left his room, situated in the 400-year-old part of the school building, chastened but greatly relieved.

Incredible to look back on those early Eton days and remember how naïve I was. I was quite a trim little chap, hard to believe now, and I had a beautiful treble voice, ending up a year in the choir as a corner-boy, which meant that I led the choir in and sang solos. But I hadn't a clue what was going on when the first of two boys made a pass at me and not much more of an idea when the second one harassed me, usually when I was trying to read the *Sporting Life*, and earnestly studying form. And I also had no idea that Jacob Rothschild, a contemporary then and still a friend now, was Jewish. I suppose I might just have recognized the fact that someone was black but, basically, to me all men were equal – a result, I suppose, of my parents' free-and-easy attitude, particularly my father's, though I hasten to add that they were both staunch Conservatives.

Another example of my attitude was that my partner at the age of thirteen in competitive doubles in and around the Frinton area was a boy called Peter Moys, who lived in a council house at Gidea Park in suburban Essex. Peter seemed to me exactly the same as us, even though he probably spoke with a London accent, and we got on well. It never occurred to us that anyone might think it odd for a council-house boy to hob-nob on equal terms, without patronage, with an Eton boy at snooty Frinton. An interesting side-light on this partnership was that Peter and I were about the same standard at tennis that year. But he

19

then concentrated on the one game, leaving school early, while I played all the other sports in their season. His tennis outstripped mine, hardly surprising since he became the country's number two or three player and was a member of the British Davis Cup team for several years.

My tennis career began, aged nine, in that first summer on the wonderful Frinton grass courts in 1945. I was brilliantly taught by the club coach, Roy Booth, even if he did insist on a somewhat exaggerated, rounded swing of the racquet on service and, to a lesser extent, on forehand and backhand. It was all good grounding though, and one could always tighten up one's shots having gained experience. The feature of Frinton tennis was the two annual American tournaments in August. These tournaments consisted of four groups according to age, and all played in their group with the winner of most games playing a final against the winners of the next group.

I chose as my partner a blonde girl who lived two houses down the road from us, Deirdre Fuller, and we won our group and both finals in the two tournaments. The finals were handicapped according to age and as we were relatively new and unknown we received our new and correct handicap from older rivals in the finals. The same thing happened the following year but by the second final this time we were not allowed quite our full allowance. As far as I can remember, we had yet to lose a game in the qualifying matches, which usually consisted of six or eight games each.

By the next year, there was open hostility towards us from over-protective parents of perennial losers but, as we had by now gone up a section, it was thought that the handicap in finals might inhibit us but it didn't and we were still unbeaten. Matters came to a head the following year when we actually found ourselves in one final playing against my younger brother Jonathan and his little partner. We were set to give away the apparently insurmountable handicap of love–30 and love–40 in alternate games, which meant that they only had to win one point out of the first three in every other game to take the game. We still won 6–love and the hostility of the crowds around the centre court was now quite open. Cries of 'Shame' and 'Play fair', echoed out from seething mothers and grandmothers as we hammered the ball past our little rivals.

When I was twelve, the club's under-sixteen boys' singles championship was reintroduced and, for once, I was an underdog in the final against a much bigger fifteen-year-old, whom I beat. When I won it the following year, there was consternation among club members as they

20

realized that the elegant challenge cup would be won outright by anyone completing a hat-trick of victories or four in all. Accordingly, and extremely unethically, they changed the rules to extend the competition to under 18s, thus allowing an over-sized sixteen-year-old called Michael Lusty to play. He could usually beat me, being much bigger and stronger, and he succeeded in doing so both that year and the following year.

This, however, left the trophy at my mercy for the last two years, when he was ineligible, and even the anti-Benson faction could hardly put back the age limit to under sixteen again even though some of them did try. So I won the championship both when I was sixteen and seventeen, and thus become the winner outright of the trophy. I was delighted since I had won a number of post-war silver-plated trophies, but this was the first large, real silver cup that I had owned.

The question of our poverty now reared its ugly head. It was made fairly obvious to my father that he was morally bound to replace the trophy and present a new one and I was told fairly bluntly that he could not afford this and I must re-present my hard-earned cup. I was very upset but reluctantly agreed. My name was inscribed on it as the donor and I stipulated that it was to be a permanent challenge trophy and could thus never be won outright. This infuriated my young brother who promptly won it three times in a row himself.

My only consolation over all this came from a kindly man, Gordon Boggon, head of an advertising agency and a generous supporter of all our activities. He quietly gave me a fiver as a reward, since he realized how disappointed I was. It was one of those old-fashioned, large, crinkly white £5 notes and I was very grateful.

As far as the American tournaments were concerned, it was put to me that partnership between Deirdre Fuller and myself should be broken. The club president was a grand old gentleman, the Marquess of Abergavenny, and it was suggested that he would be pleased if I would play with his granddaughter, Lady Marye Pepys, a descendant of the diarist, Samuel Pepys, and daughter of the Earl and Countess of Cottenham. I was pleased to go along with this diplomatic solution, particularly as the Cottenhams and their family were kind and gentle people and had entertained me to lunch many times at their Sussex home from my prep school. I liked Marye very much indeed. She was very pretty and played a fair game of tennis but not as robust as my previous partner.

Unfortunately, I did not play my own best game in the American tournament and we were beaten into second place in our section, a bitter disappointment for Marye, who quite wrongly, felt very conscious of letting me down as well as her family. In fact, egged on by the anti-Benson faction, the Abergavennys actually made me feel that I had let them down, and lot of the goodwill created by the new partnership was thus lost.

My other regular partner from then on was Jane Sheffield, an attractive girl and a remarkably powerful player for one so slim. Her parents were both good people and we all became lifelong friends. Janey and I had an entirely innocent adolescent romance and I remember taking her out to lunch at what we thought was an extremely sophisticated restaurant, the Ox on the Roof in the King's Road, Chelsea, before seeing her off on her school train to Southover Manor, near Lewes in Sussex. My future second wife and several of our best friends also went to Southover which was forced to close down a few years ago through lack of funds.

Janey later married Jocelyn Stevens who became managing director of Express newspapers and, as it turned out, my boss in the 1960s and 1970s. Janey is divorced from Jocelyn now but I see them both. She is often lady-in-waiting to Princess Margaret and still plays a very strong game of tennis. We have seldom been beaten, even against men.

Since I have stressed my father's dire financial straits, I must try to explain how we managed to afford a house in London in one of the best areas and also one at Frinton. I think the answer is that my mother, who had a little money of her own as her father was quite well off, owned the Frinton house, though they were forced to sell it soon after I left school.

All my father's ambitions at the end of my school-days were channelled through my brother and me and he was keen that I should finish up as captain of my house. Unfortunately, I did not get on well with the housemaster, Graham-Campbell; nor, for that matter, did any of the other boys. We still worshipped Whitfield and resented the austere, religious new tutor who found it difficult to unbend and communicate. He had tightened up on discipline in what had become an arrogant and riotous collection of boys inflated by success on the sports field.

The tutor refused to say all through the summer whether he would appoint me house captain although I was really the only possible choice. I had already been in the 'library', jargon for house prefect, for three halves, which made me very senior. This was a self-appointed body though, and the nomination of captain was the privilege of the tutor

22

alone. He did not like me or trust me, particularly after the school tennis incident. So my father, the mildest of men, came down one day in July to confront him.

'Either you tell me here and now whether my son will be house captain next half or I will take him away,' stipulated my father.

Graham-Campbell collapsed. 'Of course he will be captain,' he admitted. So I returned for the autumn half, mainly to enjoy myself and finish my school-days. From the first day of that final session, my relationship with Graham-Campbell completely changed and I grew to know him and like him very much indeed. It was all about trust, really. All through life I have generally behaved better with responsibility than without it and this was most certainly the case.

I had one or two racy habits to which he now turned a blind eye but basically the job went smoothly and Graggers, as he was known, and I never had cause to disagree. I would like to think that it was partly as a result of my own relationship with him, which enabled me to explain what sort of man lay behind his unbending manner to the rest of the boys, that led to his becoming much more relaxed and subsequently popular with his boys. He left to be headmaster of another public school some years later.

One of the best things that happened to me in life as a result of Graham-Campbell was meeting and becoming close friends with Col. Sir Martin Gilliatt, who has for some years now been the trusted and indispensable private secretary to Queen Elizabeth, the Queen Mother. Martin, the most perfect of courtiers, had been imprisoned in the notorious Colditz for most of the war. He was in the élite 60th Rifles, the Green Jackets, and presided over the Colonel Commandant's office of the regiment at Winchester when I first knew him.

My tutor had been in the same regiment and they were great friends so, from time to time, Martin, a man deeply involved in horse-racing would come to lunch with the whole house and we always seemed to be drawn next to each other. This suited me very well since I was already interested in racing which was to become the all-consuming passion of my life and he was able to tell me riveting stories of racecourse experiences. He was also a friend of the Royal trainer of steeplechasers and hurdlers, Peter Cazalet, whose son Edward, though not in my house, was one of my friends.

At one of these lunches, Martin informed me that he owed part of a horse called Kandy Boy running at Hurst Park the following day, and he thought that he should win.

This, to me, was real inside information and, apart from telling all my sporting friends, I had five shillings each way on the horse, the equivalent of only 25p each way now, but a fortune to me then. We clustered around our radios to listen to the racing results after the 6 o'clock news next evening and a great cheer rang down the passages of the entire house when it was announced that Kandy Boy had won at odds of 100–6, more than 16–1. I won more than a fiver, big money.

Martin then did me another favour. He was the chief selector, as it were, in his role within the regiment and he was able to offer me a place in the 60th, provided, of course, that I came through my basic training, passed the War Office selection board of potential officers, and then came through the tough sixteen-week officer's training-course at Eaton Hall near Chester, the traditional home of the Duke of Westminster but then leased out to the army. I did just manage to scramble through all these tests, and I was thus accepted as an officer, the lowliest – a second lieutenant – in the 60th where I much enjoyed my far from brilliant career, making many good friends.

Horse-racing had become my principal interest during my final three years at Eton and provided many diverting and some funny incidents. My first major touch was on Nickel Coin, a mare who won the 1951 Grand National at odds of 40–1. I had five bob each way on that one too, and that enabled me to buy a portable radio, up to then my life's ambition. It was a massive thing, a Bush, and clumsy to carry and handle, but I thought it the nicest thing I ever saw and it lasted me for some years. The win was particularly timely since we were only allowed radios in our rooms at school when we were in the house debating-society, known as 'debate', and a kind of semi-privileged middle group. The radio decision was the first popular one made by Graham-Campbell, overruling the original prejudice of his more old-fashioned predecessor Whitfield.

My mother became keen on racing too, and every April she would drive us in our old Rover from Frinton through the Essex and Suffolk roads to Newmarket for the Craven meeting, the first of the new season there each year.

I particularly remember in April 1952 making special note of two horses which ran well over longer distances at that meeting, Flighty Frances and Souepi. Flighty Frances ran a brave race to finish second and I noticed Souepi finishing like a train to be fourth in another event. I remembered these two and backed them both at Royal Ascot in June. Flighty Frances won the competitive handicap over two and a half miles,

24

the Ascot Stakes, while Souepi won the two-mile Royal Vase, now known as the Queen's Vase and, to prove my adolescent astuteness, Souepi came out at Ascot the following year and dead-heated for the Gold Cup.

I had a variety of ways of getting my bets on at school. One of the boys, Robert Frazer, whose father was, I believe, chairman of the Stock Exchange, took a lot of my bets and I gave him such a bashing at Royal Ascot in 1953 that it took him two years to pay me off. But he paid in full most honourably. He later had a somewhat chequered career, going down with Mick Jagger amidst much publicity, on an overstressed drugs rap which led to him serving part of six-month prison sentence before he became the proprietor of his own Art Gallery. Robert remained a good friend of Mick's and we thus met up again through this contact in later years. He always asked me not to mention our school connection to Mick but I could see no reason why not and the singer was hugely amused at my punting and bookmaking stories. Robert died prematurely a few years ago.

My earlier betting at school had been done with the house odd-job man. I only learnt after he had left that he had come under suspicion from Graham-Campbell for providing this service and had been sacked after refusing to reveal the names of his customers.

My other method of betting was to ring up, reversing the charges, mother's bookmaker, Douglas Stuart – motto 'Duggie never owes'. I would ring up using either the telephone in my tailor's, Denman and Goddard, or else the public telephone kiosk just across the road from my house, but overlooked by the study of the housemaster opposite, Philip Snow. There was rather more element of risk in using the telephone kiosk since it was visible to all, but they could hardly know what I was doing. However, it probably did become a little obvious when my calls became more regular, particularly during the jumping season when I was backing the Cazalet horses, especially as I darted out each day just before lunch.

There seemed no reason to fear Snow since he seemed a fairly remote individual who did not know me very well and looked more interested in the Arts than racing. It was only much later that I discovered that he had guessed exactly what I was up to from his brother, Jim Snow, northern racing correspondent of *The Times*.

We certainly had a better chance than the average punter with horses trained by Peter Cazalet who was the most consistent trainer of his time and who sent Edward a typewritten list each week with the stable's

25

runners. Inked in by the trainer was the appropriate amount of stars according to his judgement of a horse's chance. And, occasionally, when there was a change of plan he would ring up Edward who conferred with me several times each day.

In those days, there was no overnight declaration of runners and the newspaper list of probables was compiled by the Press Association in consultation with every trainer in the land. This was, all things considered, a surprisingly successful method but far from foolproof. It was abused by dishonest trainers and owners who did not want the general public betting off-course to know their horse was running. And occasionally even an honest trainer like Cazalet would slip one in because of a change of mind.

This happened one day when he had no intention of running a hurdler called Donaghmore until the morning of the race, when the old horse worked so brilliantly and seemed so well in himself that it was decided to run him. Cazalet rang up his son who passed on the message to me at our morning conference and the horse won at odds of a 100–8, more than 12–1.

Other great favourites were Monaveen, owned by the present Queen and the Queen Mother, Statecraft, Rose Park, Red Rube, and later Lochroe.

My mother and I got involved in a racing scrape which tested my father's honesty and led to a visit to the headmaster. The day we were due to return to school, the last Wednesday in April 1952, was also Two Thousand Guineas day at Newmarket. My father was working in London but my mother and I were still at Frinton and decided to drive to Newmarket for the races, after which she would put me on a train to London and thence back to Eton. We hadn't to be back until about 9 p.m. or even later

We steamed round the Essex and Suffolk lanes with my mother crouched behind the wheel of the family Rover and heaved a sigh of relief once we were through Bury St Edmunds when the road to Newmarket was virtually straight all the way. As usual, my mother really hit the accelerator pedal and the car radiator boiled over about four miles from the course. It nearly always did and we never learnt.

However, we were there in time for a losing day, the main gloom being the comfortable victory of the French-trained outsider Thunderhead II in the Guineas.

Towards the end of the afternoon, I said to my mother, 'I don't feel

26

like going back to school this evening. I'll come back to Frinton with you and we'll get Father to ring up and make an excuse. I'll go back in my own time tomorrow.' As was her easy-going nature, she readily agreed, knowing, as I did, that nothing much went on at school for the first twenty-four hours of a new half.

Just before dinner, we rang up my father and told him to contact my tutor and make an excuse that I had a touch of 'flu, but hoped to be back tomorrow. It seemed straightforward enough. A little white lie did no one any harm. We were enjoying our dinner when the telephone rang and it was my father again. 'I'm sorry but I cannot tell a lie to your tutor. I told him the truth that you have been to the Two Thousand Guineas. You will have to face the music tomorrow.'

Well, thanks a bunch. This dropped me in it from a great height and I was pretty angry with my father and a little apprehensive of the interview with my tutor, particularly in view of the racing bit. My mother was sympathetic and felt vaguely let down herself but there was nothing for her to do except pack me off on the early train to London in the morning.

I went straight from Liverpool Street station to Waterloo and hence to Windsor and Eton Riverside station, between the river and Windsor Castle. All very romantic except when you are going back to trouble. I dumped my kit in my room and then knocked nervously at my tutor's door. Graham-Campbell looked grave but said in his adenoidal tones 'I'm disappointed in you, Benson. The headmaster will deal with you in the morning.' So the buck was passed to the head man, Dr Robert Birley, and I stood in front of him for the first time. He gave me a lecture on my responsibilities and ended up by dishing out my punishment. I was to lose the first twenty-four hours of long leave, the equivalent of half-term holiday. In the summer, long leave was later than average to coincide with the Eton and Harrow cricket match, traditionally played at Lord's on a Friday and Saturday early in July. But the whole holiday only lasted four days so one day out of that was quite severe, though I suppose quite justified.

Then the fates intervened. Around the middle of the half, there was a polio epidemic and one boy died and another two were taken seriously ill. Long leave was cancelled and my punishment was forgotten. But my own punishment for my father was not. As a result of the epidemic, the whole school was placed in quarantine and parents were given the option of taking their offspring home. Naturally my parents declined this kind offer. So I insisted that my father take me out on a Saturday,

27

the day of the King George VI and Queen Elizabeth Stakes at nearby Ascot. He arrived with a magnificent picnic which I remember to this day and which we ate in Maidenhead Thicket, where he regaled me with stories of his boyhood in that very spot. I know we ate a delicious hot chicken, which my mother had managed to get into a thermos and then I confirmed the sting. 'We are going to Ascot, now,' I stated firmly. My father was extremely reluctant, since Ascot was out of bounds and racing a sacking offence. This time I was insistent, and we paid to go into the middle of the course with limited viewing facilities. I had a whale of time but my father loathed every minute, petrified that we would be caught by a master. So likely! The highlight of the day was the big race which was a repeat of the Derby finish, with the Aga Khan's Tulyar beating Mrs James Rank's Gay Time by a neck. Once again the cheeky winning rider, Cockney veteran Charlie Smirke, was able to grin across at the infant prodigy Lester Piggott, exactly the same age as me at sixteen and say 'What did I Tulyar!'

So honours were even. I had wrought sweet revenge on my father and escaped punishment as well. That was one for the bad guys.

After I left school at the end of Christmas week in 1953 I went to stay for a few days with the Cazalets at their fabulous house and stables, Fairlawne, near Tonbridge in Kent. There was another school-friend there, Robin Newman, and we were all in awe of Peter Cazalet, even Edward. He was a very good man but he could be quite frighteningly fierce and I got the thick end of his tongue while the horses were being saddled before first lot on our first morning there for standing around reading the *Sporting Life* and causing some of the horses to shy as they left their boxes.

We all rode out and it was Robin's turn to disgrace himself when his horse bolted and they careered around narrowly failing to fly into a deep hollow and scattering the orderly string of racehorses.

The trainer's main work- and schooling-rider, and number two stable jockey, was a wonderful man called Ron Harrison, who had a run a pub in nearby Plaxtol and who possessed a wonderful pair of hands. He was a particular friend of Edward's and mine and could be relied upon to impart even the stable secrets that Peter Cazalet himself chose not to divulge.

On this particular visit, we went to watch Ron school a high-class flat-racer of Lady Derby's, Sleeping Warrior, over hurdles for the first time. But even the magic of Ron's hands and all his expertise in the saddle could not persuade Sleeping Warrior to jump even one hurdle and Peter Cazalet grew angrier and angrier, shouting at the wretched Ron even though he could hardly be blamed.

Imagine my amazement, therefore, when not long afterwards I read that Sleeping Warrior was due to run in a hurdle race at Kempton Park ridden by the stable-jockey, the great Bryan Marshall. I could only afford to pay my way into the racecourse enclosure that day, inside the course rather than in the grandstand, but this was good fun during the jumping season and I was able to walk down to the first hurdle, which would be jumped again second time around in the finishing straight. Sleeping Warrior set off with the leaders, the best practice with a novice since it enables the horse to catch a clear sight of the obstacle and measure his stride accordingly. I could easily pick out the Derby colours and Bryan Marshall as the horses galloped towards me. Unhappily, as they reached the flight, Sleeping Warrior never took off and gave poor Bryan a crashing fall. Bryan was kicked in the face and his longish nose which until that moment inclined towards the aquiline was completely rearranged and to this day is concave, with a dip in the middle. I could never quite fathom why a trainer of Cazalet's ability took that chance with so reluctant a jumper.

While we were staying with him, Cazalet was going through a golden spell and my betting prospered as never before. We stayed with him through a Hurst Park meeting and a Sandown Park meeting, as well as a Newbury meeting at about the same time. The stable sent out winner after winner and I particularly remember after one of the Hurst Park days pulling all the cash out of my pockets and piling it into my hat as Edward and I sat together in the back of the chauffeur-driven Jaguar, giggling like demented idiots. An irritated Peter Cazalet, sitting up in front alongside the driver, turned to enquire what we two idiots were making such a noise about.

Dick Francis was also riding for the stable then, and I remember him winning on most of Cazalet's horses, including one called Deal Park, who scored at both Newbury and Sandown, the second time beating a horse called Stranger, ridden by Lester Piggott. Few people these days realize that Lester, to help with his struggle against increasing weight, rode for a season or two over hurdles, registering an incredibly high winning-average.

Edward Cazalet, godfather of my second son, Edward, was a successful amateur steeplechase jockey despite his gangling frame. He studied law and has now become an eminent QC.

The week before the Cazalet stay, I had gone down to Gloucestershire at the invitation of another school friend, Malcolm Shennan, to stay with his family for the two-day Cheltenham meeting leading up to Newbury. Malcolm's mother, Lilah, was extremely tough and was the queen of the greyhound world, mainly coursing, though she had plenty of success on the track as well. Her whole life revolved around her greyhounds, most of them being based on and trained at home. All of them were named with the same initials as hers, LS, an example being Latest Suspect.

I was pretty scared of Lilah Shennan, and so, too, I believe were her family, including her husband. Even more awe-inspiring, and staying there at the time, was the Earl of Sefton, a man of incredibly upright bearing, tall, austere, dignified, and handsome. He was an even more important figure than Mrs Shennan in the greyhound coursing world and it was on his estates at Altcar, just outside Liverpool, that the great annual coursing event, the Waterloo Cup, was, and still is run.

My lucky run was just beginning and as we left for the first day of the Cheltenham meeting near by, we boys were given firm instructions that the party would leave after the fourth race so that Mrs Shennan could be back home in time to feed her dogs.

Lord Sefton had a horse called Irish Lizard, a famous old steeple-chaser, and he duly won to my personal profit and delight. I collected my money from the bookmakers and also won on other races as well so I did not notice that it was long after the fourth race and, in fact, time for the fifth race before I rushed off to the car. They were still there but seething with rage at being kept waiting by a cheeky 18-year-old and Malcolm and I kept our heads well below the parapet for the remainder of the stay.

I must go back a few weeks for my final Eton anecdotes, both of them with a moral. It was the tradition, at least in our house, to marshal all the juniors – the lower boys – in front of members of the library – the house prefects – and fag them to perform various tasks. Usually, these were pretty useless jobs like taking round silly little notes to friends in other houses. I thought this a pretty pointless procedure and thought it might be amusing, instead, to hold a race of all our lower boys – two lengths of the football-pitch in the field opposite our house.

I put the idea in democratic style to the juniors, and they were more than pleased to comply, particularly when I suggested, as a reward for the winner, that he be excused fagging duties for the following week.

Normal midweek fagging consisted of running errands, cleaning shoes, or going to the shops and buying food. We all had tea in our own rooms in groups of two or three eating our own food.

So off we trooped across the road and, flanked by the other four or five members of the library, we lined up the lower boys, some sixteen of them and sent them off to turn at the other goal-post and return to the starting-line. Hard as the others struggled, there was only one in it – a pale, thin youth with a hooked nose called Watson-Gandy. He ran home some 15 yards ahead of the rest and enjoyed a week free of duties.

The following Sunday, by general agreement, we did the same thing again and my senior friends and I rocked with laughter as the little fellows, tail-coats flying or, in the case of the smaller ones, bottoms swaying, struggled in vain to keep within hailing distance of the flying Watson-Gandy, who cruised home once again.

But while I was laughing, a plan was formulating in my brain. During the week I told one of my closest friends, captain of another house, of our new entertainment with the result that on the third Sunday of the half, he brought along his lower boys to join in. This time, before the race, I took Watson-Gandy aside and said, 'I don't want you to win today. Finish with the others and don't say anything. You will still be excused fagging.' So this time, there was nothing much in it between the leaders of my boys and those from the other house and, in horseracing style, I judged that Watson-Gandy would still have plenty in hand.

On the following Sunday I invited two more of my friends who were house captains to bring along their gang of lower boys, and over the following three weeks I increased the field until some ten houses were competing and a vast phalanx of little boys were streaming up and down Master's field, as it was known. By now this cabaret had become much talked about and a huge gang of spectators turned up to watch the sport while boys were leaning out from the windows of the house alongside the field as well as the two houses across the road, one of them mine. It was incredibly funny and there was a lot of shouting and laughter. Several other house captains now approached me themselves to enquire why they had not been asked to join the jamboree. Naturally, they were all made welcome.

Unfortunately, and hardly surprisingly, the matter had by now become common knowledge among the authorities and towards the end of the week, I was taken aside by a particularly friendly master and warned that action was about to be taken to stop this activity as it was fairly generally known that I was the ring-leader. So the sting had to be brought forward a week or two. I contacted all the heads of the houses involved, told them what the master had said, and said that regrettably, this would have to be the final race. Almost as an afterthought I added to each and everyone of them. 'We might as well have a littler wager on it and run a sweepstake. Let's each of us put in a fiver.' Since virtually all the house captains would be leaving at the end of the half they could all just about afford this sum and all agreed. So, with the increased field, there was about £80 in the kitty and the trap was sprung. I did not tell Watson-Gandy of my plan but took him aside on the Sunday morning and said, 'Today's the day. I want you to show them just how good you are, win as far as you like.' I also released him from fagging duties for the rest of the half provided that he won and also added an additional incentive like a can or two of baked beans.

I could hardly contain my excitement as we congregated on the field: there were something like three hundred runners and as many spectators – half the school. We set them off and I waited expectantly, reckoning to pocket some £80 with the next 30 seconds. To my horror, as the field of black-and-white midgets thundered towards me, there was no sign of Watson-Gandy. Eventually, as they poured over the line, I spotted the little wretch, lolloping along with a beastly grin on his horrid face. He raised two fingers to me as he passed. I had been stuffed and there was nothing I could do about it.

I don't really know to this day what Watson-Gandy had against me but maybe he heard about the sweepstake and reckoned that he should have been cut in. So all my brilliant planning and scheming cost me a fiver in the end. Moral: play the game straight.

There is a postscript to this story. After I left Watson-Gandy proved himself an outstanding athlete on the track and across country. He won just about everything and ended up as a champion miler and winner of the school cross-country as well as murdering all opposition at shorter distances, too. So, to add to my fury, I had been right all along and had unearthed a champion.

My other story is much shorter. Although, in theory, you were meant to pass your trials even if you were leaving the next day, many of the lazier and more arrogant senior pupils who were leaving did not try very hard, since these exams meant nothing. Needless to say, I was prominent among those who took this point of view and made little effort to score high marks. So one morning, I sauntered down with a friend of mine who shared this philosophy and partook of a couple of cups of coffee and some sausages at the local shop before wandering into the schoolroom where we were to sit for that particular exam under the eye of a particularly weak master whom I had enjoyed taunting all year. Needless to say, I was playing it for laughs and I got plenty as I lounged in.

'Benson, you are half an hour late. This is quite ridiculous,' piped the master, adding, 'Take a Georgic and deliver it to me by midday tomorrow.' 'Why not make it two, Sir,' I responded cheekily while the rest of the boys laughed even louder. 'If you say so, two it is,' replied the master who clearly had not realized that I was leaving in two days' time.

Then the joke began to wear a bit thin. My tutor, Graham-Campbell, with whom I now got on like a house on fire, summoned me later that day and said, 'We've got a problem on our hands. I don't know what you did or said to Mr Anderson, but you seem to have upset him and hurt him most dreadfully. He tells me that he has given you two Georgics.' (A Georgic, I should explain, is a verse by Virgil some 500 lines long. Since every word is different and in Latin, it had to be copied carefully and thus took much longer than the average 500 lines normally identical. A Georgic was thus a feared punishment and two were almost unheard of.)

I had no intention of doing any of them until my tutor explained the awkward position that I had placed him in. Even though he sympathized with me, he had to be seen to support his colleague, otherwise there could be repercussions. This was indeed a tricky one, and in the end, I had to do a deal with Graham-Campbell and agree to write one Georgic if he suspended the other one. So I spent most of the following day and night peering over the dreaded Latin and copying what I regarded in those days as a load of rubbish.

Moral: don't go for cheap laughs.

One final thing must be explained about Eton. There is no Eton school tie as such and the famous old Etonian tie, so much treasured by con-men world-wide, can be officially worn only by members of the Old Etonian Association. Life membership of this body was normally paid for on one's final school-bill and most young school-leavers would rush out and buy one. But it didn't take long to work out that it simply isn't the done thing to wear an OE tie. Virtually the only men who do wear it are such unutterable bores that they have nothing else in life to talk or boast about and they hope it will attract the attention of like-minded bores in order to start up some tedious conversation.

Anyone else seen wearing one is almost certainly wearing it without authority and is highly likely to be a con-man. I lost mine 30 years ago and have not replaced it.

After an extended three months' holiday, during which I drove my parents to the brink of insanity and insolvency, I received my call-up papers to report to the Green Jackets' depot in early April.

It was during this spell that, inevitably, my luck changed but I still went racing at every opportunity. During my winning run in January, I had bet £10 on a horse of Cazalet's called Mandavee, first time out over fences, and he had fallen. Next time he ran, some weeks later, having doubtless received some heavy schooling at home, I had the princely sum of two shillings on him – all I could afford – and he won at 10–1.

Another day, I actually had my last sixpence on a horse. I rustled up just enough money for a cheap day-return ticket from Victoria station down to the new defunct Wye racecourse in Kent, my entrance to the cheapest enclosure in the centre of the tiny circuit, and a pound or so to back the one horse I specially fancied running in the third or fourth race. The horse's name was Vain Help. By the time we reached that race, though, I had foolishly frittered away all my money, except for sixpence. There was only one bookie who would take a bet as small as this. He was an elderly and very splendid little figure called Nobby and even he only gave half a betting-ticket for a wager of this size. Although Vain Help was priced on Nobby's board at 4–1, I decided that it was too risky to put my last sixpence on such a chancy horse and switched the bet to the 2–1 favourite. Vain Help won and I had to walk home from Victoria station. You might think that that sort of experience would have taught me a sharp lesson, but although I never lost as little as sixpence again, I frequently perpetrated similar stupidities but for much more money.

Army Interlude

IF, from the anecdotes related in the previous chapter, you were to come to the conclusion that I was altogether too big for my boots, you would not be far wrong. However, there is nothing like ten weeks' basic training in the Army to cut one down to size.

There were only four public schoolboys in my intake, known, just to draw further attention to them, as PLs – Potential Leaders. Most of the rest, 50 ot 60 of them, were basically East-Enders since my regiment drew most of its candidates from this area. The man in the next bed to me subsequently perpetrated a notorious murder and was convicted of it. Several of the men were illiterate as I was to discover later on in Germany when as a young officer and platoon leader, I had to write their letters home for them.

Many East-Londoners have plenty of wit and initiative and these were the ones I liked best. There was also a little Maltese man about ten years older than the rest of us who regailed us with incredible stories of his sexual exploits with his wife. 'I got fuv bits,' he would boast after his leave which, being translated, meant that he had pleasured his wife five times.

In matters concerning sex, they were light-years ahead of me, and I would listen for hours to their stories, many of which were probably quite untrue but sounded pretty impressive to me. I had not long broken my sexual duck with a prostitute who had approached me at the corner of Curzon Street and Park Lane. The area was swarming with them in those days. We took a taxi to a shabby basement flat in Victoria and, once I had handed over two pounds and been fitted with the regulation condom, now much the fashion in these Aids-fearing days, I was guided astride her body, reeking of cheap scent, and it was all over in about five

35

seconds. I felt robbed and must have looked very disappointed. 'I don't believe you've done this sort of thing before,' she declared sympathetically. My pride was hurt. 'Of course I have, often,' I replied angrily, 'I just like it this way.'

I had to try it out a few more times for either two or three pounds before I began to get the hang of it and was much improved, though far from perfected, by a long relationship with a much older lady whose cheaper services helped to take the strain off my exchequer. However, my young military colleagues had apparently been doing it with great skill and enthusiasm on a more economic basis since they were eight years old, most of them with their sisters and some with their mothers and aunts. This was somewhat shocking knowledge to me, remembering my sheltered background, but I nodded sagely at such stories, implying that much the same thing went on in Frinton too.

Ironically, it was during the tougher bits that we PLs came into our own. Incredibly, we could face physical stress and hardship much better than the others. We were only frightened of disgracing ourselves or our families by failing to maintain a stiff upper lip and complete either a cross-country run or a route march with heavy packs on our backs. I was fairly strong and fit as a keen games player but even the smallest and weediest looking of the PLs, bespectacled Willie Martineau, the only other Etonian in the intake, kept going though he was an intellectual and not an athlete. So we gained a sort of respect from the lads, whom we would try to help when they were faltering. Many of them would fall by the wayside on route marches and be taken in by kindly ladies who would feed them with cups of tea and listen to their outrageous lies about torture and physical punishment. The local MP must have been inundated with complaints from these old ladies about the Gestapo up the road.

It was not much fun with all the needless bullying, the rubbing and shining, the running and shouting, the needless profanities and not least the food. This was dreadful for the most part, with things like hearts being regarded as a luxury. Potatoes inevitably had eyes in them and were half grey and even black. Eventually the platoon democratically decided to lodge a formal protest and thoughtfully voted me the spokesman. So, rather like a latter-day and larger version of Oliver Twist, I approached the officer in charge of catering at that time, a Major Wallis of the Rifle Brigade. 'Sir,' I spluttered, 'the men and I feel that the food is inedible. We would like to lodge this complaint.' He listened without uttering a word, turned round to where the vast tubs of rotting starch were bubbling, dug a ladle into a mixture of potato and some other filth, took a bite, ruminated, and then announced, 'Good, wholesome food.' There was nothing more to be done. Tommy Wallis, subsequently promoted to lieutenant-colonel – not entirely on the strength of this gallant exploit – later became a friend of mine and nowadays he is a senior administrator of racecourses, working for the Jockey Club. He also loves his food and his son, John, has supervised catering in several managerial duties at hotels all over the world, including the Pierre in New York and the Hyde Park Hotel in London before reaching his current position as general manager of the Hyatts in the Middle East, based on Dubai.

Once we had completed our ten weeks' basic training, during which I reached sufficient shooting proficiency with both rifle and Bren-gun to be judged a marksman at both, we were given some leave before returning to do odd jobs at the depot carrying the honorary rank of acting unpaid lance-corporal. I worked in the arms store, which was a wonderfully easy job. I learnt the art of skiving from my two colleagues there, the art of doing the barest minimum of work without being found out. It was an art in which I have far outstripped my mentors in later life.

I slept in a long barrack-room with a lot of other smelly senior rifle-men and corporals and here it was that I had a second embarrassing sleep-walking experience. I slept in the second bed from one end of the room in a row of ten beds with the same amount facing on the other side of the room. One night, I was wandering around in my sleep when, subconsciously, I tried to get back into the second bed from the end. Unfortunately, as was often the case when sleep-walking, I was disorientated and tried to get into the second bed diagonally opposite my own.

I was awakened with a start to the angry cries of a particularly repulsive and aggressive elderly corporal who thought I was pressing my attentions upon him. I have never moved so quickly, and fled back to the other end of the room and my own bed before the lights could be turned on, feigning deep sleep. They never found out who it was though I was viewed with some suspicion for a while.

Eaton Hall was constructed in the strange, mock Gothic architectural style of London's St Pancras station, but when I finally arrived there in midsummer, we officer cadets were housed in prefabricated cabins outside the railings of the main house and of decidedly no architectural interest at all.

37

Basic training was a cakewalk compared with this 16-week course, the worst four or five days of which were spent in the hills and bogs of North Wales. The advantages, though, were that we were all kindred spirits with a common objective, that several of my friends there owned cars, and that we had a certain amount of free time to go into Chester for dinner and at weekends even go further afield to the races. Quite often I also went dog-racing at Chester, which primitive or not satisfied my wagering needs.

The trouble with horse-racing was that it started too early and we never came off duty to get there in time for the early races. I once arrived at Haydock Park just before the last race and on top of that backed a loser, while on another occasion we arrived at Manchester for only two races. Unfortunately Chester racecourse had no Saturday dates in those days and only staged the famous three-day May meeting, still one of my favourite race weeks. I arrived at Eaton Hall too late for that meeting in 1954 and wouldn't in any case have been able to get off mid-week, which would have been tantalizing. I was able to get in almost the full quota of races on other Saturdays at two little jump meetings, Uttoxeter and the oddly named Woore Hunt. The last named, like Manchester, is now defunct.

I also developed a passionate relationship with a pretty local girl named Lesley, but unfortunately this failed just short of the ultimate goal despite many cinema and back-alley clinches. Still, I survived somehow until about four days from the end of the 16 weeks by which time I had been accepted as an officer by the 60th, due in no small part to the efforts of Martin Gilliat.

However, there was one final problem. Under-officers were appointed from among the cadets to assist the permanent staff in matters of discipline and minor administration. It was a position which neither my friends nor I aspired to as usually the under-officers were over keen, obnoxious, and natural informers. The worst of these lived in an adjoining hut and all of us under his jurisdiction resolved to teach him a lesson before we left. So between us we devised the simple but effectively unpleasant plan of lobbing a thunder-flash into the bathroom while he was taking a bath. A thunder-flash makes a loud enough bang during tactical exercises in the field but in an enclosed bathroom it is positively deafening, though, in theory, it should do no actual structural harm. The plan went well and we all rejoiced at the mighty explosion followed by the scream of terror. Unfortunately, several of the staff heard the commotion. The unpopular under-officer was only too keen to squeal and point his finger at everyone he could think of, and an inquiry was set in motion.

We were very lucky. The Commandant of Eaton Hall apparently recommended that the entire remove of officer cadets should be returned to their units without commission, a ludicrous over-reaction. But those responsible for such decisions up at the War Office refused the recommendation, pointing out that it had cost the Army quite enough to put the 50 or so of us through the 16-week course without wasting the whole investment on one isolated prank.

I then joined my regiment at Munster, near the Dutch–German border. It was an icy winter in Westphalia, and Munster is a boring place at best. But my fellow officers, including John Leon, were a lively lot and, of course, it was a pleasure to be treated as an adult again. I had command of a platoon of about fifty men, including experienced NCOs, and it was faintly ridiculous that a spotty nineteen-year-old should be in charge of the welfare and military education of grown men. I had to solve several appalling family problems though I took advice on these from one of my corporals who was a particularly intelligent man.

Imagine me, with my almost non-existent real-life sexual knowledge, trying to solve the problems of a man whose wife was being unfaithful to him with his next door neighbour back in West Ham. I discovered a popular way of solving this sort of poser: give the man a weekend pass on compassionate grounds together with a free travel-voucher. I don't know what this did to the domestic lives of the citizens of West Ham but it earned me a few favourable points.

My Company commander was a Major Edwin Bramall, a good soldier, a fine cricketer, and a very nice man. It must have seemed idiotic to a man with his ability and war record to have young officers like me acting on his behalf but he never showed it. We were all awed by his ability and terrified of botching any of his instructions. He subsequently became Chief of the Imperial General Staff, then Chief of Defence. He was knighted and quite recently made a life peer.

One of the advantages of being in the Army in those days was being able to make use of the officers' clubs, particularly in Germany. I went to Hamburg for a long weekend of mischief with a couple of my colleagues and the officers' club there was the famous Four Seasons Hotel, now fully restored to its five-star glory. We paid the paltry sum of 7s 6d a night, while a large gin or brandy cost sixpence.

The delights of the notorious Reeperbahn came much dearer. This street of clubs and tarts provided practically every known entertainment

39

and perversion, and was a 'must' for young soldiers who wanted to find out what life was all about. I found out in the back of a taxi.

Other simpler experiences while I was based in Munster included a journey across the Dutch border to visit Arnhem, scene of the tragically disastrous airborne landings in 1944; a regimental point-to-point where I met many old school friends from other regiments stationed in Germany and drank two bottles of kümmel on my last day before returning home; and a week's course for officers adjoining the appalling Nazi concentration camp at Belsen. The feeling of horror as one wandered around mounds of grass bearing little plaques stating '500 men and women are buried here' and much greater figures, is indescribable. No birds sing there.

I returned to Winchester for my last nine months and very pleasant it was. I was in time to attend many deb dinners and dances during the summer of 1955 and life was not too taxing. We had a visit from the Queen and somewhere I have a photograph of myself hidden within a group of about 200 officers and Her Majesty. That summer I also opened the bowling for the regimental cricket team with Ted Dexter's brother-in-law at the other end. I finally left the Army in April 1956 and had to face up to real life.

Joining the *Express*
and My First Marriage

I LEFT the Army on 5 April with, as usual, a pathetically small bank balance. What I received then and the small amount I had managed to save would, I calculated, last me about six weeks. So I had until the middle of May before I would have to restructure my professional aims. I had made up my mind to become a racing correspondent. It was, of course, one thing to decide to become one, quite another thing even to break into this tiny field of endeavour. Nowadays, I would not even be able to get my own son into the profession without his serving a long apprenticeship probably compiling births and deaths and serving as general dogsbody on a provincial paper, or perhaps joining the Press Association in a junior and menial role.

My father might have wanted me to follow his footsteps into the law, but he never put any pressure on me and did not seem to think that the expense of my Eton education, which had cost him so dear, would be wasted in my declared field. As a matter of fact, Eton turns out as high a percentage of racing correspondents as it does Prime Ministers, bankers, and stockbrokers. At one time about 20 years ago the Press Room on the racecourse consisted of about one-third old Etonians.

One such was the famous Clive Graham, the 'Scout' of the *Daily Express* and paddock commentator for BBC television. My uncle and godfather, Jack Hawkins, had once obtained Clive's autograph for me on a day out at Newmarket and the great man had added a tip below his signature – Constantia, a well-known filly who promptly lost next time out. I was delighted with the autograph and not upset by the dud tip. My only contact with Clive was that I had become friendly with his personal assistant, Dan Abbott, a vast man standing some 6 ft 5 in and built to match. But Dan, good friend though he was, and still is, was in no hurry

41

to bring an ambitious young man into the firing-line of his own profession.

However, I had an immediate stroke of luck. I had a friend of about my own age, Lady Zinnia Denison, who had inherited quite a lot of money and was ever ready to spend it. One of her first ventures was to buy the title and become proprietor of a magazine called *The Londoner.* Through my school-friend Roger Gibbs, I was awarded the post of racing correspondent on the strength of absolutely no experience. This enabled me to telephone racecourses, announcing who I was, or else getting one of my girl-friends to masquerade as my secretary, and obtain a free pass. Sometimes I would try it at the complimentary entrance without a preliminary phone call. Sometimes it worked and sometimes it didn't, but every time I got in free it was a bonus. I wrote the sort of pompous little articles that, at the time, seemed frightfully good but in retrospect made me squirm.

Another stroke of luck about the same time was that I discovered that I had been placed on 'The List', a list of eligible bachelors suitable for deb dances, dinners, and even weekends. The list was basically compiled and run by an old lady called Lady St John of Bletsoe. Betty Kenward, the ageless Jennifer on *The Queen,* also had something to do with the list, I think. How anyone could have described me as eligible, I can't imagine, but there I was receiving invitations right, left, and centre from very grand people whom I had never met. I don't have to underline the advantages. Apart from meeting lots of girls, it saved a fortune in restaurant bills.

It was the beginning of the season and by May, though there was no sign of a job, I was enjoying a life of racing at the London courses during the day and eating, drinking, and dancing most nights. But it still took money to exist and my capital, by now down to two figures, was diminishing each day.

Fairly early in May, I went to one of Lady St John's balls at Londonderry House, just off Park Lane (and now a hotel). As I wandered idly in the drinking-room beside the ballroom, I spotted the mother of my best friend at school, Julian Mardon, in animated conversation with none other than Clive Graham. What an opportunity! For Dulcie Mardon was not only the mother of my friend but she had also introduced me to her niece, Carole Master, whom I was to marry two years later.

This was the opening that I needed. I minced over, greeting her effusively, and she, in turn, was equally effusive as she introduced me to

42

Clive, doing much of my own dirty work for me by adding that I was a racing fanatic and was dying to follow his profession.

Clive was, as always, pleasant and polite and, when I explained my ambition, invited me to write an article on a racing subject and send it around to him at 24 Draycott Avenue, his Chelsea residence. That to me seemed the breakthrough though, in retrospect, I should have realized that Clive must have said that sort of thing before and could hardly create jobs even though he did in fact have a considerable amount of advisory clout on the *Express*. I danced with my future aunt with double enthusiasm that night, principally because she seemed to have provided me with the key to my ambition, and also because she was incredibly glamorous which had presumably lured Clive to her side in the first place.

I duly wrote another pompous boring little essay and sent it around to Clive and there ensued an ominous silence of some ten days. Then, at around midnight on Saturday, 17 May, the telephone rang in our Cliveden Place house and, by good fortune, I was there and awake, chatting and drinking with my parents. It was Clive and he was fairly terse. 'Go around to the *Daily Express* at 4 o'clock tomorrow afternoon and there might be something for you,' he instructed.

I needed no second bidding, though there was one minor problem. I had been invited down to Oxford that Sunday for a party on the river and I was much looking forward to it. But it wasn't difficult for me to make a decision and I picked up the telephone first thing in the morning to cancel. Dan Abbott had also been invited to the same party and, unknown to me, had also received the same telephone message from Clive the previous night. Dan went to the party and I went to the *Express*.

At 4 o'clock, I was guided up through the middle of the vast news-room at the busiest time to present myself to the Sports Editor, Bob Findlay. He presided over the sports department which was situated then, and still is, on the far left-hand side of the news-room. He greeted me in his kindly, Scottish brogue. 'We want an easily digested form-guide, not too technical, that our racing readers can understand. Think you can do it?' I nodded enthusiastically.

I was given sheets of paper and carbons and told to write clearly and legibly and get started. The race-meetings for Monday were at Alexandra Park and Leicester so I wrote a brief form summary for each of the 12 races, underlining a selection. They decided to put a round black blob against my form selection for each race on the card.

They seemed satisfied with my first attempt and, to my great pride, I was able to open the back page of the *Daily Express* next morning and see my first attempts at national journalism in print. Furthermore, the *Express* then had a circulation of more than 4 million copies a day and was probably read by nearly a quarter of the entire nation.

It was a miracle. My starting salary was £12 a week for an experimental three-month period. And, when I successfully negotiated this trial, I was put up to £18 a week. When Dan heard all about this, he could hardly have been overjoyed though to his credit, he never made one unpleasant remark to me and our friendship continued unchecked and indeed, even burgeoned. But he must have been pretty annoyed with himself at his decision to go to the party since, with his experience as Clive's assistant, he might well have had an edge over me.

Since that time Dan and I have often discussed the whole saga and we both agreed that, for better or worse, the fates produced the right result. Dan left racing on a full-time basis when he moved on from his job with Clive but he is still a familiar figure on the racecourse. He and his wife, Sue, are often to be found at the stables of either Guy Harwood or John Dunlop helping out with owners and running syndicates and the like. In a small way they have also been quite successful owners.

I should explain, incidentally, that *The Londoner* was, by now defunct. It did not last very long and doubtless my own lack-lustre contribution was a factor in its demise. Zinnia survived, though, and greeted the vicar or registrar on several occasions, making it difficult for me to keep track of her as her name changed from time to time. Still, Lady Zinnia is a fairly unusual prefix to any surname and she can be tracked down in the gossip columns over the years.

The *Daily Express* in those days was a fine, thriving organization. Lord Beaverbrook, the proprietor, was world famous for his drive and personality and it was no coincidence that Winston Churchill had appointed him Minister of Supply during the war. Lord Beaverbrook quite simply got things done.

His son, Max Aitken, was an attractive man and a Battle of Britain war hero. He ran the organization with his father in the background but was always under his shadow. Arthur Christiansen, the editor, was another legendary figure in Fleet Street, who would patrol the entire editorial staff, including the sports department every afternoon between about 4 and 5 o'clock, even though his duties as editor were onerous. Thus I, a very junior 20-year-old, would be greeted virtually every day –

I worked a six-day-week – as was every other member of the department, by the great Christiansen, or Chris as he was universally known. I should add that I already knew Chris from Frinton since he had a house at Holland-on-Sea a mile or two up the coast and was a regular figure at the golf club, mostly at weekends. But, while this may have made a slight difference to the warmth and depth of his daily conversation with me, he would still have greeted me as he did even the youngest sub-editors around me.

The irony of this is that, once he retired, and I became more senior in what were to be my 30 years on the paper, I never again had the same rapport with any of the many subsequent editors and, in some cases, none at all. As the effectiveness and efficiency of successive editors diminished, so in most cases their accessibility lessened and virtually disappeared. And so, not by coincidence in my opinion, the paper declined to its present position and circulation of much less than half its 1956 sale. I say all this in a spirit of sadness since, even to the end, my memories and experiences with the *Daily Express* were mostly happy ones and I left of my own volition and with no acrimony. But it was largely the ineffectiveness of both successive editors and managements which prompted me to apply for and receive the voluntary redundancy terms which were offered to reduce the work-force in April 1986. I left just over one month short of my full 30 years, having succeeded Clive Graham as the 'Scout' on his premature death in August 1974.

For the first few years, I did my quota on the desk as a racing sub-editor as well as writing the form-guide each day. But after only a couple of years, I was also promoted to write the column 'Bendex' as well. This had nothing to do with its closeness to my own name but was an inherited column which had also at one time been written by Clive himself. It was a short step then to deputize as 'Scout' for Clive when he was either sick or on holiday and, for a while, I also had an additional weekly racing gossip-column, 'Racing Roundabout'. So in the late 1960s and early 1970s I sometimes made as much as four different contributions to the racing-page, either under my own name or a pseudonym.

None of this was allowed to intrude too often into my active social life. In fact, the job was complementary to my private life and the two fitted hand in glove. For instance, it was a privilege to be paid for travelling around the country, staying with friends at often great country houses for the race meetings at York, Chester, Cheltenham, Newbury, Ascot, Ayr, Doncaster, and Newmarket.

Indeed, it was a curious double life I led in those early days. I went into the office most days since the form-guide was reasonably complicated to compile, and I had to write with one hand while turning the pages of the form-book with the other. I never mastered the art of typing and neither did Clive nor our other famous colleague, Peter O'Sullevan. Occasionally when Clive had had a few drinks at lunchtime, not an infrequent occurrence, and he was waiting for his secretary, Betty Watts, a not inconsiderable toper herself, he would mutter an oath in that clenched-teeth manner of his and belt out an abusive message on the typewriter, using one finger with great force. Except when I was required to work late on the racing-page as a sub-editor, I would leave the office at about 7 o'clock in the evening, having gone in at about 3.30, and nip home to bath and change into my dinner-jacket or quite often white tie and tails. Then it was a dinner-party and often a dance.

Surprisingly, bearing in mind the morals of young girls in the mid-1960s onwards, it was extremely difficult to get beyond the kiss-and-cuddle stage with debs during that era. One or two of them supplied the full service but they quickly became marked women and had to retire to the country in semi-disgrace at the end of the season or else be perpetually marked as wanton women. Maybe I was just unlucky but I don't recall getting lucky with a deb in 1955 or 1956. I was sometimes dated up for the weekend by one of the certainties and would be looking forward to holing up with her in her flat, but then I would get a much more glamorous weekend invitation, and even if sex was off the menu, I would ditch her.

In spring the following year, as I embarked on another season of freebies I also started dating my future wife, Carole, with whom I had originally had a fairly long schoolboy walk-out before we had gone our separate ways. She was, you recall, the niece of Dulcie Mardon, who had introduced me to Clive Graham.

Carole had always been pretty but had blossomed during the period we had not seen each other and was now a model at the well-known fashion house of Victor Stiebel. I started going down to her family home again at Witley in Surrey. Her father, a somewhat austere man, tolerated me mainly because he was mad about tennis and we played together. He beat me one day and I never heard the end of it. Her mother, like her aunt, was very good-looking too and it was this that swayed me to consider marriage, even though I was still only twenty-one. Father, whose bark was a lot worse than his bite, was chairman of Friary Meux Brewery, based in Guildford. So, from time to time, when he was in a generous mood we would have excellent wine. And, as a clincher, her mother was an excellent cook whose lamb stew has never been equalled in my considerable experience.

By Royal Ascot time we were getting close to engagement but I had accepted an invitation to stay in a house-party given by Major and Mrs John Wills who lived near by. Their daughter Susan had also become a friend of mine. I was not sure how long the invitation extended but Carole had made me promise to come back on Thursday evening to take her out to dinner and spend the weekend with her. So I was none too popular when I announced that I would have to leave the party after racing on Thursday. I am glad to say that the Wills family did not hold it against me and I am still on good terms with Jean Wills, a close friend of my second set of in-laws.

It was as a result of leaving this grand house-party that Carole and I became engaged, she reacting to my proposal with the rather girlish reply, 'I'll think about it. I might.' She did not think long as she considered that this somewhat ungallant answer to my offer of commitment was an acceptance. Maybe she should have thought longer. She notified her mother, who was duly over-excited but we all agreed that I would have to break the bad news to her father and duly arranged to go down there the following weekend.

Subsequent history indicates that he knew full well the situation but he gave me one hell of a run about before I was able to corner him and notify him of my intentions. However, he could think of no valid objection except on a point of finance, a subject close to his heart, and he made it a condition of sale that we must wait nine months until the following May and I had to save £20 a week until then.

This was a particularly tough period. A nine-month engagement is no fun at all and there were several rows. My own family took a benign view of the situation, though they rightly thought and advised that I was much too young. They were never ones for laying down the law and were not overwhelmed when my father-in-law to be spelt out to them his terms and then asked them, 'What are you going to do about it?' My parents were so poverty-stricken, as usual, that they could offer nothing tangible but fortunately my future father-in-law volunteered to buy us a small house in Chelsea or thereabouts. So we approached the happy day, buying a tiny house, 2 Guthrie Street, a cul-de-sac just between the Fulham Road and Sidney Street in Chelsea. It was just what we needed and we were very lucky.

I had been saving diligently when I went, the week before our

47

wedding, to Newmarket to stay with new friends Tom and Solna Jones for the Guineas meeting, Wednesday until Saturday. My old school-friend Colin Ingleby-Mackenzie was also in the party and I remember he and I sharing a bathroom in which our host had thoughtfully placed a bottle of champagne on the edge of the bath.

It was that sort of week with parties overnight and silly games played after dinner. It was also extremely hot that year – the hottest spring week I can ever remember. To give an idea of how sunny and hot it was, I was able to use sunstroke as an excuse for not returning to London on Friday to do my work in the office. On ordinary days I could dictate over the telephone to special copy-takers, but on Friday evening I had to produce form for all the Saturday meetings, the busiest day of the week, and it was very unpopular indeed for me to put this marathon piece over the telephone. My sunstroke was, in fact, a hangover pure and simple, exacerbated by the sun perhaps, but somehow I struggled through the form for about twenty-four hours. We all had a wonderful time with endless laughs. Tom was a generous host and Solna an even more generous hostess since she paid most of the household bills and it was her house. Her father was the kindest of all men, Stanhope Joel, by now restricted to only ninety days a year in England having gone to live in Bermuda and Jamaica for tax reasons.

Thomson Jones, still a young and relatively new trainer, had devised a showy way of parading his horses after racing that week. Normally, owners and friends would go round stables in the evening, following the trainer from box to box while each horse stood with the rug off and was commented upon and admired. Tom's system that week was much more spectacular. He put out some chairs on the lawn for those too old or drunk to stand and circulated the butler with glasses of champagne or any other drink required. Then each horse was brought on to the lawn and paraded for general perusal.

It seemed like a throw-back to Edwardian style, or had he picked it up in Chantilly? Anyway it was most enjoyable as well as instructive though, sadly, it was never repeated since Solna quite reasonably banned it on the grounds that the horses' hooves cut up her lawn.

There was only one thing wrong with this idyllic week – my last full week as a bachelor – I could not back a winner. I lost and lost and lost and, as my nest-egg so diligently saved began to dwindle, I became more desperate. Tom himself trained a flying two-year-old and we tried to land a coup. The colt was called Harry Goldmine, named by Stanhope Joel after a ridiculous tabloid newspaper report containing some

48

rubbishy gossip about Tom and Solna, making reference to Solna's fortune and her marriage to Tom. Harry was Tom's actual Christian name though no one ever used it except tabloid newspapers. We all kept very quiet about the horse and went for a major touch at odds of a 100–6. He made a gallant effort to win, disputing the lead inside the final hundred yards, but was just run out of it by a good horse of Harry Wragg's, Simpatico.

By Saturday I was desperate but the bad luck continued when I made one final despairing plunge in the final race, a sprint. I backed a very good and very fast horse, Drum Beat, but even he could not make it and I drove home to London with Colin in a state of depression. I had blown the lot and had only a few pounds to lay my hands on. Then I cheered up. 'I've just remembered my grandfather's wedding present. He always gives his grandchildren £100 as a wedding-present,' I said. I had also taken the precaution of checking with my parents that the letter, written in his well-known handwriting, had arrived.

I could hardly wait to get my hands on the blue envelope and wrenched it open. There was a cheque inside all-right. I hardly bothered to look. After all, it was a formality. But then I opened the cheque and froze with horror – it was made out for £25! This was a disaster and I had virtually lost another £75.

The wedding was to be on Thursday at Oxted in Surrey. The choice of venue was dictated by my father-in-law's uncle, Charlie Master, also a past chairman of the Brewers' Society. He had lent his house near by for the reception as he had done previously for my wife's twenty-first birthday ball. We had booked to go for our honeymoon to a conservative, pleasant hotel in Palma, Majorca where the entire family of in-laws had holidayed for the past few years. We had paid for our air tickets but I still had a serious cash-flow problem. This was not eased on the first day of the Chester meeting, which ran from Tuesday till Thursday of the fateful week, when I backed a horse called Pundit, owned by Max Aitken's wife Vi, and ridden by the great Australian jockey Scobie Breasley. Pundit started at 5–1 and beat the favourite Prince Moon, ridden by Lester Piggott by an easy three lengths. To my horror though, Piggott lodged an objection and was awarded the race with Pundit disqualified and placed last as was the custom in those days.

I was now down to less money than I needed for the honeymoon and there was only one last hope. Tom Jones trained a three-year-old filly, Diplomatic Bag, owned by Solna, and she was due to run in the 3.15 race at Chester on the Thursday with the wedding scheduled for 3.30.

Diplomatic Bag was expected to win and I put my last £20 on her.

Having had lunch with my best man, Julian Mardon, Carole's cousin, and the ushers at the local pub, I organized a human chain to run from the church down to the telephone kiosk. One of my *Express* colleagues, Leslie Nicholl, was a guest at the wedding and he volunteered to ring the racing-desk at the office and get the result as it came over the tape-machine.

I stood nervously at the top of the aisle, awaiting the result. The congregation, mostly older relations, were rather touched by my nervous state. They would have been less moved had they known that it was a horserace at Chester that was causing my condition rather than the forthcoming nuptials. Then, only minutes before our own personal off, the news came buzzing through the human chain – Diplomatic Bag had won at 3–1. Mafeking had been relieved. I was momentarily disappointed by the price which I expected to be 7– or 8–1 but a win of £60 plus my stake of £20 was more than enough to cover immediate expenses and the honeymoon. Things were very cheap in those days.

This cheered up proceedings no end and I was able to turn around and greet the bride with a beaming smile which, once again, touched the congregation. Carole knew from my face the good news and I whispered almost too audibly, 'she won at 3–1', earning a frown of displeasure from my father-in-law who was leading her to my side.

So the wedding and reception were a huge success though I did have to ask the driver of the limousine taking us back to London afterwards to stop and buy an *Evening Standard* to confirm that Diplomatic Bag had not only obliged but had not been disqualified either.

We were to spend one night in London at the Hotel Meurice, situated above the famous restaurant, Quaglino's where we were thinking of dining. We sped to our room, intent on consummating the marriage and were interrupted by the telephone. 'This is the housekeeper. Can I come and turn down your bed?' she asked. 'I'm afraid you're too late,' I replied. In the evening we decided to go downstairs to Quaglino's and joined our families at dinner, much to their surprise.

The honeymoon in Majorca went smoothly, too, with hot sunshine throughout, though I got too confident one day before the end of the fortnight, stayed out on the beach too long, and suffered mild sunstroke.

My father-in-law had asked me to give up betting but I merely agreed to reduce my stakes and the very first Saturday back from our honeymoon I had three ten-shilling doubles and a ten-shilling treble, total investment £2, on three horses which all won. My luck had clearly changed and I won enough to buy us a radiogram, a combined radio and record-player for our drawing-room in the new house.

Registering My Colours

It was quickly accepted by my new family that racing – and betting – were an integral part of my life. My wife was as keen as I was and she encouraged me in the natural progression to ownership.

In the early autumn of 1960, Thomson Jones mentioned to me that the owner of a useful three-year-old flat-racer called Prince Igor wanted to sell and asked me whether I would be interested in buying the colt as a potential hurdler. I was interested but could not afford the asking price of £1,200 on my own so I approached my friend Lord James Crichton-Stuart, whom I had known for a year, to suggest that we went half-shares. The deal was done and I quickly registered my colours, plain peach jacket with a green-and-white quartered cap.

Prince Igor did well schooling over hurdles at home and the day dawned when he was due to run for us for the first time at Doncaster. Lord Jim was unable to attend because of his banking duties so Tom Jones and I were driven up at break-neck speed by the trainer's new young Irish assistant, Hugh McCalmont, who was due to ride for the first time on his own horse, Speedwell, in another race.

Prince Igor's reputation had preceded him and he started favourite. I had a good bet and was full of hope as he set off in front, jumping boldly at the first few flights of hurdles, until to our horror he fell, still leading, out in the country. Ironically, young Hugh and Speedwell led all the way in their race to win handsomely and his jubilation was such that his driving on the way home was little short of suicidal and we once found ourselves on the wrong side of a dual carriageway down the A1.

That was on a Friday and Jones, undeterred by this set-back, elected to run Prince Igor in a small race at unfashionable Warwick only eight days later. The horse showed no ill-effects from his fall and could hardly

52

be said to have had a race. As it was a Saturday, both owners and their wives piled into my car for the drive to Warwick and, to our amazement, Prince Igor started an even shorter priced favourite this time at the ridiculous odds of 6–4 on. Still we were looking forward to a win but to our immense disappointment the horse finished a moderate fourth and we thought the end of the world had come.

Shortly afterwards, I encountered one of my habitual financial crises and had to approach Jimmy, somewhat shamefaced, to break the news that I could no longer afford to maintain the partnership. He very sportingly agreed to buy out my half-share at par, £600, and I was out of racing.

The rest of the Prince Igor story can only make me laugh or cry. He came out in January, carrying Lord Jim's colours, at Doncaster again and won by 8 lengths. He reappeared at Haydock and this time scored by 12 lengths. He was then second in a high-class race before Jim for some inspirational reason decided to sell him at the Ascot Sales where the horse fetched £2,000 to the bid of David Crossley-Cooke. Two days later the horse went lame and never did much again.

There are two interesting sub-plots to the story of Prince Igor. Firstly, that tiny race at Warwick in which he so disappointed us by finishing only fourth turned out to be one of the races of the season. The winner, a French horse called Cantab, may only have been making his first appearance over hurdles but ended up the season unbeaten, the champion of his age-group and winner of the Triumph Hurdle at Hurst Park. The second horse that day came out next time and won a handicap against more experienced horses by no less than 25 lengths while the third also ran up a sequence of four wins directly afterwards. We had caught not one tartar but three as Prince Igor's subsequent form proved.

The other sub-plot was that the horse's purchaser, Crossley-Cooke refused to pay for him because of subsequent lameness though amazingly he kept him in training and actually ran in one or two races. He rode him himself. The British Bloodstock Agency, who had actually bought the horse on his behalf at Ascot, sued him for payment and the case came up some time later in the law courts.

A few weeks before the case, Lord Jim approached me and asked me if I would give evidence instead of him for the BBA: 'After all, you knew the horse as well as I did, if not better, and you know that it was not a crooked deal. But it would not look good for me in my position at Coutts to be seen involved in a case like this.'

Ironic that I, who had lost money on the horse, should end up giving

53

evidence about him on behalf of Jimmy, who had done well both in prize money and in capital profit. I didn't mind, however, since Jimmy had played very fair with me. I told the court that the horse had run regularly virtually every month for something like a year and a half before he was sold, proving his soundness and ability up till then. It was an open-and-shut case, and the judge found for the BBA against Crossley-Cooke, who had behaved extremely stupidly. Next time he appeared in court he received a two-year suspended sentence. He got himself into all sorts of trouble afterwards, to no one's surprise.

Our eldest son, Harry, was born on 23 October 1960, my twenty-fifth birthday. Among his godparents were Colin Ingleby-Mackenzie, who was to achieve fame the following year by leading Hampshire to the County Cricket championship; Nicky Mountain, who had introduced us to Sally Crichton-Stuart and her husband Lord Jim; Solna Thomson Jones; Virginia Walwyn, wife of Peter Walwyn; and my wife's brother, Melvyn. We also amazed the in-laws by adding a Greek Orthodox godfather, Constantine Dracoulis, who shocked us later by becoming the only Greek shipowner ever to go broke.

It was that year that Peter Walwyn started out as a trainer. Having tasted ownership with Prince Igor, I was eager to continue and I now made up my mind to plunge into the yearling market, though I did not really know enough about the make and shape of yearlings. At the Newmarket sales I studied them all with Carole – as keen a racegoer as I was – and fell in love with a chestnut filly with a huge white blaze on her face and white socks. She was by the stallion, Solonaway, out of a mare called Miss Gammon and I determined to buy her. At 680 guineas, she was mine for a minute at least – a long time in the sale ring. I don't know why the auctioneer waited so long but, eventually, another bidder came in, the well-known Epsom trainer Staff Ingham, and he and I carried on. Subsequently another trainer, the veteran Reg Day, nodded at 1,800 guineas which was too much for me. I had been looking around frantically for a close friend who might have come in half-shares with me but to no avail.

Reg Day trained the filly for the elderly Mrs Magnus Castello who named her Sweet Solera. Two years later Sweet Solera won both the One Thousand Guineas and the Oaks, the two Classics for fillies only. I have never again been as close to a owning a winner of that calibre.

Instead, I bought another filly with just as good a pedigree, by Petition out of Aleria. She went to be trained by Peter Walwyn, at

54

Windsor House in Lambourn. I couldn't think of a name for her but a week or so later we were invited to dinner at Cherkeley, near Leatherhead by Lord Beaverbrook. He took a great liking to my wife, while I sat next to Lady Beaverbrook and mentioned my yearling filly. She took down the breeding and a few days later sent a postcard with three suggestions on it, one of them Ambition. So that was it, Ambition, and the name turned out to be the best thing about her. She never won a race. The other yearling which we bought for my father-in-law, Jack Master – whom I had seduced into racing by then – was equally well named: Petit Poussin, being by Big Game out of Spring Chick. But here again the name was better than the racehorse and she was about as useless.

Peter Walwyn, however, did well with others of that first crop, among them Golden Wedding and Be Hopeful, and later went on to be champion trainer more than once, winning the Derby in 1975 with Grundy and many other great races. In fact there is a strong body of racing opinion that the greatest race ever was when Grundy beat Lady Beaverbrook's Bustino in the 1975 King George VI and Queen Elizabeth Stakes at the Ascot July meeting. Lady Beaverbrook had by now become heavily embroiled in racing as a successful owner.

The saddest and cruellest racing moment during that period was at Ascot in July 1960. Our friend Constantine Dracoulis had a horse running in the fourth race and invited my wife, whom he admired enormously, to accompany him into the paddock. The jockey was Manny Mercer, one of the very best, and elder brother of Joe Mercer, who went on to become champion jockey many years later.

Manny knew my wife and I and teased her as he doffed his cap to the owner. 'What are you doing in here? I'll report you to the stewards,' he joked to Carole. The horse did not win and half an hour later, Manny was jogging down to the start in front of the stands for the next race when his mount, Priddy Fair, reared up and fell back against the rails, crushing Manny's head against the upright. He was killed and the last race was abandoned as a mark of respect. Manny's brother Joe collapsed when he heard the news and my wife was distraught.

Poor Dracoulis was not the luckiest of owners. He did buy a good horse called Primera, who won him some useful races, but then he decided to sell the horse and Stanhope Joel came along and bought him at the end of July. Primera promptly came out at York in August and, in the hands of Lester Piggott, pulverized the opposition in the valuable Ebor Handicap, carrying top weight. Dracoulis who was in Greece at the time, consoled himself himself with a bet of £6,000, though he only received the starting price of 6–1 rather than the 10–1 and better which had prevailed till just before the off.

There was a classic Piggott story after this race. Primera had usually been ridden up till then by Willie Snaith, a cheerful little jockey who had been one of my earliest and best friends when I went into racing journalism and who had alsc been delighted to ride Diplomatic Bag and save my honeymoon. Willie was a good, hard-working jockey who enjoyed plenty of success but he was none too elegant and it was decided to replace him with Piggott.

Despite the disappointment of losing such an important winning ride, Willie was his usual cheerful and sporting self after the race and congratulated Piggott in the weighing-room. 'Hang on,' said Lester, 'do me a favour. I haven't got any money on me. Can you go and buy a case of champagne for me?' It was the tradition for winning jockeys to buy their colleagues champagne after a big race. Willie willingly bought the crate but there was no sign of any repayment during the next two weeks or so by which time the story had come to the ears of Stanhope Joel, the owner.

Lester went to Stan's office in the West End of London to collect his present and when he counted the money, he found that there was the price of a case of champagne missing.

'Here what's all this?' protested Lester in an angry mumble, 'it's not all here.'

'Oh yes it is,' replied Stan's son-in-law and racing manager, Paddy Brudenell-Bruce, who was handling the transaction, 'we've given the rest to Willie for the champagne.'

'No, no, no. You've got it all wrong,' protested Piggott, 'he wanted to buy it himself.'

Poor Dracoulis. When his shipping company collapsed, most of his colleagues and relations involved got out without losing all their money. But he lost the lot, being an honourable man and having signed various guarantees. He has lived in relative poverty ever since.

I have mentioned my association with Lord James Crichton-Stuart and our partnership in Prince Igor. His wife, Sally, I had met in Hampshire in 1959 and we got on well from the start. Our friendship lasted through incredible circumstances for more than 29 years.

Before I met her, I had seen Sally in the distance at various race meetings and also spotted pictures of her in the gossip columns and the glossies and had not been over impressed by her celebrated looks. To be highly critical, she was in the later stages of puppy fat in those days and I did not expect to be bowled over by her. So it was not so much her looks that impressed me when we first met that October weekend but her character. Her sense of humour was highly developed and she was very funny. My memory of that weekend was that she and I laughed and laughed. She laughed at my jokes and I laughed at hers. Some of them were pretty silly but we laughed all the more. What better basis for a relationship?

Soon Lord Jim, Sally, Carole, and I were inseparable, going out anything up to four times a week and meeting for the races as well.

Lord Jim was a decent enough fellow and I was always fond of him. But he could be dour and his preoccupation with making money was time-consuming and a slightly boring topic of conversation. There was no malice in him though, but I must admit it was slightly hard on my wife, as Sally and I did tend to monopolize each other's attention while Carole had to listen to long financial tales from Jimmy. Incidentally Jimmy, almost universally known as Lord Jim, subsequently became a director of Coutts Bank until his sudden and premature death a few years ago.

During the first year of our friendship, Sally was fining down, the slightly bloated look which hid her classic features melted away. Apart from myself, her closest friend and admirer at that time was David Niven, who spotted her charm and potential even before I did and who kept in touch with her all his life.

What kept the communal friendship going was Lord Jim's new-found enthusiasm for racing and he also became fascinated by the outgoing character of one of my closest friends Thomson Jones, the Newmarket trainer universally known as Tom.

The summer of 1961 was a golden one for me. I was happy with my baby son Harry, my friendship with Sally Crichton-Stuart was still going strong, and I hit a golden streak. My winnings for the season hit £10,000 in May when I had £300 each way at Sandown Park on a horse called Persian Lancer, owned by Stavros Niarchos who won at 10–1. Niarchos had come into racing for the first time as a diversion and his racing manager was Lord Belper, a great friend of mine then and brother-in-law of the Duke of Norfolk.

Ronnie Belper, who had lost an eye in a shooting accident, had been single since his wife Zara had divorced him and married the Royal steeplechasing trainer Peter Cazalet. We spent many uproarious weekends at his country pile, Kingston Hall, near Nottingham. Ron was a 'words more than action man' where ladies were concerned in those days but his favourite pastime was to rush up, accompanied by other male house-guests if possible, to give what he called 'hardship' to the female members of the party. This consisted of grabbing the lady of the moment, carrying her to the bed followed by some fairly harmless fumbling and then leaving the room again. 'Hardship' was timed to take place when the girls were changing for dinner and would thus be wearing only a dressing-gown, a towel, or perhaps underwear.

One evening Ron suggested to two of us, myself and Colin Ingleby-Mackenzie, that we should join him in a 'hardship' raid on an attractive girl little known to any of us. When we entered the girl's bedroom with the usual cries of 'Gotcha', or some such foolishness, we found her bedroom empty but there were watery sounds from her bathroom within. Ronnie motioned Ingleby behind a curtain and myself into the wardrobe, where he joined me. We stood like schoolboys in the darkness with the door open only a tiny crack, with Ron's one eye looking out. The wretched girl returned to her bedroom and stood admiring herself in the mirror, her towel dropping to the floor. Before we had a chance to pounce, however, the door of the bedroom opened and in walked the other member of the house-party who had been absent when our plan was formulated. He was not unexpected and glided over the girl to be greeted with a passionate embrace.

At this moment, Ron could contain himself no longer and tumbled out of the wardrobe with a mighty shout of triumph, stumbling towards the appalled and embarrassed couple and followed by myself and, from behind the curtain by Colin, both of us feeling ashamed of ourselves. The girl burst into floods of tears and gave vent to her anger on the wretched boy-friend. 'You knew, you knew,' she howled at him, beating him with her fists. And he was practically in tears, too, as in vain, he protested his innocence in the plot.

We all slunk out, Colin and I feeling by now like complete worms, and inevitably dinner was a somewhat down-key event that night. Next morning the girl packed her bags and left.

My wife had a theory that she put to the test with Ron. There was an element of risk involved but she was determined to try it. When it was her turn for 'hardship' and Ron burst in on her, she greeted him with a warm smile and said, 'Come Ron, come and get me. I've been waiting for this.' She sank back upon her bed, arms open with only a dressing-gown between her and a ghastly fate. But she was right. Ron

58

turned tail and fled and never bothered her again. It was the struggle he enjoyed, not the conquest.

Another time when we stayed there for the St Leger meeting at Doncaster, Lindy Guinness was among the guests and I introduced her to a bookmaker who happily took her 10s or £1 bets and gave her generous odds. I was beginning to have difficulty getting my bets on with this bookmaker as I was currently too successful so I devised a plan. I had a strong tip from a trainer for a horse running in the first race on the third day of the meeting and I instructed Lindy to go up to the bookie and place £100 each way. 'Don't worry,' I explained as she looked horrified. 'I will have £99 each way on it and you have £1 each way.' We watched as she placed the bet at odds of 4–1, and the bookmaker looked surprised though he had to take it. When the horse came home a winner, he looked up at the stand and saw us all laughing and cheering. He was furious but could do nothing about it.

Back in those days of 1961, I approached Royal Ascot with confidence as I was still winning and invested each week in stocks and shares. My stockbroker, Ian Cameron, only bought me the best and most sensible shares and I was building up a nice little portfolio. We had also purchased a new and bigger London house in Milborne Grove between Fulham Road and the Boltons, an upmarket residential area. I remember paying £11,000 mostly from the sale of our Guthrie Street house.

The bookmakers regarded my winning streak as a flash in the pan and were anxious to do business with me as my stakes rose and rose. But I was not doing particularly well coming up to the third race on the third day of the meeting, the Gold Cup. Cyril Stein, managing director of Ladbrokes, took an active part in those days in overseeing the betting both on and off the course. Now he is a City tycoon, immensely successful, who is more involved in the many other divisions of the Ladbroke Empire. But this June day in 1961, he approached me and said, 'What do you want to back?' I replied that I thought the favourite, Puissant Chef, was a certainty. 'He's 6–4 on,' said Cyril. 'That's too short for me,' I replied, to which he responded, 'You can lay 5–4 on, with me if you like.' I gave in and bet £1,250 to win £1,000 odds of 5–4 on. Puissant Chef ran abysmally and could finish only fourth.

I was not too upset by this as I could well afford it and we decided to go up to Stanhope Joel's box in the grandstand for the last two races. Ted Dexter, the England cricket captain, and a good friend of mine was also in the box. The bookmakers are also represented up in the grandstand behind the boxes where they do a roaring trade during Royal Ascot. I fancied a horse called Kathyanga in the Chesham Stakes and lazily asked my wife, who was going back to the bookmakers to make her own bet, to put £500 on for me with Ladbrokes. Ted Dexter went with her.

When she came back to the box she mentioned that the Ladbrokes representative, the elderly Arthur Burnett, had only laid me half my bet, £250, at odds of 2–1 but that she had put on the other half at the same odds with William Hill. We both thought this was rather odd since the firm's principal had only minutes earlier been inciting me to bet and happily taken £1,250. It didn't add up as my credit was good.

Kathyanga won which put me in the mood to have swipe in the last, the very tricky King George V Handicap, in which I fancied a horse called Vinca. This time I went down to Ladbrokes myself and placed £200 each way at starting-price and another £200 each way at Tote odds, which you could do in those days. Vinca won at 100–7, while the Tote paid more than 18–1. I collected about £8,000.

The next day we approached with supreme confidence. Stanhope Joel, whom we joined for lunch, and with whom we spent most of the day in his box, expected to win two races with En Tor and Silver Tor. He had already won the first race on the previous day with Bun Penny. All three were trained by his red-faced Irish trainer, Brud Featherstonhaugh.

En Tor, a two-year-old, won early on in the afternoon and I also backed the 10–1 winner of the tricky Wokingham Handicap, Whistler's Daughter. I plunged heavily on the easiest winner of the day, the previous year's Derby and St Leger winner, St Paddy, in the Hardwicke Stakes and finally in the last race of the day the stage was set for Silver Tor in the famous sprint, the King's Stand Stakes. Silver Tor duly stormed home and I had enjoyed my best ever day, netting well over £30,000. I received cheques the following week for £42,000, mostly from Ladbrokes – a lot of money in those days particularly as I was earning something ridiculous like £2,000 a year.

Incidentally, when I retold this story in slightly compressed form in a page of my Royal Ascot memoirs in the *Sporting Life* on Wednesday of the meeting in 1986, an angry letter was subsequently printed from a reader. He complained that my story was clearly a pack of lies since how could a racing correspondent earning £2,000 a year be betting in such figures and winning so much. The idiot had completely overlooked the

60

fact that gamblers play up their winnings.

There are two postscripts to this glorious week. The following Monday Cyril Stein phoned me and asked me to come to his office to discuss a matter of great urgency. He suggested a time which I could not make but I agreed to see him at about 3 o'clock, since I was having lunch at Buck's Club only two hundred yards from the old Ladbrokes' office in Old Burlington Street. 'Can't you discuss it on the telephone?' I asked. 'No, it's too important,' he replied tersely.

I lunched well as usual and rounded off with several glasses of the club port. So I was in good shape to face up to Cyril when I staggered into the Ladbrokes' office at the appointed hour. I was not overjoyed to be told that Cyril was not yet ready to see me since he had made such a point of the issue, but I filled in the time by strolling into the racing-room, which I did quite often as a favoured client, and studied the form for the meetings at Leicester and Folkestone, humble fare after the great Royal Ascot meeting. I picked out four favourites running at quarter-hour intervals and, still being kept waiting, placed a £100-yankee on them. A yankee consists of six doubles, four trebles, and a four-horse accumulator on the quartet – eleven bets – and if they all win you hit the jackpot. They did all win and I had netted something like another £8,000.

I then appeared before Cyril. He looked angry. 'Why did you use Ted Dexter's name to bet on Kathyanga last week?' he asked. I was dumbfounded. Equally angry, I countered, 'I don't know what you are talking about. I most certainly did not use Ted's name nor did I need to.'

But Cyril persisted. 'Arthur Burnett tells me that you tried to put on £500, getting your wife to use Dexter's name to obtain a better price. I believe him.'

Cyril was in no mood to examine the total lack of logic of such a ploy. Why should I have to use someone else's name when earlier that day he himself had been enticing me to place a big bet and at attractive odds? I was livid but he would not listen to the truth. It was obvious to me that Arthur Burnett, who was elderly and fairly doddery, had mistaken the name Benson for Dexter, particularly as Ted had been placing his own bet at the same time. The fact that Ted's bet was only £20 made it all the more anomalous.

Cyril was wholly unreasonable and ended the meeting by saying, 'I don't want you to be able to say that Ladbrokes have closed your account. From now on you can only have a bet of up to £10 to win. Nothing larger. No each way. No doubles, trebles, and accumulators. No Tote odds, no racecourse prices, just starting-prices.'

61

That was it. But I had the last laugh. 'You are quite wrong in this matter. But I must tell you that your rudeness in keeping me waiting has cost you another £8,000,' and I told him about my winning yankee.

That night I went to a cocktail party up near Lord's Cricket Ground and I regaled all and sundry with this story. Suddenly, in walked Dickie Gaskell, a good friend who now betted on the rails for Ladbrokes since they had taken over his own Stratford-based company. Poor Dickie. He was always having to face up to complaints from his many friends who were Ladbroke punters and this was a tough one for him. Basically, Dickie was scared of Cyril and although he promised to see what he could do, and expressed outrage, I knew it would be hopeless.

Through all of this, Sally and I remained as close as ever and she came with me after lunch one day in July 1961 to my favourite jeweller, Richard Ogden, in the Burlington Arcade off Piccadilly to help me choose a birthday present for my wife. I was still at the peak of a golden spell of luck then, and I was prepared to be generous even though I wasn't getting on all that brilliantly with Carole.

Sally was wearing a very simple dark-blue suit, very plain and she looked magnificent. Richard Ogden thought so too and was enthusiastically trying his fine antique pieces on her to see how they looked. 'You should be a model,' he commented prophetically since Sally did become a successful model two or three years later.

In the end I could not choose between two wonderful items, a diamond necklace containing three sapphires set in a triangle and another more simple sapphire necklace, so I bought them both.

When I presented them to my wife she was indeed delighted as she should have been but her first words were a trifle bitter: 'Just wait until I show these to Sally. She'll be green with envy.'

The other postscript is that I went into the big Goodwood meeting at the end of July winning £96,000 on the season and keen to break through the £100,000-barrier. Inevitably, my luck changed and I lost about £12,000 at the meeting. I was too stupid to stop and by the end of September I had lost the whole lot and more since I had to sell all my newly acquired shares at a loss, the market having gone down steadily during July, August, and September. I was in at the peak and was selling at anything of up to a third off the top.

Ladbrokes got none of these losses, of course. It all went to other bookmakers. And I was set for a long period in the doldrums. The irony was that Cyril and I then met and made up our differences. It was too late for him to get his money back but we have remained on good terms ever since.

That year, still in the money but only temporarily, I decided in August to go to Deauville for a fortnight's holiday. By then I had bought a new horse, Kopa, in France and he was due to run in Deauville on the Saturday at the beginning of our holiday. There was one snag. Stanhope Joel was due to host one of his wonderful parties at Newmarket that night but I solved that one by chartering a small plane to take us to Deauville for the day on Saturday, return to Newmarket that evening and then take us back to resume the holiday the following day. Simple when you've got a little cash.

But Saturday did not turn out so well. The horse ran badly and I was terribly sick in the aeroplane even though the journey to or from the north of Normandy did not take much more than an hour. What with this and Saturday night's party with the champagne flowing, I was not feeling too good as we made the return trip to Deauville. I was like a sheikh with his harem since apart from my own wife, I also took Sally and another Sally, wife of John Bardsley. Their husbands were due to join us in Deauville some time later. As we walked into the old-fashioned airport building, we were welcomed by the single Customs man who remembered us from the previous day. As I returned his greeting, I keeled over in mid sentence, hitting the ground with such a force that my arm was bruised for days afterwards, and lay there blue in the face and rigid. I naturally gathered all this information from the girls later on.

The 'harem' was much alarmed, the more so when the local doctor arrived, took one look and muttered 'cardiac' as he injected me straight into the heart. I was about one-quarter conscious while he was performing this terrifying deed but I can still remember the blast of his garlic breath. I was placed on a stretcher in a makeshift ambulance and driven, together with the girls, to the Normandy Hotel, where we were due to stay, rather than the hospital. As one tends to do when recovering from some shock incident, I was feeling somewhat light-headed and did not really appreciate what had happened. I remember being carted into the hotel on the stretcher and catching sight of the well-known racehorse owner Gerald Oldham, a friend of mine who was standing on the steps looking at me in horror. 'Don't know what they're doing. There's nothing wrong with me,' I assured him jauntily.

I rested up in my room for the rest of that evening but felt fine the next morning so we continued our holiday. And what a holiday it was since I was constantly escorting round what the French called 'Les trois belles Anglaises'. The centre of life in Deauville then, as now, was the racing and the casino, plus some light sea-breezes at cocktails by the beach and an open-air lunch, and occasionally after racing, the polo.

Gregory Peck was there that summer, at the height of his fame, with his new French journalist wife. He became friendly with us though not as friendly as he would have liked since his wife was very jealous of my 'harem'. But I did have an amusing incident with him at the races one day. We all had tickets which took us freely into all enclosures including the area behind the winner's enclosure where the jockeys weigh in and out and owners and trainers meet up to discuss their business. I had just walked into this area one afternoon when there was a commotion behind me and I turned to see the gateman, who never even asked for our tickets firmly blocking the way to Peck and booming 'Non, non, non, pas ici.' I was appalled to see the great man practically being manhandled so I doubled back, took him by the arm and mumbled in his ear, 'Just say "Proprieteur Anglais",' so Hollywood's number-one star was forced to approach the recalcitrant gateman and mouth in that inimitable deep American drawl, 'Proprieteur Anglais'.

My racing luck now began to fail me while Lord Jim's fortunes maintained an upward trend. It was during that summer that Tom Jones went to Ireland and bought two three-year-olds, one of them, called Rubor, for £2,000 which was intended for me and the other, Wild Fast, for £3,750 for Jimmy. However Lord Jim, although a rich man, pleaded that he could not afford this animal and so Jones asked me to get him out of a hole and switch. I was going through my short flush spell and thus agreed.

The day came when the two horses, who were trained to take part in similar kinds of races, were to have their first run in England. Tom had decided to put Rubor, belonging to Lord Jim, over hurdles at once and ran him in a race at Newbury called the Freshman's Hurdle, for which he also saddled the favourite, Grey Gauntlet. He thought my horse Wild Fast would benefit from a run on the flat before being put over hurdles and he entered him for the last race on the same card, a 12-furlong event for horses which had never won. The price Tom had paid for Wild Fast, I should emphasize, was based on potential rather than achievement so far.

The eternal foursome, Jim, Sally, Carole, and myself decided to travel down on the race special from Paddington which stops right by the paddock and takes just under an hour. There was much laughter and joking as we enjoyed our lunch on the downward journey in our reserved seats, most of the noise emanating from Sal and me.

Rubor was not in the least bit fancied – neither was Wild Fast – but Jim kept mumbling, 'I think I'm going to win today. I feel it in my bones. I've told everyone at the bank to back him.' This was ridiculous because Tom had stressed the fact that Rubor was only running to gain experience and was to be ridden by an unknown rider called Curren while the stable jockey, Johnny Gilbert, would be on the much-vaunted Grey Gauntlet, who had some good form in Ireland. To add piquancy to the story, I was racing manager for the owner of Grey Gauntlet, Major Douglas Vaughan, who ran a plantation in Jamaica and was unable to be present that day.

I need hardly tell the rest of the story. Grey Gauntlet came to the final hurdle with the leaders and looking a sure winner but was out-speeded on the run-in by Rubor. And Jim had a fiver on the Tote which paid odds of more than 60–1.

And this was meant to be my horse! I was pleased for Jimmy and put up with his gloating during the longish gap before my race which was the last on the card. After all, perhaps Wild Fast could do the same as Rubor, as Tom had been telling me he was the better horse. But Wild Fast could not do the same, nor could he even finish second, third, or fourth. He tailed in plumb, bang last in a field of about twenty runners. My cup of woe did indeed flow over. On the journey back, I could hardly eat the delicious tea which was one of the features of those race trains. Even I, the greatest of losers, found it hard to raise a smile, and my wife, not quite such a great sport, was in a downright sulk.

Sally was totally sympathetic and did her best to support me while Jim chortled and gloated his way through his tea and most of ours, too. 'I told you I'd win,' he kept repeating, impervious to the fact that this is quite the most irritating remark that can be made by one racing-man to another in such circumstances.

Rubor went on to greater things while Wild Fast continued on his trail of disaster.

Poor Jim. He was never really the right man for Sal as even his closest friends and relations would surely admit. They were very young when they married and Sal had tried to get out of it shortly beforehand. Jim was a simple soul and could not control the pressure of handling a desperately attractive, bright, and outgoing wife. Inevitably they separated though, as Jim was a Roman Catholic, it took a long time before he would agree to an annulment. Happily he found the right woman the second time round – Anna Rose Bramwell, sister of Michael Bramwell, director of the National Stud at Newmarket. They were very happy and had three children.

It was certainly no fault of Sally's that her marriage failed. They were just incompatible. She and I continued to see a great deal of each other through perhaps not quite as much as we went our separate ways from time to time. One of the last things my wife did while we were still married was to set up Sally with her own model agent, Peter Lumley, the top man at the time.

Adverse Fortune

THE experience I had with Rubor and Wild Fast should have signalled to me that my golden summer was at an end, and indeed it wasn't long before I was in financial difficulties again. My father's death on St Andrew's day, 30 November 1961, at the age of sixty-five, naturally deepened my gloom.

I was upset when I got the news that afternoon. I was having a drink at about 5.30 with Colin Ingleby-Mackenzie at his house in Dovehouse Street, Chelsea when the office rang. It was Leslie Nicholl, the man who had conveyed the details of Diplomatic Bag's victory at my wedding, who had taken on the unpleasant task to break the bad news to me. Colin was very sympathetic, the more so since he knew my father, whom he called 'The Guv'. Our two fathers had been old friends and fellow members of the Union Club.

Colin and I were due to go to dinner that night at the Hyde Park Hotel – a B. G. Whitfield's old boys' annual reunion. We decided that it would be best for me to go since Whitfield had been a good friend of my father's. The news would have ruined his evening so we resolved not to tell him until the next day. To carry the verbal load to cover up my subdued mood, Colin insisted on sitting next to me throughout the reunion.

The trouble came on the publication of my father's will. When he died, I owed the bookmakers quite a lot of money but I was able to say to them, 'Sorry boys, but my father has just died and you know that wills take some time to sort out. Lay off me and you will all be paid as soon as possible.' However, I soon discovered that all I was getting was his opal tie-pin and his guns, which one of my half-brothers lost anyway. My brother received his fob-watch and that was it. However, I kept my head down until one evening six months later I was idly thumbing through the *Evening Standard* in the underground on my way back from Fleet Street when I noticed a column headed 'Wills of the day', and, to my horror, spied the desperate message – after two or three estates valued at about the million mark – 'Stephen Benson, Recorder of Abingdon, Deputy-recorder of Oxford, of 21 Cliveden Place, London SW1 – nil.' It was like a football result and it was there for all to see. All did see it and the first bookmaker was on the telephone as I walked through my front-door.

I was desperate and it was Stanhope Joel who came to the rescue. Having a drink with him in the Connaught Hotel one evening, he commented that I looked a bit low and I admitted that things were bad.

'Come and have lunch with me here tomorrow and we'll all go down on the boat-train to Southampton and you can tell me all about it,' he suggested.

So I travelled down on the train with 'The Squire', as we all knew him, and his benign wife Gladys, known affectionately as Ma. We went up to their spacious state-room abroad the QE2 and Stan gently established that £11,000 would save my bacon. 'You'll get that next week. Pay me back whenever you like if you can.' I should add that, unusual in this sort of situation, Ma Joel had been well aware of what was going on and seemed to encourage it. This was typical of her generous spirit which is seldom the case with a wife if she hears that her husband is about to part with money to anyone but herself.

This was an enormous load off my mind and, sure enough, the money came from his London office next week. I repaid the office in small instalments over several years until I had reimbursed nearly £10,000. Then one day I ran into Stan in Deauville and I reiterated my gratitude to him for saving me, mentioning that I had repaid nearly all the capital. 'Good Lord,' he said, 'you've done quite enough of that. I'll let the office know.' And I never heard another word. Whereupon Stan ordered a bottle of his favourite champagne, Veuve Clicquot, which we finished without any trouble at all.

There was never a better host that Stan Joel. In the early 1960s, we would go and stay with him in Jamaica at his house in Ocho Rios, midway between Kingston and Montego Bay. Sometimes we stayed in his main residence, Content Hill, a few hundred yards inland from the sea, and at others at the beach house, Clearwater, which was almost equally comfortable and in some ways more convenient. Stan bought the Sans Souci Hotel just down the road and did a deal with the famous Cipriani in Venice to try and reproduce the food and service of the

Italian hotel in a Jamaican atmosphere. Although Sans Souci was not bad, and we had some fun there under the new arrangement, it never really worked because the Jamaicans weren't able to live up to the standards of the Cipriani.

I remember one year at Clearwater when the England cricketers were in Jamaica and several of them came over for the day, among them Freddy Titmus, who had lost a couple of toes in a boating accident, and Geoff Boycott, who must have been on his first tour. Contrary to his later dour image, Boycott was enormous fun and made non-stop jokes.

Stan was a cricket enthusiast and had a box at the famous Sabina Park ground in Kingston. One day he was wearing his favourite bright-red trousers and he walked around the perimeter of the ground in front of the teeming hoards of local supporters. 'Look out, boys, here comes de new ball,' shouted a local comedian.

I was always rather saddened by the manner in which Stan spent the last years of his life. He was the most English of Englishmen and his pleasures were all to be found at their best in Britain. He loved racing, shooting, cricket, wine, women, and song. In his case the wine was Veuve Clicquot and the song could mainly be heard at parties, of which he gave a great many. He was a bringer of happiness. So he missed a lot of enjoyment when he decided, because of his three daughters and their families, to become a tax exile. He still used his 90 days a year in England. In the second half of the 1960s, he was taken ill here and was wrongly advised by lawyers that he could go into hospital on compassionate grounds even though over-running his time allowance. Too late it was discovered that the lawyers had boobed or that the Inland Revenue had changed its mind. Stan came over to Europe and was all set to fly from France to see his filly, Lupe, run in the Oaks. As she was about to leave for Epsom, his advisers telephoned advising him against coming, so he was unable to watch Lupe win and could come no nearer home that Deauville and Paris for the rest of his life. I would meet him on the racecourse or in the casino but he was always keen to hear the news from England and sad that he was no longer part of the scene. Gladys Joel was taken seriously ill and remained in Bermuda for the last years of her life. I am not sure that she fully took it in when Stan died some years before her.

We were staying with Stan and Gladys in Jamaica in January 1961 when the first-ever James Bond film, *Dr No*, was being made just up the road. I remember meeting Sean Connery in the evenings, and also his glamorous co-star, Ursula Andress. She was unknown until then but made a great impact in a memorable scene when she emerged dripping from the Ocho Rios sea. We would have dinner with one of the locals, Blanche Blackwell, where Connery would eat his chicken squatting on the floor in a most unlike-James-Bond fashion.

Blanche's son, Chris Blackwell, who had been to Harrow, was the local technical adviser on that film and later went on to found Island Records, a prosperous music business. His first protégé was the little black singer Millie, but he made his fortune with the aid of the great reggae singer Bob Marley. He also had Stevie Winwood, U2 and Bryan Ferry recording for him.

One year I did not stay with Stan was January 1962 when I went with Colin Ingleby-Mackenzie a little further down the coast to Port Maria to write his book. Colin had made his name as captain of Hampshire county cricket team when they won the championship in 1961 and was something of a national celebrity. Since he and I both suffered from the same sickness – betting on horses – we thought it would be a good idea to cash in on his celebrity and write a book. It was to be published by my own organization, Beaverbrook Newspapers, who did that sort of thing in those days, and serialized in the *News of the World,* who also offered Colin a contract for a weekly column.

To find the necessary peace and quiet, we stayed at a banana plantation owned and run by Major Douglas Vaughan, a somewhat severe figure who was also Stan's agent in Jamaica and a great racing man. He had owned a horse, First of the Dandies, which had finished second in the 1948 Grand National and had appointed me as his racing manager. His son Charles, known as Jeremy, won the 1961 Grand National with Nicolaus Silver.

When we arrived at the plantation, Douglas dropped a bombshell. 'I think I should tell you that I am divorcing my wife and citing Lester Piggott.' I was astounded because although I knew his wife Golly, and thought her attractive enough, I had always regarded her as a considerably older woman and Lester was almost exactly the same age as myself. I muttered something about not thinking this a very good idea but Douglas seemed determined. He did in the end drop his threat to cite Lester but went ahead with the divorce.

Lester's attitude to me did seem to change for some years and I only discovered something like a decade later from our mutual friend Charles St George that Lester had always believed that I had grassed on him. Far from grassing, I knew nothing about the situation and was so naïve that I would not have believed it anyway. Charles also told me, incidentally, that Douglas had tried to join him with Lester in the lawsuit.

The book was written in unorthodox manner, but Colin and I quickly realized that the faster we got the job done, the more time we would have to play. Douglas arranged for a tall blonde Canadian called Myra to perform the secretarial duties. Each day, Colin and I would enjoy a massage, half an hour each, while we discussed the day's topics and I took a few notes. I had already conducted a few interviews with relevant characters, usually cricketers like Denis Compton and Dennis Silk, the headmaster of Radley, before we left.

Then I would retire to the end of the swimming-pool and dictate to Myra who would take it all down in shorthand. Colin had little to do but fool around with my wife in the swimming-pool and occasionally answer my shouted questions or come over and make rude remarks.

By the first Friday night, Myra left for the weekend with 28,000 words in shorthand which she promised to type up by Monday morning. On Monday we waited in vain for her but there was no sign of her and we grew more and more worried. 'Come with me,' growled Douglas, our host, 'I'll flush her out.' We went to a little village of huts where Douglas stormed into several but drew a blank. Then Douglas came out of another pre-fab with a triumphant glint in his eye. 'We've got her now,' he said. We motored to a run-down shack overlooking the sea and there she was, drink-sodden, my precious notes scattered around the floor and her local lover cowering in the darkness. Douglas was rough and tough as she floundered drunkenly, trying to make some sort of sense and grab her clothes.

Whatever he did or said did the trick. Myra arrived at the side of the pool an hour later, very sheepish, took more dictation and within two days she had caught up with all the typing and never gave us any more trouble.

We finished the book in two weeks and three days, giving us some time to play. One evening Douglas took us over to Kingston to have dinner with the local bookmaker. Colin took a great liking to the extremely attractive, dusky hostess whom we took to be the wife. Clearly his interest was becoming too close for comfort and the host invited him to his study where he had something to show him. The bookmaker, Merrick Watson, unlocked the drawer of his desk and brought out a large revolver, which he smoothly extended towards Colin. 'This is how we deal with unwanted intruders out here,' he said, looking menacingly towards Colin. The message was loud and clear and

71

we left the house soon afterwards.

The book was named *Many a Slip*, an apt title in every respect suggested by Stanhope Joel. It did not do terribly well and we only made about £1,000 out of it but we got a further £5,000 from the *News of the World*. We put the whole £6,000 in a new account, Coverpoint Enterprises, in Colin's bank alongside Harrods, but I was forced to withdraw my 25 per cent, £1,500 within days to pay the more pressing bookmakers. Colin's £4,500 lasted a little longer, and the Coverpoint Enterprises account must rank as one of the shortest and least profitable in the history of Lloyds Bank.

The decade which had begun so well for me was now in full decline. The year 1962 saw my financial troubles becoming almost insupportable. We were involved in a horrendous car crash in the South of France from which we were lucky to escape with our lives.

It all started when Mark Watney, an attractive, amusing friend of mine popular with almost everyone, rang up from Cap d'Antibes in the south of France and suggested that we went down there and joined him at the Racquet Club, down the road from the famous Eden Roc. The Racquet Club was associated with a club of the same name in Miami and was owned by a tennis fanatic, Roy Evans, the man who invented the Jeep. Mark had worked out some deal for us since we were desperately short of money and part of that deal was that I should play tennis every evening with the proprietor against opponents chosen by him. He was a strange, chunky little man who lived Spanish hours. He would stay up very late, accompanied by his extremely nice blonde girl-friend, and not re-emerge from his quarters until about 4 p.m. the next day.

It was all very well being Roy's partner but he was not all that good, being already in his fifties and far from a natural athlete, and however well I played, we were sometimes beaten. He did not like that one little bit and I always had to take the blame. Still, it was a small price to pay since it was a friendly little hotel with all the facilities that we needed.

One day we ran into Jimmy Goldsmith, who had chartered a yacht and was cruising around the area. Jimmy, whose father, Frank Goldsmith owned the Carlton in Cannes, is half French, completely bilingual, and a good man to be with. He asked us to join him in a three-day cruise. We recruited Sally Crichton-Stuart, who happened to be in the south of France at the time, Mark Watney, and another girl. We set sail westwards and decided that it would be amusing to visit the nudist island, the Isle du Levant, a few miles off the coast from Lavandou. We arrived off-shore at about midday and the men decided to take the dinghy to the beach to examine life among the nudists and also to book somewhere for dinner that night.

So Jimmy, Mark, and I strode ashore, feeling very self-conscious as it was compulsory to strip off and we stood out like sore thumbs with our white bottoms. However, we quickly got the hang of things and even managed, entirely due to Jimmy's grasp of the language and natural command, to book in for dinner at the only hotel on the island in the tiny built-up area, Heliopolis, and also to charter the only taxi to meet us at the jetty at 7.30 and take us up the hill.

The arrangement all went smoothly. In the evening it is generally conventional to wear normal casual clothes – shirt and trousers or even a dress for the girls – though some of the hard-line residents stick to what is known as 'le minimum' and is just that.

The taxi turned out to be a left-hand drive Land-Rover but two of us fitted in front with the driver and the other four sat in the back. The journey up and the dinner all went well and, as I had volunteered to pay, I had a certain amount of money on me which proved vital later. When we had finished we piled back into the Land Rover and two or three locals perched themselves on various extremities, one on the front, two on the tail-board to hitch a lift down the hill.

My wife and I sat alongside the driver in the front and I remember vividly that he had a strange, half-smile on his face. When we were all aboard, we told him to go and, without saying anything and without switching on the lights or the engine, he let off the hand-brake and started coasting down the heavily rutted and stony road. From front and back we told him to stop, in the case of Jimmy in commanding French, but he took no notice and we started picking up speed as the road became steeper. It was winding, too, with a precipice down on the left and a sheer wall to the right with only the sea at the bottom.

The noise by now was considerable, with the wheels banging the ruts and stones making a fearful clatter while those in the back were still shouting instructions. I was obviously frightened but was desperately trying to figure out a way of stopping the car before it was too late. But I would have had to stretch across my wife to reach the wheel and wrenching that would have been hopeless and possibly fatal. There was no escape. The driver still had his fanatical half-grin and seemed in some sort of trance as he hung grimly to the wheel.

Finally, there was a louder clatter, the car seemed to leap in the air and there was a great crash as we turned over. I remembered nothing more for a short period, probably a minute or two, and then became aware of being half-trapped underneath the Land-Rover which had overturned. I crawled around for some seconds, shouting out names, but could find no one, the dreadful realization dawning on me that I might be the only one alive. I then managed to crawl out, stood up to find a battlefield scene with people groaning and crying, several lying by the roadside. I could see Carole and she looked all right as I walked towards her. She turned and saw me and let out a great gasp of horror. Only then did I realize that I was drenched in torrents of blood: there was a gaping hole on the right side of my head and an ear was hanging off.

Two of the hitch-hikers were in a bad state and Mark Watney was in terrible pain with serious chest injuries. The rest of our group were more or less all right though Sally had a badly bruised arm. I was particularly worried about my wife since she was pregnant but she was made of stern stuff and, when she had landed on top of the driver when we overturned, had punched and kicked the living daylights out of him so that he had run away into the night.

I lay down again on the side of the road, my shirt ripped off as attempts were made to control the flow of blood. I must have passed out again because when I came to I thought I had gone to heaven. Leaning over me was a woman with an enormous bosom practically touching my chest. She was a local, of course, wearing 'le minimum' but my loss of blood prevented me from taking much further interest in her charms. Eventually an army ambulance arrived from the military base on the island and Mark and I were put on board. We each thought the other was dying as we trundled up the hill again. Once there, I had a thickly padded bomb-dressing strapped to my bleeding head and ear, which was almost cut clean in two. The others went back to the boat to summon assistance from the mainland.

Meanwhile, we waited at the army base for what seemed an eternity but was in fact about two and a half hours. It took Jimmy some six or eight telephone calls to doctors on the mainland before he could persuade one to come out in a motor-boat and collect us. All the others thought it was a practical joke since the idea of a car crash on the island seemed quite ludicrous.

We were finally taken back to the quay and loaded gingerly aboard the speed-boat. Poor Mark was in terrible pain and his chest bone, the sternum, was sticking out, completely broken. But my blood made me look worse and I was taken aboard on a stretcher while he had to walk.

When we docked at Lavandou, I was supported firmly by each arm to go to the waiting ambulance but I first had to request a pause to relieve myself against a wall, a natural reaction in cases of injury and shock. I started off and it went on and on and on. People around, and my two supporters began to mutter admiringly and by the end of this marathon performance, I received a spontaneous round of applause.

We were taken up to the hospital in the little town of Hyères and were placed side by side on trolleys in a corridor. I had on only a pair of beige trousers and the zip had burst during the accident. My shirt and shoes were gone by now. After a while, Mark was wheeled away and I was left all night, very frightened, while I heard the ringing chimes of a clock outside my window every quarter of an hour from 2.30 onwards. I suppose I got some sleep but I was confronted at around 8 o'clock in the morning by a hatchet-faced matron figure who demanded, 'de l'argent'. It was then that the good fortune of my electing to pay for dinner became evident as I fumbled in my pocket and found a 500-franc note, about £40, which I handed to her.

This seemed to satisfy her but some half an hour later she returned, equally hatchet-faced and said in French, 'That was for your friend. We want the same for you.' This time, frightened and injured as I was, I lost my temper in my illiterate French and she retreated. I had assumed that Jimmy would have made the necessary arrangements, but as is often the case, the message had not been received.

Soon after 9 o'clock I was wheeled into a bright room which was presumably the operating theatre. To my fury, I was then made to wait for half an hour while one of the hitch-hikers was brought in and given attention first. One of his buttocks had been sheered clean off and this was sewn back on again.

Finally, I was wheeled centre stage whereupon the door opened and in walked about a dozen young men – local medical students as I later discovered. They were followed by a young man in his late twenties, wearing jeans and an open-necked shirt showing an extremely hairy chest. He came over, looked down at me, and gently unwrapped and took off the bomb-dressing on my head. As it came away there was a great gasp and cries of 'Oh la la' from the students as they recoiled from the gory right side of my head.

The hairy-chested doctor began sewing, without anaesthetic which I later discovered was correct procedure in such cases. It lasted an eternity and my most frightening moment was when he forced the needle through the cartilage at the base of my ear to sew that together. I

75

thought he would pierce my eardrum, remembering my small son's nanny's experience in the war. She had her eardrum pierced by a doctor in Canada and was deaf thereafter.

The doctor finished his work on me and I was finally wheeled back to a proper bed in a private room. When my wife and friends came to visit me soon afterwards, I suffered from a fit probably caused by a combination of the trauma and lack of sleep and had to be held down by about four doctors and nurses while I thrashed around.

When I got back to London some eight days later, my own doctor took out the stitches and there were eighty-six of them – the work of a master. My luck had been in. The young doctor, so casually dressed, who had operated on me was a brilliant young plastic surgeon from Paris, Dr Tallent, and he had been down there to give a lecture to the students gathered around me. He had certainly lived up to his name, and I would like to thank him now. You have to look very close at the side of my head and ear to see any sign of a scar.

Unfortunately, poor Mark's luck had been as bad as mine was good. His doctor or surgeon did not do a good job. His sternum was put together and six broken ribs were also diagnosed. But two broken vertebrae near the nape of his neck went unnoticed and thus he remained in agony when we were taken by ambulance down the coast to the Sunny Banks Anglo-American hospital in Cannes. When we arrived there, the door of the ambulance was flung open and we were confronted by a very English matron: 'Well, well, well. What have you two naughty boys been up to then?' was her opening sally.

We stayed there for a few pleasant days and I was soon fit enough to be flown back as a pampered invalid passenger to England and my own bed and doctor. Mark was meant to stay on for some while but, against advice, discharged himself although, because of his undiagnosed vertebrae, he sat and walked with his shoulders at a crazy angle, still in enormous pain. When, finally, he was correctly diagnosed, he was made to wear a plaster cast around his neck and shoulders which he hated and removed most unwisely a lot of the time.

He never fully recovered from this injury which affected his whole sunny nature. His moods became variable and, about a year later, he had a ridiculous tiff with his girl-friend when she was not ready to go out to dinner at the right time, went back to his flat off Grosvenor Square, and blew his brains out with a shot-gun.

My wife showed no ill-effects from the crash and our second son, Edward, was safely born on 26 February 1963. His only problem has been with his eyes from time to time and doctors have agreed that this could have been triggered by the accident, even though it occurred seven months before this birth.

Mark and I, through his English lawyer who practised in the south of France, tried to sue the owner-driver of the Land-Rover, who turned out to be also the owner of the hotel. We got absolutely nowhere though the wretched man was taken to court and fined the massive sum of 10 frances – less than £1! We were, I suppose, lucky to have survived and achieved as much or as little as we have. Sally became a good wife to the Aga Khan and a good mother to their three children. My readers in the *Daily Express* may have had cause to regret my survival but Jimmy Goldsmith (for some time now Sir James) is one of the world's richest and most successful business men, head of an empire which stretches across the globe.

By Christmas 1962, it was clear that we could no longer afford the house in Milborne Grove and we were forced to sell it privately to the widowed Lady Hesketh, who allowed it to be used as a London pad for her son Alexander and some of his relations and friends. She gave us £18,750 which showed us a good profit and enabled us to purchase a less attractive house but with a suitable garden for the children near the Berrystede Hotel at South Ascot, only a couple of miles from the racecourse.

The move to Ascot was the beginning of the end of our marriage. I was offered a job as a sort of greeter by John Mills, the owner of the famous restaurant club, Les Ambassadeurs. The club had a popular disco night-club, the Garrison, in the basement while, on the first floor was an elegant casino, Le Cercle. Since I went to these three places as a customer so often, John offered me no less than £100 a week to attract my friends to the building where I could eat free as well as entertain. This fitted in with my life-style to perfection and the money was a godsend.

I had a soft spot for Les A, since it was the favourite restaurant of my parents and family, as was the old night-club upstairs, the Milroy. As a treat I had been allowed to both places as a schoolboy from the age of about 12 wearing my smartest blue suit and I also had special dispensation from the distinguished head-waiter, Mr Williams, who had a mane of white hair, to collect autographs form the endless stream of Hollywood celebrities who would lunch and dine there. One night alone, I secured the signatures of such all-time greats as Spencer Tracy, Joan Fontaine, and Clark Gable as well as the slightly less eminent but still as exciting, Zsa-Zsa Gabor. I was always very polite and discreet and never suffered a refusal. However, it was a close-run thing with Gable, probably the biggest catch of them all. I had been eyeing him and waiting my time to strike when, suddenly, he got up and left. I had to rush from my table and only caught up with him as he was strolling up the street towards the Dorchester Hotel. He had an extremely attractive girl with him. 'Excuse me, Mr Gable,' I panted, 'could I possibly trouble you for your autograph.' The great man groaned. 'Can't you leave me alone, I must have some peace.' I looked crestfallen. The girl spoke, 'Aw, come on Clark, he's very young.' So Gable relented and signed. I thanked him politely and remain for ever grateful to the unknown girl-friend.

It was considered somewhat infra-dig at Eton to collect autographs but most of my friends were quite impressed by my collection, which included such as Winston Churchill and other household names, apart from those I have mentioned like, Humphrey Bogart, as well as all the great sports stars, including Don Bradman, the finest batsman of all time.

Royal Ascot in 1963 was almost as much as a downer as 1961 had been an upper. As we now lived close to the course, we gave a small house-party – small since we hadn't many spare rooms. By farming out the children we were able to have two couples to stay, as well as my old, faithful butler, Beard, in the attic. Beard was an amazing man. He started life as a tailor's presser but had always enjoyed a flutter on the horses. One day, when Clive Graham was tipping three horses a day in his Bendex column in the *Daily Express*, Beard backed all three and the whole lot won. He threw in his job and rang up Clive to announce, 'I've made enough money to chuck a job I hate. Let me come and be your valet for nothing.' This was obviously an offer made in the euphoria of the moment but Beard started working for Clive and, through him, met others in the racing world who appreciated his services. He worked in various private boxes for the well-known professional punter Alex Bird, and he was butlering for Tom Jones that fateful week at Newmarket before I got married.

He visited me once a week to press my suits and trousers and clean my shoes, and, this particular Ascot, he was a live-in butler and presser during the evenings and early mornings while, during the day, he went to serve in the Crosse and Blackwell box at Ascot. Beard was one of the nicest men I have met and totally trustworthy.

By the Thursday of the Royal meeting, I was going down the drain again and decided to risk all on one last major gamble. The horse selected for the job was a filly called Prophetess, trained by a good friend of mine, Teddy Lambton. Teddy always told me when he fancied one and he reckoned that Prophetess would win. She was running in the last race of the day, the King George V Handicap, the same race in which I had had such a touch on Vinca two years previously.

I went up and down the rails, visiting all my bookmakers and putting £200 each way here, £300 each way there until I had a total of nearly £2,000 each way on her at an average of 6–1. I had kept a little wad of cash on me to pay the week's expenses, including Beard, and this came to something over £200 so I went to the Tote and had a final £100 each way in cash.

From the start of the race, which was run over a mile and a half, Prophetess and another horse much bigger than her, Master Cappelle, raced clear and battled it out, neck and neck, well in front of the rest of the field. It was an unusual situation in such a contest but, coming into the straight, it was clear that nothing would catch the two in front and neither would give in. There was a moment when she got her head in front but in the last 100 yards, the bigger, stronger colt just edged her out, and although it was a photo-finish I knew we were done for.

I made a bolt for the car in order to be home before my guests. The disappointment only just began to sink in when I sat down in the drawing-room and worked out what might have been. The difference of that photo-finish going against Prophetess was nearly £14,000 even though I did not lose on the bet, actually winning about £1,000. But worse news was to come. There had been an objection and the stewards considered the case for nearly half an hour before finally allowing the result to stand. One of the stewards came up to Teddy Lambton afterwards and said, 'Bad luck. If that had happened anywhere else but Royal Ascot we would have disqualified the winner.' Apparently the winner had hung and slightly impeded Prophetess all the way through the final furlong, just taking the filly's ground. Since she was much the smaller of the two, it might well have made the difference between victory and defeat.

I went up to my dressing-room to take off my tail-coat and trousers and put on something more casual, leaving them on the bed for Beard to press when he returned a little later. I carefully emptied the pockets of my trousers first and, as usual, put my money and valuables on the dressing-table. I also put in the same pile the two £50 Tote place tickets which were worth £250. I put the win tickets in the wastepaper basket. The plan was to collect the Tote money before the first race on Friday, quite normal practice.

Beard came back and did his stuff. He left fairly early on Friday morning for the Crosse and Blackwell box since he had to prepare for the guests. When I went upstairs to change at around midday I could find no trace of the two successful £50-place tickets and was extremely concerned as they represented my cash float and I was relying on that money. I searched high and low but to no avail so I had to wait until after racing for Beard to return to find out where he had put them. When I asked him what had happened, he put his hands to his face. 'Oh, no,' he groaned, 'I thought they were losing tickets and I had never seen such big figures. I took them as a joke to show my friends working in the box, pretending that I had lost. I threw them in the pig-swill bin.'

This was the last straw but I could not be too angry with Beard since he was so upset himself and felt that he had let me down. However, we did search in our own dustbin to find the two corresponding win tickets, which were useless but which had a code of assorted letters printed on them. I then wrote to the Tote explaining the situation and enclosing the win tickets to show the code. I did not expect much luck though, as the win and place pools were separate.

Everyone who knew the story was convinced that Beard must have cashed the tickets except for a handful who knew him and myself. I never had any doubt whatsoever that he was telling the truth and one day, several weeks later, I received a letter from the Tote saying that their place pool on the last race at Ascot on Gold Cup day had £250 left, the proceeds of a £100 bet and they therefore enclosed my money in full.

Sometime after this, particularly with my job at Les A, I started to stay up in London mid-week more and more. During the winter I took a room in a flat in Egerton Gardens owned by my old friend Lord Brooke, whose marriage had recently failed. Brookie, heir to the Earl of Warwick, who now lived abroad, was always pleading shortage of money so he was glad to let the room to me for a not unreasonable rent while the other spare room in the flat was rented out to Tommy Wertheimer, who lived in France and was only an infrequent visitor to London.

I stayed up more and more, partly in the line of duty but also because I was too tired to drive down to Ascot late at night. By April 1964, relations between my wife and me were fairly tense. We went up to the Grand National as usual and stayed at the Adelphi Hotel with Tom

Jones and his friends. We were one of the main groups there that year while the other leading group was headed by the great trainer, Fulke Walwyn. Although we were rival parties in some ways, we were good friends too, and were delighted when Fulke trained the Grand National winner, Team Spirit.

Early in April, Fulke hosted a celebration dinner-party at the Berkeley Hotel in London, situated in those days just down the road from the Ritz. We enjoyed the evening, but some ten days later when I was in Brookie's flat I began to feel below par with a sharp pain behind my ear. Next day my face was swollen and there was no mistaking that I had mumps. As the news spread, reports started coming in from other members of the dinner-party and it soon became apparent that something like 15 out of 20 people who had eaten at the Berkeley had mumps too. One of them was the jockey, Dave Dick, and another was the young amateur champion, Sir William Pigott-Brown, of whom I had seen a lot during my night-rounds in the previous year or so.

William did not start off so painfully as me and although he had a grand London flat in Wilton Crescent, he asked if he could come round and move into Egerton Gardens in the second spare room. Brookie agreed so we started a sanatorium with my landlord, a great hypochondriac, nursing us since he had cupboards in his bathroom full of medicines. We had plenty of brave visitors who felt they were immune from mumps and by the end of a week we were beginning to feel quite chirpy, and I remember shouting home a two-year-old called Streetfighter, who won by five lengths. Streetfighter was owned by Magsie Kindersley. She and her husband Gay had also been at the fateful dinner and contracted mumps though not so badly.

Just as William and I thought we were on the road to recovery, the second phase began and this was a wholly different ball game. Every gland in my body swelled and I developed a temperature of 104 degrees. I had pancreatitis as well, and I could swallow and digest nothing. I could not even hold down water. I was so ill that the fact that my testicles swelled up like melons was the least of my worries. William had the same problem and one of them never returned to normal size and has been known as Mumpy ever since.

On the Monday evening my wife came to see me and conferred with the doctor before going out to dinner. I thought this was somewhat callous of her since he told her that I might well die within the next few hours. All of this medical activity excited Brookie as we had a nurse day and night, being too ill to move to hospital. But he also became rather ill himself that week as he had fallen while riding at the weekend and painfully chipped his shoulder-blade. 'Nobody takes any notice of me,' he complained.

My doctor also discovered that some other patients of a colleague of his suffering from mumps had also dined at the Berkeley on the same night and, following up the matter, he discovered that an under-chef had gone down with the disease a day or so later and had obviously contaminated all our food.

Gradually, we recovered and when we were well enough, William and I went down to his new house near Blewbury which was full of builders but was just habitable. He had bought the house and the adjoining stud, and we were to have many happy times there over the next fifteen years.

We were still desperately weak though, and decided that we needed sunshine so we booked to go down to Marbella for three weeks. My wife than gave me an ultimatum. If I went to Marbella, that was the end for us. I argued that I needed to recuperate and William and I went down there early in May. Dave Dick and his girl-friend also joined us to recover from his less severe bout of mumps and William had a lady with him as well. As we recovered our strength the great question was: Were all our spare parts in working order?

It was all right for the others. They soon felt strong enough to try it out with their companions but it was not so easy for me, and although I got close with a slightly cross-eyed German diplomat's daughter I had to wait until we got home to check the system out and find everything satisfactory.

Carole stuck to her ultimatum and we made fairly civilized attempts to conclude our divorce without upsetting the two boys who were very young. The divorce went through later that year and I was a bachelor again, a state which lasted thirteen glorious years.

The Profumo Case

IN the spring of 1963 I became indirectly involved in events that led to a national scandal, a scandal which led to the resignation and disgrace of the Secretary of State for War, John Profumo.

It became a regular habit of several of my friends to enjoy long lunches at the Mirabelle in Curzon Street, mostly at the invitation of, and hosted by, an American called Tom Corbally – so long that we were often still drinking when the cleaning staff came in to vacuum the carpet and floor around us, preparing for the evening customers.

No one seemed to know much about Tom who was something of a mystery figure. He was very good-looking and fortyish then, with a hint of grey in his hair – now completely white, incidentally. His main distinguishing feature was his extremely deep and resonant voice which frequently attracted the stares of customers from other tables. He had been married to Gorgeous Gussy, a glamorous American tennis-player who had created a sensation at Wimbledon in the 1950s by wearing frilly knickers under her skirt for the first time on Centre Court. She competed at Wimbledon both under the name of Gussy Moran, under which she made her name, and later as Gussy Corbally. By the time I met Tom, however, Gussy was out of his life and they were probably divorced.

Tom came from Eastern USA but had developed some decidedly European tastes and lived for a while in London. The air of mystery about him was heightened by the fact that he always seemed to have limitless amounts of cash but never wrote a cheque. He was extremely liberal with that cash and usually picked up the bill, adding a generous tip which ensured him a good table, and he also paid his gambling losses promptly, though if they ran into the thousands, he would have to drive back to his flat just off Grosvenor Square to draw from his seemingly endless cash supply.

His favourite after-lunch tipple was a stronger version of the traditional Stinger. Whereas the normal Stinger consists of a smallish glass of white crème de menthe – it can be green – topped up with a little brandy, Tom insisted on what he called a 'Special', which was a huge tumbler or balloon brandy-glass equally filled with crème de menthe and brandy plus a few chunks of ice. 'None of the cissy *frappé* nonsense,' he would drawl. The drunker he got, the deeper the voice and the slower the drawl. He would often fall asleep and once, when he rang me up in the middle of the night from the famous Hotel du Cap d'Antibes to invite us down to stay, he fell asleep and all I could hear, however loud I shouted, was resounding snoring. Extremely expensive snores they were too, since he presumably did not hang up until he woke up.

One evening I went round to his Duke Street flat, no more than a hundred yards from Grosvenor Square and just short of Oxford Street on the other side, for a few drinks and a gossip. As we chatted, there was an urgent and insistent ringing on the door-bell. Insistent because Tom never moved very quickly and it took him about a minute to reach the door. In strode a dapper man with swept-back hair and glasses and a voice about as deep as Tom's. He was English, and Tom introduced us. His name was Stephen Ward.

'Do you mind if I hole up with you here for a bit. I've got this girl staying with me in my house and some lunatic black man is after her and has fired a volley of shots through my front door. The place is swarming with police and I need to lie low. Don't want to get involved in that sort of thing, do we old boy?' he finished, turning towards me.

The lunatic black man's name was Johnny Edgecombe, who worked in some nightclub, I think, and he had become infatuated with the girl in question, whose name was Christine Keeler. That incident triggered off the whole Keeler–Profumo affair which nearly led to the downfall of the government and certainly led to the disgrace of Jack Profumo and several other people too.

Ward was still there when I left the flat and I saw him on numerous occasions, always there, as the plot thickened.

Basically Ward, who affected grandoise manners and mannerisms, practised as an osteopath but got his kicks from providing girls for those higher placed on the social scale than himself. He was lent a cottage on Lord Astor's Cliveden estate on the Thames beyond Maidenhead and he would bring down girls there every weekend, and sometimes in mid-week as well, to entertain visitors, many of them from the great house at Cliveden. Thus he was in close touch with Bill Astor, son of the legendary Nancy Astor who succeeded her husband, the late Lord Astor, as MP for Plymouth for so many years. Through Bill Astor he also met the Conservative Minister Jack Profumo (married to the actress Valerie Hobson) and many other well-known people, including a Russian diplomat. And it was the latter that caused the trouble.

As the Keeler–Edgecombe case developed, police and the newspapers became more aware of the strange involvement at Cliveden and the names of Christine Keeler and Mandy Rice-Davies became household words. Profumo's involvement became the subject of considerable gossip, so much so that he was forced, firstly, to make private denials to the Prime Minister, Harold Macmillan, and then actually stand up in the House of Commons to make a formal denial.

It was lying to both his party leader and to the House which really earned him most opprobrium. Eventually, when it became clear that he had been involved with Keeler who had herself been involved at the same time with the Russian diplomat, so that national security could have been at risk, Profumo had ignominiously to resign. He disappeared from public life and subsequently devoted himself to charity work.

Profumo's chief tormentor in the House of Commons was the Labour MP, Col. George Wigg, who hounded him from the start to finish with a rare moral fervour. George Wigg later became chairman of the Horse-racing Betting Levy Board, the statutory body which raises money from the punters via the bookmakers for the subsidy of racing. Ironically, he was also involved in a rather unpleasant case of his own later in life.

Lord Wigg, as he became, was a difficult customer, to say the least. He did some good things when serving his term on the Levy Board, notably servicing Stanley Wootton's astonishing gift of a large chunk of Epsom Downs to the Jockey Club and also tweaking the tail of that August body from time to time. But, on the other side, he was often viciously unfair to the Jockey Club as well as inaccurate. He was an inveterate litigant, an implacable enemy, and I found him extremely unpleasant. So too did Clive Graham, only more so, and Clive was not a man easily incensed. I once made an appointment to interview him in his London office. His secretary, Valerie Frost, had previously worked with Clive, Peter O'Sullevan, and myself at the *Daily Express*. I went with an open mind to obtain Wigg's views and record them accurately. I was subjected to a tirade of abuse and invective about Clive Graham and Beaverbrook Newspapers, notably the *Evening Standard*. He continued a recital of hate against the paper boasting how comprehensively he was suing it, and he continued on these lines, snapping out references to himself in *Hansard,* until I could take no more. I shook hands, left the office, and did not print a word of the interview. I suspect that he would have been waiting to read it and would have pounced on anything minutely inaccurate, or with which he was in disagreement, to resort to further litigation against my employers.

Meanwhile, the Profumo case developed and Stephen Ward was arrested and tried for living off the earnings of prostitutes. He was convinced that he was the victim of a conspiracy of silence but still expected several of his important friends to give evidence on his behalf. Hardly anyone came forward and he became increasingly paranoid though not actually without justification. With the trial reaching its end, he took an overdose and died later in St Stephen's Hospital.

Both Keeler and Rice-Davies became national and to a certain extent, international celebrities while the lives of most of the men involved were ruined. Christine Keeler, the major figure, gradually slumped into a low-profile life of obscurity and relative poverty whereas Mandy Rice-Davies basked in the limelight and appears to have prospered.

At some stage of all this, my friend Tom Corbally disappeared having tipped off the authorities about Profumo's involvement with the Russian diplomat. He returned to America without saying a word to any of us but moves around freely these days, visiting England and France.

The author in cheerful mood, pre-war in Hyde Park.

The author with younger brother and parents on the sea-front at Worthing during prep - school days, 1948.

(Above left) The author and brother Jonathan cricketing on the beach at Frinton.

(Above right) The author, aged about fifteen, posing by the famous Wall at Eton.

63.

WHISTLER (P. Nelson) The champion 2-y-o sprinter. Obviously only really makes 5f. Met his only defeat of the season when beaten 2 lengths by Bebe Grande in the Gimcrack Stakes, at York in August. By Panorama, out of Farthing Damages, by Fair Trial. Received 9-4 in the free handicap. 16 hands.

PINZA (N. Bertie) A good strong colt who won 2 races at 2-y-o. Was surprisingly beaten by Neemah at Ascot. By Chanteur II, out of Pasqua, by Donatello II. 9-2 in free handicap. 16+ hands.

A significant page from the author's neat 1952 racing notebook, compiled at Eton. The two horses mentioned, Whistler and Pinza, went on to become champion sprinter and Derby winner respectively.

Dominick Elwes painting the Earl of Suffolk and Berkshire in full hunting regalia. Mickey did not like the painting and it ended up with Charles St George.

Dominick Elwes and friend.

Lord Lucan, in patriotic pose, beneath the Red Ensign, on one of his yachting trips.

A pen, ash, wine and coffee drawing of my then girl-friend Charlotte Curzon, made by Dominick Elwes on the back of a Mark's Club menu. Dominick enjoyed making this sort of picture when he was in the mood.

The Countess of Suffolk holds Lady Camilla Bingham, Lord Lucan's younger daughter. This photograph was taken by Lucan himself barely three months before he disappeared.

The author posing with top racehorse owner Charles St George at Newmarket. The rather embarrassing long hair seemed pretty smart in those days. *(Daily Express)*

A human pyramid on the lawn at Sir William Pigott-Brown's Berkshire estate. From bottom right, Bryan Ferry, the author, black model Mynah Bird; centre, right, Jerry Hall, left, Wendy Stark, one of the queens of Hollywood, and top, another black model, Alva.

Bryan Ferry with Jerry Hall, Mustique 1976.

Author and wife examining local sea-trophies, Barbados 1978.

Vincent O'Brien (left) and Robert Sangster outside the Lyford Cay Club, Nassau, January 1978.

Wedding picture together with sons Harry (right) and Edward (left), 26 October 1977.

Unofficial christening photograph of daughter Honor, aged five and a half months, taken during Ascot week 1981. Father (left) and mother (second right) with two godmothers, Phillipa Courtauld (second left) and Sally Aga Khan.

Exhausted in more ways than one on Macaroni Beach, Mustique. Captured by Patrick Lichfield.

The great Blushing Groom after winning the Group One Prix Morny in Deauville, August 1976.

A New Centre of Operations

AFTER Carole and I went our separate ways, I moved in full time to Egerton Gardens. Lord Brooke and I, though dissimilar in temperament, never had a quarrel. We had no lift and we lived on the third floor so it was quite a plod up the stairs. This had one advantage as far as I was concerned. If a lady agreed to struggle up all those stairs, she plainly wasn't coming up for a cup of coffee or to see my etchings.

My career at Les Ambassadeurs had come to a halt a month or two earlier as John Mills had decided that I was not justifying my £100 a week plus food and drink. This was no fault of mine since I tried my best, but I wasn't prepared to push my friends too hard to do anything that they didn't wish to. Mills would never admit it, but I think he probably expected me to bring in more punters for the gambling-club upstairs. He did not tell me that the arrangement was coming to an end, and I continued to perform my duties for some time after he stopped paying me. We picked up our friendship though, and we remained friendly till he died. He was a particularly noticeable figure in Monte Carlo where he gave fabulous parties during the Grand Prix weekend.

My centre of operations now switched to 44 Berkeley Square with the Clermont Club from the ground floor upwards and Annabel's in the basement. I was a founder-member of both.

I first met John Aspinall in the summer of 1961 when we sat at the same table at a dinner-party given by Constantine Dracoulis in his Lowndes Square flat. Aspers leaned across the girl between us and said, 'I hear you have made a lot of money on horses. Well done. I love to hear of the bookies being crushed.'

We chatted throughout the evening and he suggested that I should come to one of his celebrated private gambling-parties, which switched

87

from venue to venue but were of questionable legality. The police eventually caught up with Aspers and his indomitable mother, Lady Osborne, known to all as Lady O, and they appeared in front of the magistrates at Marlborough Street. As a result of this case, during which Aspers and his counsel showed up the ludicrous anomalies of the gaming laws, the law was changed to permit closely controlled casinos to operate.

So all those who have put away a fortune from running casinos in London have Aspinall to thank, a fact that several of them conveniently forgot when he applied for a licence in the mid-1970s and again in the early 1980s. Greed and hypocrisy go hand in hand where many casino promoters are concerned.

Although the Clermont was not the first casino to open in London, it quickly became the most fashionable and popular. There was always a steady stream of foreign notables but the mainstay of the business in those days were the British upper classes, particularly the aristocracy. It was as if the owners of stately homes the length and breadth of the country, and Scotland and Wales too, had at last discovered a much-needed outlet. Once the Clermont was under way, and Aspinall had started giving his parties there, he and Mark Birley, who had previously worked as an advertising executive in J. Walter Thompson's four doors up the road, planned to open together a night-club downstairs.

Excavations began to dig out the area which is now Annabel's but which was to begin with only the Clermont's cellars. Then Aspers ran into a cash-flow problem since he needed all his resources to run the Clermont, which temporarily was going through a difficult period, and Birley was left holding the baby downstairs. Under some pressure, Mark was able to find some other backers and continued to create his masterpiece, which he named after his wife and which remains the most elegant and popular night-spot in the world.

When Annabel's opened, it was not the instant success which some people now believe. It was one long struggle for Mark and his brilliant head-waiter, Louis who, together with his right-hand man, Freddy, had been lured from the Mirabelle, then the most successful restaurant in London. Many a night I was one of only a handful of patrons, most faithful of whom was the London-based American, Bobby Sweeny, the great amateur golfer. Bobby was number one and I reckon that I was number two though Mark's backers turned out to support him and their investment as often as possible.

In fact, so badly was Annabel's going at that time it was decided to change the whole character of the place by putting more emphasis on the food, which had at first been secondary. Originally they even experimented with the French custom of closing on Monday nights. Gradually, however, quality came through and Annabel's began to fill up night after night with diners and dancers while George Hobart's bar was also thriving on its own. George was another great character, extremely keen on racing, who had joined Annabel's from Jules Bar in Jermyn Street. George frequently put on bets for us and was a friend of many of the jockeys who for many years had frequented the Turkish baths next to Jules Bar.

During my first bachelor summer of 1964, I would lunch at the Clermont nearly every day and was generously treated by John Aspinall. I entertained so many ladies that one day it was decided to have a 'Bird of the Year' lunch to which I would invite about a dozen girls. Aspers approved the idea and agreed to give the lunch which would be held in the garden outside the restaurant. He even agreed to buy some expensive jewellery to award as prizes. The names of the girls were to be put in a tombola and the draw would be conducted by the head-porter, Pearson, one of a dying breed who had come on from a similar position at White's.

The day dawned gloriously warm and sunny and I had a string of calls from men friends who wished to participate. The news of the lunch had leaked out and the ordinary restaurant was packed with spectators, mostly older women who came to criticize. At the last moment Aspers lost his nerve and decreed that the names of all the ladies in the club must be included in the draw for the prizes, as he feared problems otherwise.

Pearson, who always conducted such draws, did not quite understand the situation though I vainly tried to tell him to favour the numbers and names of my girl-friends. However, it was too public and too late, and I could not make him understand so I had to grin and bear it as I read out the name of the first prize-winner, Ellie Shapiro, wife of the then director of Laurel racecourse near Washington. John and Ellie were on their honeymoon and he was a good friend so I was not too disappointed by this. Second prize went to one of my girls and then Pearson drew out the name of one of the toughest spectators and critics who, luckily, had left the room. 'Oh, I know where she is, I'll send for her,' blurted out Pearson only for me to hiss in his ear, 'For Christ's sake put it back and we'll draw another one.' To my horror the same name came out again and this time I snatched it from him and said, 'Disqualified for absence,'

89

quickly drawing out another name myself.

I stayed with Brookie until the following summer, normally weekending with William at his rapidly improving country retreat. He was adding to the facilities all the time and had a fine swimming-pool, a sauna, a games-room, and croquet lawn with adjoining trampoline. He also had a tennis-court which, of course, suited me very well. I was always given the main guest bedroom which had one snag to it – a two-way mirror through which William and his friends could peer from a sort of cupboard in his dressing-room. It was all right as far as I was concerned because I knew about it from the first day I stayed there and the first thing I did when checking in was to hang a jacket or dressing-gown over it. But many an unsuspecting couple were watched during the following years. However, I won't reveal the names of either the watchers or the performers.

One Sunday in June 1965, I played in a cricket match with Phillip Martyn and we drove back together to London. He invited me to move into his very smart flat in Bolebec House near the Carlton Towers Hotel, thus beginning a new era of my life. I think he meant the arrangement to be a temporary one, but it became permanent, so permanent that when he left the country for Switzerland and then America he sold it plus all the contents to me. Phillip was establishing himself as a successful backgammon player and the game was becoming increasingly popular and played every day at the Clermont. I would just watch him and the other players, day after day, never participating. But one day, sometime later, I decided to take it up and soon found that, even as a learner, I was able to win. My newly discovered skills meant that I spent more and more time at the Clermont Club. Aspers would also ask me down to his country estate to stay from time to time.

Apart from gambling, John Aspinall's great obsession in life is animals and he has developed probably the two finest private zoos in the world at his house, Howlett's near Canterbury and, later, at Port Lympne, a few miles further down the road on the coast. Aspinall's special interest is in gorillas and tigers though he also concentrates on helping to save endangered species. He gave a ball in July 1986, for instance, which like all his parties was glamorous and awe-inspiring, purely to celebrate the arrival from the Far East of a rare rhinoceros. No one, even his enemies, can doubt the sincerity of his relationship with the animals as he puts himself at risk, year after year, wrestling and playing with them, particularly gorillas and tigers. I have lost count of the times that he has limped into the club with cuts, scratches, strains and the most horrendous bruises from his friendly encounters.

There have been some terrible tragedies there, too, probably inevitable since he does his best to treat his animals as naturally as possible. Two of these, both some years ago, concerned injuries to young people. On one occasion, Robin Birley, who was about 12 years old and the son of Mark and Lady Annabel Birley was down there with his mother. They were watching Aspers play with a female tiger and Annabel begged him to let Robin, who was tall for his age, join in. It all looked so easy. It was Robin's tallness that caused Aspers to give in to Annabel's persuasion. Animals can be excited by children, as my daughter found out from behind a cage there a couple of years ago and had to be removed swiftly on the instructions of Aspers and his wife Sally. So Robin was allowed in and, suddenly, the tigress turned on him and clamped her jaws around his face and head. Aspers lept on her back and hauled with all his might on her jaws but cried despairingly to the keeper, who ran for help, 'I can't budge her.' Then miraculously, the tigress moved her jaws for an instant to adjust her hold. It was an instinctive bid for the jugular but that instant allowed Aspers and the keeper to prise her mouth apart and release the boy. His head injuries were terrible, and he still bears the scars though he is a well-balanced young man with a good sense of humour who lives a happy life.

One touching anecdote connected with this incident concerned a visit to the injured boy in hospital by two lawyers acting on his behalf. They started asking him questions about the accident. 'Hang on a second, why are you asking me these things?' enquired the boy. 'It's all right, we are on your side. We are going to represent you in court.' Robin snapped back, 'I'm not saying anything. I don't want Mr Aspinall taken to court and I don't want any money. He saved my life. Will you please go away.'

The other sad incident which did lead to court proceedings concerned the very pretty young model Meryl Lamb, who was a weekend guest of Aspinall's half-brother, James Osborne, while Aspers himself was abroad. As the tigers looked so tame she put her arm through the bars of their cage. One of the tigers fastened on to her and ripped the flesh and sinew from her elbow downwards. She had terrible injuries and sued, but no negligence was proved and she lost the case.

More recently, Aspers suffered a triple blow when two of his keepers were killed in separate incidents by the same tigress and a third keeper was killed by an elephant. These disasters led to public hostility against Aspers, who was deeply upset and blamed himself particularly for the death of the second keeper as he had decreed that the tigress should not be put down after the first incident. This time he took a rifle and shot her himself. She had climbed impossible-looking inward-curving bars of the cage to get at the keeper, who was preparing her food in a second enclosed area. He colleague shouted a warning too late for him to escape.

It was, incidentally, at Howlett's around 1967 that my own riding career ended. I was with a couple of friends staying the weekend with Aspers and he suggested that we went for a ride across the park. I was mounted on a fairly senior mare and was warned that she was liable to swerve at the slightest thing. All went well and we were galloping across a field towards a couple of trees, with me at the rear but perfectly happy, when a small gorilla jumped from the tree just off our path, and my mount, not unnaturally, shied. I fell out of the back door and landed flat on my back. I was totally winded and lay there feeling paralysed. The young gorilla stood staring at me, laughing, I swear. I thought I had broken my back but I was lucky and was only winded and badly bruised. It took some time to find me and then more time to collect me in some form of wagon.

I had plenty of time to think and decided to hang up my boots. After all, I lived in London, did not hunt, and rode only occasionally, though I had ridden intermittently since the age of six or seven in my Bude days.

One of my kindest friends in the early and middle 1960s was Earl Beatty, whose father was an admiral and one of the most renowned sailors of the First World War. When I first met him, David Beatty was nearing his sixties,but he was young in mind and body, kept himself in remarkable condition, and seemed to prefer the company of people younger than himself. He must have been at least 30 years older than me but we all got on well and soon he married a very young wife, Diane Kirk, and they lived in some comfort and splendour in a lovely house, Chicheley, near Newport Pagnell only a few miles off the M1 motorway. They were thus only about an hour from my area of London and they used to give wonderful weekend parties to which I was a frequent visitor.

But David, like his father, was also a keen sailor in every way and he had a distinguished war record during which he reached the rank of

Commander. He was a member of the Royal Yacht Squadron and had his own motor-yacht, the *Sea Huntress,* which was a converted warship. He later sold this, having commissioned a brand-new boat, the *Diamira,* the name a combination of Diane, his wife's name, and Miranda, that of their daughter. I spent many happy trips aboard both *Sea Huntress* and *Diamira* and David had the knack of running into interesting and glamorous friends in the Mediterranean. It was with David and Diane on different cruises that we bumped into Richard Burton and Elizabeth Taylor, docked next door to us on a huge chartered boat in St Tropez on their first honeymoon; Aristotle Onassis and his mistress, Maria Callas, aboard his yacht, *Christina,* and also on his private island, Skorpios; and Stavros Niarchos with his fabulous sailing-boat, *Creole,* and on his island, Spetsipoula.

Onassis was a particularly charming host while the allegedly temperamental Maria Callas could not have been more attentive. She was in charge of providing refreshments and I well remember her making sure that my glass was never empty. We sat and drank before lunch around an amazing, small mosaic swimming-pool and after lunch Onassis himself took us on a guided tour of the boat. He had some fabulous paintings on board but the one he was proudest of was by Winston Churchill, a gift from the great man who had been a regular guest on board.

The hospitality on the Niarchos island was well up to standard too, and I remember being particularly impressed by the revolving table which enabled the food to be circulated. I got to know Niarchos much better later, particularly when he became more heavily involved in racing at his second attempt.

On most of my trips with the Beattys, I was a spare man, though I did occasionally take a girl-friend. Once a companion was laid on for me during a cruise around the Greek Islands, in the shape of Princess Sylvia Djorjadsky, who was at least thirty years older than me and who had been in her time Lady Ashley and then the wife of Clark Gable. Still a bright blonde, though of considerable age, she certainly had a story to tell, particularly when she had had a few cocktails. She and I became conspiratorial friends. She had quite a thirst on her and made me responsible for filling her glass at all times, even if it had to be done in secret.

David could not be described as a mean man – he gave endless hospitality – but he was touchy about drinks, which he liked to control himself. So Sylvia arranged to bring her own case of champagne which I had to help her smuggle aboard. As a result, she felt quite justified in ordering me to open a bottle of her champagne whenever she felt like it and sharing it with anyone around. Curiously enough, David was not always happy about this.

David seemed most at home in the old port of Antibes, where he always based his boats. We spent many happy evenings touring the little restaurants and drinking-places in Antibes, particularly Chez Felix by the harbour entrance, while we discovered a delicious restaurant in the square, Taverne de Provence, which mysteriously moved one year, turning up on the old sea-wall near Paul Gallico's house and now subtitled, as it were, Les Vieux Murs.

It was with David that I first visited Sardinia when the development was just starting. We got caught by a sudden storm not far from the Cala di Volpe when well away from the main boat, with only a dinghy to hand. David bravely insisted on leaving the rest of us where we were in relative safety while he went off alone to return to the boat and get help from the crew. We were mightily relieved when they all hove back in sight. We also had a nasty moment when swimming in the Gulf of Corinth and became surrounded by huge, grey jellyfish cutting us off from the boat. Somehow we managed to avoid being stung, which was just as well since they could inflict painful injuries. We spent much of that trip spotting those same jellyfish, though I never saw them again during later visits.

We also paid visits to Rome since there were good boat-repair yards in the waters near by. Altogether, I have good cause to be grateful to David and Diane.

Sadly, we were not on such good terms when he died which was not entirely my fault. On probably my last trip on board the *Diamira,* I took a girl with me and David took an obvious liking to her. Subsequently she and I fell out and there was no love lost between us. David started seeing her as his own marriage crumbled, but I was not aware of this. One evening he invited me to have dinner with him alone at Grosvenor House. During the course of a perfectly pleasant evening, he slipped in the loaded question under my guard. What did I think of this girl? I told him and it was not complimentary. His face fell and I realized that I had put my foot in it. We parted that evening on courteous terms but he obviously reported back my comments to the girl and we were never really friends again for the fairly short time that he lived afterwards.

One of my last memories of the happy days with David was when we were cruising of St Tropez. We had quite a boat full including Brian

Alexander and the Earl of Lichfield. We were anchored about 400 yards off a small rocky island, just a hill sticking out of the water, lunching, drinking and swimming. Patrick Lichfield, always competitive, challenged me to a race from the boat to the top of the hill on the island and back. I should never have accepted the challenge as I was older and overweight. But I was a little fitter than I looked, having played a lot of tennis and I always considered myself an athlete so I foolishly picked up the gauntlet. I led swimming ashore and was still in front until half-way up the hill by which time my feet were being cut to ribbons by stones and spikes. Determination kept me going though Patrick padded by and I suddenly realized that he was wearing light gym-shoes. He had out-smarted me, thinking ahead and knew that the island would be hard on the feet. Instead of accepting the inevitable, I plugged on to the top and had to make the equally painful downhill journey before struggling exhausted and bleeding back to the boat. Still my pride would not allow me to accept a lift in the Boston Whaler dinghy which had been sent by friends to fetch me and I completed the full course. But I was half-dead and it took me some time to recover. It also taught me a sharp lesson both about my own pride and Patrick's scheming mind.

My final memory of drama with David and Diane involved a flight down to Nice to join the boat and stay for the weekend in May in Monte Carlo for the Grand Prix motor-racing. I had been carrying on with a girl whose demands on me had been very exhausting. Fond of her though I was, I felt the need for a rest and kept my impending trip to Monte Carlo a secret from her.

At this period of my life, 1966, I was burning the candle at both ends and in the middle as well, going out every night, carrying on with my girl-friends, and often staying up all night playing backgammon. As a consequence I was in a constant state of exhaustion. This lunatic existence undoubtedly led to an epileptic condition, which had been dormant since those blows to the head at school, and aggravated by the car accident.

On the morning of the flight I arrived at London airport to join David and Diane. I had left it rather late, but excused myself as we were about to board to make a telephone call to the girl to tell her of my plans. The Beattys being rather grand had a man who escorted them at the airport and they sent him with me to the telephone kiosk.

I got through to my girl-friend and broke the news that I was disappearing for a fortnight – Monte Carlo being only the start. She started screaming hysterically. At that moment I completely lost my

95

memory, due to my epileptic condition, and the courier started banging on the door. I said to the hysterical girl, 'It's no good screaming at me. I don't know who I am but there is a man banging on the door and he has come to take me away.' The man led me in a semi-conscious state to the aircraft where I was placed next to a stranger, facing David and Diane. There were some planes designed like that in those days. By chance the stranger happened to be a doctor and he understood my condition. I have no recollection of the first three-quarters of the journey but just as we were flying over the Alps, I vaguely remember Diane asking me basic questions about myself and, by the time we landed at Nice, I had a fair working knowledge of myself. Apparently the doctor had been most helpful in this line of therapy and, by the time we reached the boat, I was more or less all right though still feeling a little groggy, probably due to sheer over-tiredness.

I had many attacks of varying intensity during that eight-year period and an ECG showed that I did have a small smudge on the left side of the brain. I went on a course of pills, Epanutin, and these, together with a general slowing down of the hectic tempo of my life, finally cured me. During this period, for obvious reasons, I had to give up driving.

I had several dramas when I keeled over in public places. One of these was when I was walking down Sloane Street and I came to in St George's Hospital. Another was when I went down standing by the backgammon table in the Clermont, hitting my arm and head when I collapsed for good measure. On another occasion I had been given tickets by the England Test captain Ted Dexter to watch the match at the Oval and I lost my memory for virtually the whole day, coming to my senses during the late afternoon, too late to go. The amazing thing was that I never missed producing my copy for the *Daily Express* though I suppose it was possible that they were rung up when I was unconscious and may have filled in for me. I don't remember!

It was quite eerie too for witnesses of my turns. I remember causing great mirth at the breakfast-table staying with Tom Jones at Newmarket when I went pale, broke into a cold sweat, and lapsed into one of my memory losses, though still conscious. Thankfully, that is all in the past, as is my other affliction, asthma, except when I am in contact with cats which I avoid.

My worst ever asthma attack was when I was staying with my uncle Jack Hawkins, my mother's brother, and his wife for the South of England Junior Tennis Championships at Devonshire Park, Eastbourne in August 1951.

Their house was at Willingdon, about eight miles inland from Eastbourne. One night my asthma became so bad that I could not breathe indoors and had to be moved to a camp-bed in the garden. It was very unpleasant and the next morning it looked as if I would be unfit to play in the tournament. Their local doctor was a balding, bespectacled, benign middle-aged Irishman, who inspired confidence. I went to see him in his surgery and told him of my history of hay fever and asthma. I also told him that I had a headache. He made me lean forward and place my head between my legs. He then grasped both sides of my head and neck and made a sudden wrench to one side, then the other. I was taken completely by surprise and there was a loud cracking noise in my neck at each movement. When I stood up, my headache had gone and I felt as if my head was pounds lighter. My asthma quickly got better, too, though I suffered from it intermittently until much later, particularly in hot and dusty conditions.

The doctor's name was Bodkin Adams and he was the darling of his many elderly lady patients who lived in that part of the world. Many of them left him money in their wills and, more particularly, cars. He was fanatical about cars, drove an old Bentley most of the time, and had a collection of six or seven, including sports cars. Not long afterwards, having improved my health, he was arrested for murder and was the central figure in one of the most celebrated cases at the Old Bailey. Eventually, after a long trial, he was acquitted but much of the evidence was very damning and most people considered him guilty.

My view, and more importantly, that of my uncle and aunt, was that he was careless with the quantities of drugs that he prescribed and administered. He practised a kind of euthanasia, administering heavy sleeping-draughts and pain-killers according to the pleadings of his patients. My verdict: a kindly man at heart but sometimes foolish and lacking in judgement.

The case boosted the name of my colleague on the *Express,* Percy Hoskyns, who was about the only newspaperman or policeman who publicly believed in the innocence of Dr Bodkin Adams. Percy was chief crime reporter and his reputation was greatly enhanced. He also founded and ran the Saints and Sinners Club which puts on so many lunches and dinners to support children's charities.

Apart from these two afflictions, both happily things of the past, I have been generally fortunate with my health – touch wood! Most of my sudden illnesses have been quite dramatic though. The mumps was one such. I also suffered a severe bout of poisoning emanating from an abscess under a hollow tooth which blew up to such an extent that I had to retire to bed and miss both the Cheltenham and Grand National meetings in March 1980.

Most dramatic of all, perhaps, was when I went from Barbados in January 1977 to spend a few days in St Moritz with the Aga Khans in their rented house. I had a pain in the lower front of the shin-bone of my left leg as we travelled to St Moritz via Zurich, but it was not too bad and felt as if I had rapped it against a low, sharp edge of a table. We had a low glass-top table in my flat where we had spent the one night *en route*. The next morning, however, the leg was swelling up and there was a livid red mark which was becoming more painful. Sally insisted on taking me down to the hospital at the bottom of the hill and the doctor immediately became very serious and ordered that I lie with my leg up while they took blood tests. Privately, he told Sally that it was thrombosis, extremely dangerous since if the blood-clot moved and reached my heart it would be fatal.

Meanwhile the nurse was trying to extract blood from the inside of my wrist and making a terrible mess of it. It was extremely painful as she chopped away with her needle trying to find a vein.

Sally showed all the qualities of a true friend. She rang up, using all her clout and, with the help of her own doctor in London and his influence, booked me into King Edward VII hospital (Sister Agnes). She got hold of K's pilot in Paris and asked him to bring their G2 jet to St Moritz at once and fly me to London airport. This was all achieved in a matter of hours and, with ambulances, nurses and doctors, I was in my room at Sister Agnes by early evening.

The nurses and doctors there were shocked by the Swiss butchery to my wrist but even the experts who came to take frequent blood samples sometimes had difficulty in getting any out of me. I was a reluctant donor. Eventually we found a rich seam near the top of my forearm. My blood had to be thinned to help dilute the clot and I stayed very still in my bed for some days before I was deemed fit enough to be operated on. The specialist, Mr Cocker, was going to remove veins from the leg, cutting at the groin, taking out the vein which included the clot. He did a brilliant job though the operation had to be delayed while my blood was artificially thickened again having been previously thinned down.

That ends medical history – not too bad considering my state of overweight and the high-speed life I have led, though I have latterly become a diabetic, luckily without major complications.

Thirteen Glorious Years of Freedom

HAVING been a relatively slow starter as far as girl-friends were concerned I certainly made up for lost time during the thirteen glorious years between marriages. I was married when I was twenty-two and engaged for nine months prior to that so that by the time marriage to Carole came to an end in May 1964, I had only enjoyed a handful of relationships. Perhaps it was all for the good since it is easier to appreciate your freedom when you are a little older and a little more experienced.

However, in common with most bachelors, I did not have many long-running affairs. Nevertheless, with only one exception that I can think of, I remained on the closest of terms with all my ex-lady friends which ultimately gave me a substantial bank to fall back on.

I was pretty spare, when I first met Sue Aylwyn, a successful fashion model known as the 'Queen of the catalogues'. This was because she was very popular with photographers and clients who compiled mail-order catalogues. She could be seen gracing the pages of limitless brochures sent out by Gratton Warehouses, British Home Stores, Littlewoods, and the like.

When I met her, she had just ended a close relationship with Robin Douglas-Home, nephew of the Prime Minister Sir Alec Douglas-Home and also of the playwright William Douglas-Home.

Robin's younger brother Charlie, like Robin himself, had been at Eton with me, the one a little older and the other a little younger. Charlie was a scholar at school and later joined me on the *Daily Express* for a while before going on to be editor of *The Times* before his cruelly premature death in 1985.

Robin was also something of an intellectual though he squandered his talents to the popular media. He had a whimsical little-boy-lost manner which he kept to the end but he was loved by many women. We used to laugh when he came to do his studies under my tutor at Eton and he used to play up to this reaction. He, too, became a chatty columnist for the *Express* and wrote a number of books. He was a friend and admirer of Frank Sinatra about whom he also wrote and developed a close friendship with Princess Margaret, a frequent visitor to his cottage at Pulborough in Sussex.

His relationship with Sue was a stormy one since, I suspect, she could be very stubborn and he irritatingly unreliable. One of the things we had in common was a love of gambling, but in his later years his betting on horses became totally erratic and often ridiculous. He was, in short, a mug punter. I remember him ringing me one Sunday, the day of the Prix de l'Arc de Triomphe in Paris, which was due to be televised by the BBC with Peter O'Sullevan doing the commentary. He asked me to ring O'Sullevan and arrange for him to put £500 on a horse in the big race for him.

'That's impossible,' I said. 'Peter's already at Longchamp and he's much too busy to run around putting other people's bets on for them.'

'Don't worry,' responded the amazing Robin, 'there must be a telephone number for him in the grandstand. Just ring him up and I'm sure he'll put the bet on.'

He was genuinely annoyed when I repeated that the whole thing was impossible. During the same period, when he ran out of credit and was also extremely hard up, he persuaded many of his women friends – quite a few of them married – to place bets of up to £500 and even more on their own accounts with firms like Ladbrokes, William Hill and Heathorns. He convinced himself, and also the poor girls, that this would cost them nothing as he would pay if the horses lost and it was therefore quite different from borrowing money. The problem was that he often couldn't pay and this caused a lot of trouble. Tragically, he died in his little cottage having taken an overdose of sleeping-pills on top of endless bottles of vodka.

Sue and I lasted some four years before we decided that if we progressed nowhere by the Grand National of 1969, we would call it a day.

The National weekend was chosen as that was one of her favourite outings of the year, and we had a particularly enjoyable time at Liverpool, surrounded by our usual racing friends, before returning to London on Sunday and parting after dinner.

100

I am not a great student of astrology but it is more than coincidental that both my first wife and Sue were born under the sign of Leo and were both strong domineering women while I am a Scorpio and also like to be the boss.

During those four years, we travelled around a lot and I remember a silly little episode while staying at the British Embassy in Paris one weekend. My visit to the Embassy took place during the period that Christopher and Mary Soames were in residence, stemming from my close friendship with them and their five children, all of whom have been brought up by the Nanny who had previously guided me and my young brother through our early formative years.

Christopher Soames was a successful and popular ambassador to France, and an inspired appointment by the Socialist Prime Minister Harold Wilson even though Christopher himself was a Tory and an ex-Cabinet Minister. What made the Embassy even more welcoming for me, and led to plenty of jokes, was the presence in a matriarchal position of Nanny King and also of the butler, François who had previously been head-waiter at the Clermont Club. So, despite the grandeur of the surroundings, I felt very much at home in the Embassy. When we arrived that weekend, we were taken to our rooms and along the passage were doors bearing the names of the guests. Accordingly I stopped by a door marked Mr Charles Benson and the convoy then proceeded to inspect Sue's quarters and install her. To our great amusement, the card on her door bore just the one, stark name – Sue. The young Soames and I thought the whole thing a huge joke but when Mary Soames heard about it she was livid about such an insult and tracked down the wretched secretary responsible, who had, of course, not known Sue's surname.

Some of the greatest days at the British Embassy were Arc de Triomphe Sundays when the Soames gave magnificent lunches, usually for 120 guests. If the weather was fine, which it often is on the first Sunday in October, the lunch would take place outside in the garden at tables with about ten places each. All the members of the family hosted a table and so did the redoubtable nanny. I suppose there must have been some sort of protocol governing the placings with, maybe, the grandest members of Royal families, politicians, and aristocrats at either Christopher's or Mary's table, but I can remember some pretty high-faluting names at Nanny's table where I was always drawn by special request. It was one of the great sights of Paris, when lunch was announced, to see Nanny scurrying around grabbing important people

101

by the elbow and saying very firmly, 'My table for lunch, please.' The food there was always magnificent and it was usually partridge at the Arc lunch, no mean achievement for so many people.

Whenever I was there on my own the wine and liqueurs – supplied and paid for by Christopher himself lest any tax-payer should complain – were magnificent. I remember Christopher and I polishing off a nineteenth-century bottle of Calvados, one of his particular favourites and them moving on to the 1910. Mary Soames, youngest daughter of Sir Winston Churchill, and author of a marvellous biography of her mother, is, quite simply, one of the nicest and finest people I have ever known. I have never heard her say an unkind word though she could, of course, be gently critical of bad behaviour. One hopes that she saw none of this from her five children though she would have had to look in the other direction on occasions. All five are full of character.

Like many good women, including my mother and my present wife, Mary was prone to be teased by her husband in particular and her family in general. I remember one evening at dinner in the Embassy when she and Christopher were due to go to a ball afterwards. She looked extremely pretty but her hairdresser had planted a crown of white flowers – lillies, I think – in her hair and those were the object of continuous derision. I thought she looked marvellous but I was in a minority. In the end, she was so upset by the continuous ridicule that she refused to go to the ball to the relief, I suspect, of Christopher.

Christopher was knighted and later made a peer as he continued his political career. But he was subject to long spells of ill-health in later years, bravely borne until his death in September 1987. He became quite a successful racehorse owner, taking over the famous colours of Sir Winston Churchill, chocolate and pink, which were once carried by two very brave horses, the grey Colonist II and High Hat. The latter had the distinction of beating the greatest post-war filly, Petite Etoile at Kempton Park in 1961.

My other relationship which lasted some two and a half years and included three holidays in Mustique was with the beautiful, blonde Lady Charlotte Curzon, daughter of Earl Howe.

Lord Howe was a fanatic about cars and motor-racing and his dapper, bald figure could frequently be seen crouched in the raciest of sports cars, something like a Ferrari or a Maserati. Charlotte herself always drove a Lotus and she cut a particularly spectacular figure behind the wheel of her Europa, painted in the John Player Special colours, black with gold lines. She had this for much of the time we were together though I had some difficulty in getting into it.

Her parents resolutely refused to have me into their house, Penn, near Beaconsfield in Buckinghamshire or indeed have anything to do with me at all. I can't say I blame them since I was hardly the prospective son-in-law that they must have been seeking: twelve years older than their daughter, penniless, divorced, and with two sons.

None of this, however, made any difference to Charlotte, who, behind her meek-and-mild exterior was an extremely determined young woman. Her determination got her into some unfortunate situations from time to time.

Our relationship started after we had spent Christmas week with different partners at William Pigott-Brown's house in the country. I and the rest of the party seemed to enjoy ourselves more than she did that week, but before we went our separate ways, she intimated that we should make dinner date a week or so hence. Despite the differences in our characters, we struck up an immediate rapport. Matters came to a head when I invited both her and another young girl whom I had been dating to Jimmy Goldmsith's ball in the Ritz Hotel. The décor was exotic and the food superb, but the high-spot of the evening was when no less than five bands marched in, having flown in in a specially chartered Boeing from New Orleans. They were led by the old, grizzled members of a traditional New Orleans jazz band, headed by the baton-twirling leader.

I was loving the music and danced as much as I could with my two girls, who were seated on either side of me. Jimmy had encouraged me to bring them both and I thought there would be no difficulty in keeping them occupied but they received surprisingly few offers to dance and soon we were three of the only dozen or so people left in the room.

When we returned to the front door of my block of flats, the younger girl became, not unreasonably, upset at the presence of Charlotte, who stood her ground. As I was unable to give an assurance that I would not continue to see Charlotte, the other girl took her leave despite my soothing words. She was quite right but, in fairness to myself, I had always told her that I could not see her exclusively.

Charlotte came with me to Mustique a fortnight later, where we met both Bryan Ferry and Mick Jagger, and I narrowly escaped drowning for the first of two separate occasions on the island. Our house that year was the smaller of two owned by the Guinness family. It was possible to walk down a small cliff and cross over some rocks to a tiny beach. This was not, however, one of the recommended beaches, but could be used for convenience. One night after dinner when several of us had had too much drink, we decided to take a midnight swim there and all went reasonably well as we staggered down into the water. It was a shallow entrance to the sea, surrounded by slippery rocks. We swam beyond them but, after a while, the others swam back round the rocks and returned to the house with the exception of Charlotte who stayed on the beach. It was a totally dark night and I suddenly realized that in my drunken state I could see no way back. I eventually hit the rocks and tried clambering up them only to slither down again. Charlotte grew desperate, trying to talk me into the right spot, but although I could hear her and needed her guidance, I found it impossible to home in on her instructions and continued to slide on and off the rocks which were covered with seaweed and slime. Eventually, of course, I crawled ashore but it was another lesson learned.

On that side of the tiny island there was the massive wreck of the liner *Antilles*, which had run ashore there one night, split in he middle and burnt out. No one had been drowned and most of the passengers and crew had been taken ashore on Mustique. Not the Captain, however, who had broken all instructions and fled to another island. The French Government was embarrassed about the whole fiasco and sold the hulk to a speculator. He tried to salvage the lead and other valuable materials on board but was, in turn, killed when piloting his own Cessna when it crashed while the salvage-boat was overloaded and sank. The wreck, with its crack down the middle, made an interesting tour though the creaking noises within the hull were eerie and rather frightening. Bryan Ferry recorded them and actually used them in the backing for one of his records later on.

The other time that I nearly drowned in Mustique was two years later and it was a much closer thing. Charlotte and I were sharing the Gingerbread House with Bryan and Jerry Hall, who was on the scene by then. The four of us decided to go down to Pasture beach, an attractive little bay with waves coming in from the Atlantic. This is the only beach on the island which has no reef to protect it and there is a clear notice up to warn of the danger.

But I knew better. I thought myself a strong swimmer and was used to body-surfing though in waves no bigger than those of my days in Cornwall during the war. I decided to fool around in the surf without getting out of my depth. Charlotte went for a long walk along the beach collecting shells and Bryan and Jerry were fooling around on the beach

104

not far away, probably no more than 40 or 50 yards from me.

What I had not bargained for was the way in which the sand beneath the water undulated, often by as much as two feet. So one minute I was standing only waist high between waves and the next I was up to my neck. What with this and the very strong undertow, dragging me out, I was suddenly in trouble. I started taking in water as I struggled to stay afloat with the undercurrent towing me one way and the waves pushing me the other. The intake of water and the effort involved in swimming soon sapped my strength and I really thought I was going to drown. The ironic thing was that I could still see Bryan and Jerry so close yet completely unaware of my problem. It was just as well that they did not know since they were weaker swimmers than me.

My mind was still working clearly and I had already figured out the danger to Bryan and Jerry and I had time to think of one final plan. I was strangely unfrightened by the prospect of impending death, just as I had been in that headlong plunge in the Land-Rover in the South of France 14 years earlier. The thought suddenly came to me: force my whole body as high in the water as possible and the waves would sweep me in, nullifying the undertow. And so it worked. I was able to stagger ashore and collapse on the sand, completely exhausted. None of the others had any idea what I had been through. Curiously enough, although I felt no real fear when I thought it was all over with me, I remember being filled with anger at my own foolishness and at the prospect of ruining other people's holiday and letting down my sons. And I am no sort of hero.

It was on the second of those three trips to Mustique with Charlotte that we met the notorious model Vicki Hodge and her boy-friend, the equally notorious John Bindon. He had already done time in Maidstone jail and had a number of convictions under his belt though these were nothing compared with his later exploits when he killed a man, stabbing him to death, and narrowly escaping a murder conviction by pleading self-defence. Bindon was also a film-extra and sometimes slightly more than that, so his name figures on the credits of several films made in the 1970s.

Charlotte ran into Vicki first and reported back to me that she had asked her to invite me as a newspaper man to be discreet about her presence on the island. I was furious at this request which was all the more impertinent in view of her own behaviour with Bindon there and her subsequent revelations to the press, particularly about her sordid affair with Prince Andrew in Barbados, revelations which she sold for money.

As a holiday companion, Bindon was quite amusing and I actually got on well with him. He delighted in telling us stories of his criminal past and of life in prison. He was proudest of all, though, of his enormous penis, which he would delight in exposing to literally anyone on the island. He would hold it in the palm of his hand and swing it around, encouraged by Vicki, the woman who wanted me to be discreet. On one occasion he even flashed it for Princess Margaret and the island's owner, Colin Tennant, seemed to regard the act as part of the regular Mustique cabaret. On another occasion, Charlotte and I had drinks with the proprietors of the *Washington Post* aboard their small yacht moored offshore. To the amazement of the Americans, Bindon circled the boat in a small motor dinghy, pulled down his pants and started swinging his dick like a lasso. They were appalled and I had some difficulty in explaining away my so-called friend.

Back home, my relationship with Charlottes's family was impossible. When all is said and done, I was doing Charlotte no harm and was certainly introducing her to a wider circle of friends. But they resolutely refused to meet me or let me into their house. By contrast, Lady Howe's sister, known as Auntie Flo by Charlotte, was all over me on her visits to this country from South Africa. She lived in Durban, was a bastion of local society, and was always inviting us to go and stay with her.

I ran into Lord Howe twice while I was with Charlotte. On the first occasion we were staying for the weekend near by and Charlotte suggested that we went for a ride down the long drive and circled the house so that I would at least know what it looked like. I had a brand-new dark-brown Rover, recently supplied by the office, and I was rather proud of it. Unfortunately, as we were leaving the drive, we came face to face with Lord Howe in his low-slung sports car. Charlotte leaned across me and they conducted a perfectly friendly conversation though he didn't actually say anything to me. His last words to her were 'What a perfectly dreadful car' and he zoomed off in a cloud of dust.

The second occasion that we met was at Silverstone during practice for a big race there. Lord Howe, having been a racing-driver himself and son of an even greater one, was vice-president of the RAC and president of the British Racing Driver's Club so he never missed any sort of motor sport if he could help it. We were walking across the infield when we ran straight into him and this time Charlotte had to introduce us. Lord Howe gazed at me for a second and said in a not unfriendly tone 'horses'. That was all, just the one word. I was tempted to reply 'cars' but decided against it. As they chatted for a while, I glanced away and spotted, standing near by, the former world motor-racing champion, Denny Hulme, whom I knew quite well. I wandered over to talk to Denny and then I had a thought. 'Would you like to make an old man very happy?' I asked, adding 'Lord Howe, president of the BRDC, is over with my girl-friend, who is his daughter, and he would be thrilled to meet you.' Denny was pleased to oblige and, sure enough, Lord Howe was thrilled to bits to be talking with one of his heroes. An ironic situation.

I did get as far as the door of Penn on one other occasion and caused a fair amount of consternation. It was a Sunday morning and Charlotte and I were flying down to Sardinia for a holiday. She decided to spend Saturday night with her parents but said it would be all right for me to pick her up there as she would be ready to open the door herself at 8.30. In those days I had a green Ford Escort – it was just before the advent of the brown Rover – and I drove up and rang the bell. While I was waiting for her to appear, I opened the luggage-boot ready for her suitcase and, feeling through my pockets, I found a set of keys, which I took to be my flat keys and threw them idly into the boot, since I would not be needing them on holiday. Charlotte arrived and we put in her luggage and slammed the boot. I went back to the driver's seat, fumbled in my pocket for the car keys and brought out my flat keys. I had locked the car keys in the boot which opened only on one of them. It was a Sunday morning and there was no way that we would get hold of a garage to come out and force open the boot in time to catch our flight. Equally, I was unwilling to miss out on any part of our holiday, since flights to Sardinia were difficult to book at that time of year. We decided to go without luggage and make arrangements for the car to be collected the next day and the cases sent on to us. The Aga Khan household always stocked plenty of spare washing and shaving-kit and I had already been lent or given his shirts and trousers in the past as we were much the same fit. Sally would look after both of us and we could buy anything else while waiting for our gear to arrive.

So Charlotte rang for a taxi to take us to the airport and I saw Lord Howe looking testily out of the door as he spied my plebeian Ford parked right outside. I rang up Billy, a particular friend who had for years parked cars at the Clermont and Annabel's and who often did private jobs for me and many of my friends, particularly 'Lucky' Lucan, and, explaining my plight asked him to deal with it. Billy told me later that he had enjoyed his meeting with Lord Howe who had been very friendly towards him, relieved, no doubt to be ridding himself of the impediment outside his house. And the suitcases arrived in Sardinia two days later.

It wasn't until some 18 months after Charlotte and I had drifted apart that I was to meet Lord Howe again.

Charlotte had taken up with George Wright, a small-time criminal and car-dealer with three convictions and a short spell of prison to his name. George was regarded as a sort of tame bad-egg by some of his West End friends but even Charlotte's close friends, as well as her parents, were appalled when she took up with him. She became quite frightened of him in due course, particularly after his displays of violent temper. Once he loosed off both barrels of her shotgun inside her little mews house between Belgrave Square and Eaton Square. The first shot went through her bedroom door and the other one went out of the window peppering the walls of the Belgian Embassy.

This was a serious offence and the brave George quickly lost his bravado, hiding in the attic and leaving Charlotte to face the music with the police. Incredibly, she protected him at great personal risk and lied about his whereabouts to the police. He got away with it because of her. Another time when she was trying to give up seeing him, she joined a group of us in Annabel's after my birthday dinner upstairs in the Clermont. I was sitting opposite her with my back to the room when I saw in the gloom her face tighten. I looked over my shoulder and there was George standing menacingly over us all. He demanded that Charlotte dance with him. To humour him, I offered him a drink and several of us tried to calm him down. But he demanded his dance. To prevent a further row Charlotte agreed, but came back alone to the table in tears. He had been twisting her arm and pinching her viciously. He disappeared for a while but then returned, obviously the worse for drink and, when she refused to dance with him a second time, he suddenly swept the bottles off the table and started smashing glasses with his hand. He was hustled away by waiters and one of the members of my party, who knew him better, joined him at the door to escort him to hospital since there was blood pouring from his hand and an almost severed finger.

This led to the only disagreement I have ever had in more than twenty-six years of friendship with Louis, the master head-waiter at Annabel's. Louis suggested that it was my fault for causing the fracas while I retorted that Wright should not have been allowed in as he was not a member and was most definitely not invited.

The following year, George Wright was found dead in his bed in mysterious circumstances. It was never clear whether he had taken an overdose, whether accidental or not, or whether it was the result of his having swallowed, as a typical act of bravado, a gold chain from around his neck. There were also suggestions of foul play and dark hints that there may have been people who wanted to get rid of him.

His death made front page news in most of the papers, especially the tabloids since most journalists seemed to know of his association with Charlotte. Her name, and that of her family, were dragged through the mud. Charlotte returned from a skiing holiday and more publicity was given to her association with him as there were numerous pictures of her at the funeral in the popular press.

At about this time, I received a telephone call from Lord Howe. Would I meet him for an urgent discussion at his London house in Pittshead Mews? The house backs on to what was then the Curzon House Club and is now the Aspinall Curzon. The club had been the family home at one stage. This was an amazing development. How could Lord Howe want anything from me whom he had so resolutely banned from his life only a year and a half previously?

When I arrived he greeted me warmly within his somewhat diffident limits, sat me down and poured out his heart. 'You understand the newspapers,' he began. 'What can I do to stop the family name being dragged through the gutter press. Why has my daughter done this to her mother and me?' he continued. 'We have given everything to her and her sister. We have always done our best for her and welcomed her friends to our house.' At this point, sorry as I was for this obviously bewildered elderly gentleman, I could contain myself no longer. 'Lord Howe,' I interrupted, 'I sympathize with you but I cannot allow you to make a remark like that in front of me, of all people, having banned me from your house for nearly three years.' He held up his hand. 'That was nothing personal, I assure you. It was just that we are a totally motor-car family and you are a horse man. It was no more than that.' I was hardly mollified by this ludicrous explanation but I let it pass as I felt genuinely sorry for him.

In the end I gave him the best advice that I could, which was to say absolutely nothing to any pressman ringing up and to advise his wife and family to do the same. The trouble had been that, in his innocence, he had already given honest answers to scandal-mongers who had got through to him, the same answers that any slightly old-fashioned father would have given about a man such as George Wright becoming mixed up with his daughter. He was quoted as saying that he was glad that Charlotte was rid of Wright which was exactly the reaction of most people. But the tabloids, as usual, were able to twist this to an attack on a wealthy aristocrat speaking ill of the poor dead car-dealer who had dared to cast his net above his station.

That was my last contact with Lord Howe.

However, Lord Howe's name helped me just once, though he did not know it. Charlotte and I were staying with Simon and Philippa Courtauld for a weekend which included a ball given by Lord Fermoy, uncle of the Princess of Wales. We enjoyed the party, where Prince Charles was present though not his future bride who was much too young, and it was daylight when we decided to drive back. Charlotte and I were the first of our group to leave even at that hour and we set off for the shortish journey, which involved joining the M4 at exit 14 and coming off at 13. Charlotte was driving me in her black Lotus and exactly midway between the two exits we ran out of petrol.

As we stood helplessly on the hard-shoulder, waiting for our friends to come by and pick us up, a large police Jaguar drew up and two policemen got out, not particularly pleased to see us. We explained our dilemma. They did not seem prepared to take positive action to help. 'Aren't you a member of the RAC?' demanded one of the policemen to Charlotte. 'No, but my daddy is president. Is that any good?' replied Charlotte in her most demure terms. Funnily enough, she was not trying to flex her muscles. That was the way she was and she genuinely thought that this was a relevant answer.

It certainly worked. The policemen roared with laughter and made space in the back of their car which had no real seat but was filled with cones used for cordoning off sections of blocked motorway. They lifted us back to the Courtauld house, and we clambered out thanking them profusely as they lectured us on the strict necessity of collecting the car first thing in the morning. It was already first thing so we took this to mean second thing. They would alert the necessary authority to the car's presence but we must move it by midday. We asked them in for a drink or a cup of coffee and they were just declining politely when there was a roar of swirling gravel from the drive round the corner of the house and a convoy of three cars screeched to a halt with figures tumbling out in various states of sobriety. I rushed over to my host to explain the situation advising him to go quietly but he insisted on coming over and congratulating the policemen personally, insisting that they came in for

110

some sort of beverage which they did under such pressure. We were able to persuade some unlucky member of the group to wake up early enough to take us and a can of petrol to collect the car in the nick of time and thus Lord Howe had saved the day.

But, of all the trips we took together, the most dramatic was abroad the QE2 for the Dunhill International Backgammon Championship. This was the brainchild of Patrick Lichfield who organized it together with Dunhill, who put up the prize money and most of the expenses, and Cunard who provided accommodation aboard their flag-ship. The plan was to promote the world backgammon championship, the competition being restricted to thirty-two players. In effect, for publicity purposes, they invited about twenty-six of the world's best players and threw in six other invitations for people like Clement Freud, the writer, television personality and Liberal Member of Parliament; Victor Lownes, head of Playboy Clubs in Europe; Michael Pearson, somewhat fluky winner of the first-ever Clermont Club championship, son of Lord Cowdray and a familiar name in the gossip columns; and myself. I got in purely because I was also invited to conduct the auction on the first evening, the day before play began. I did quite a lot of these auctions before backgammon and tennis tournaments and also at charity lunches and dinners and do even more these days.

At the pre-tournament party at Cunard's offices in London, I first met Victor Matthews, the managing director, who was running his company's side of the action. I remember chatting to him at some length and getting on well, which was fortunate for me since he later became proprietor of the *Daily Express* and was therefore my boss. He told me later that he had disliked most of the backgammon players whom he had found arrogant and stand-offish.

We were all flown, together with the organizers, journalists and other permitted hangers-on, to New York, where we stayed for one night in an hotel before embarking. I was allowed to bring Charlotte, presumably because she was a friend of Lichfield and was titled and looked good, which suited the sponsors.

The auction went well and I raised plenty of laughs. I tend to insult each player before selling him, and also anyone else in the room including bidders, and most of them know this and seem to enjoy it.

In fact, as a rule of thumb, the more I insult someone the more I like them. Clement Freud, whom I knew fairly well from the racecourse, obviously did not realize this. When I came to sell him off, I described him as just about the worst player in the tournament, a statement which

111

would have met with full agreement from just about every other player. So when someone bid a modest £200, I quickly knocked him down saying amidst roars of laughter, 'That's more than enough.' It was the smallest price of the evening with the favourites going well into the thousands of pounds. I only went for £500 pounds and took a fifth myself with four friends.

I had long forgotten about my remarks on Clement Freud's ability when about ten of us sat down for lunch. We could choose our own companions and tables but we were virtually all friends. Suddenly, as we were just beginning our scrambled eggs, the safest lunch to order, Clement loomed up and glared down at me with his red-rimmed watery eyes. 'How dare you say such things about me at the auction?' he boomed. 'I was chosen to play on merit. I am a public figure and I have told my constituents that I have taken this week off because I am one of the 32 best players in the world. Your remarks will be reported and will undermine my credibility.' And he stormed off.

The whole table was flabbergasted at this pompous outburst but we all roared with laughter. Clement was duly beaten in the first round that afternoon and did not speak to me for the next four days.

We were to play one round a day starting on that Wednesday afternoon and evening and I was on a winning streak. I beat one of the favourites, Gino Scalamandre, in the second round on the final throw, which caused him great rage and fury though he overlooked the fact that he had been incredibly lucky to get that close. I then had a fairly kind third round against Victor Lownes, who had knocked out a better player in the early stages and thus I was through to the semi-finals. My training programme was unorthodox and indeed unique. Nearly all the other players stuck to backgammon in the evenings and through the night, playing for money and with great intensity among themselves. Apart from the tournament, however, I did not look at a backgammon board and spent night after night in the night-club mostly at the bar, surrounded by Charlotte and all the other girls in the party. I did quite a bit of dancing as well, and each morning Charlotte and I staggered back to our cabin any time between 3.30 and 5. There was a very good cocktail bar on an upper deck where the barman was a wizard with reviving Bullshots and Bloody Marys.

There was also a casino on board but the manager did not seem to know much about us – or perhaps he knew too much – and he kept credit very tight and the limits too low for most of us. One camp-follower, Robert Millbourn, who had paid his own way just to be part of the action, had to beg for more credit after he had lost his cash. 'I'll give you another £500 if you streak around the casino,' said the manager, thinking he was joking. To his amazement and to that of the other players in the casino, Robert stripped stark naked and ran round the entire circuit. He enjoyed himself so much that he also did it a second time.

The ship's newspaper was reporting the backgammon in glowing terms but, back at home, Nigel Dempster was running a vendetta in his column in the *Daily Mail*. The reason for his fury was simple. He had originally been invited on the trip but had been turned down when Michael Pearson had stipulated that it was either him or Nigel. The organizers had decided in favour of Pearson so Lichfield had to break the news to his friend Dempster who took it badly, so everything that went wrong on the trip was reported by Nigel. No one knew how he was getting his information which was fairly accurate though slanted and exaggerated. For instance, we had complained about the food, which was duly chronicled, but had otherwise enjoyed ourselves enormously, which was not. The main suspect was Taki, a rich Greek and a great sportsman who was also beginning a career as a writer and journalist. Taki liked nothing better than to stir up trouble and, apart from conducting a widely noticed ship-board romance with a married lady which would have made much better copy, he was leaking daily to Dempster over the ship's telephone. It was his idea of a joke though the sponsors did not see it that way.

At the semi-final stage, some of the group opened a book on the outcome and I was nominated outsider of the four players left at odds of 9–2. Barclay Cooke, who played in the other semi-final, was hot favourite. All the battle-hardened professionals on board seized on these odds and backed me to a man. They knew that there was very little between the four of us and, although I was only an amateur, I played quite well and had a good temperament. The bookmakers were Victor Lownes, the American writer Jon Bradshaw and – surprise, surprise – Clement Freud.

I won my semi-final and the captain asked Charlotte and me to his private cocktail party that evening. Freud was there and, to my amazement, he approached me. 'I'm in trouble and I need your help,' he started, eyes more watery than ever. 'I'm one-third of the bookmaking syndicate and we've laid you to lose us well into five figures. What should I do?' I was flabbergasted by this extraordinary approach and didn't know what he could want. I decided to be flippant and it seemed to work as we were back on speaking terms. That night I drank more than ever, leaping around the dance floor with my bevy of ladies and even a few of the other players on this occasion. 'I'm a finalist,' I would chant from time to time and this would be taken up by the others. I was escorted to my cabin later than ever with one or two of the others walking me to the door to make sure I didn't get into any more trouble.

I still felt fine for the final which was against Barclay Cooke. It was first to reach 29 points and we were at it, neck and neck for four and a half hours. Barclay, abstemious at the best of times, drank two or three glasses of water but one of my Greek friends, Janni Zographos, nephew of the head of the legendary Greek syndicate in the French casinos before the war, started supplying me with glasses of champagne. We reached a score of 28 all and I dramatically threw the doubling cube into the crowd. This had to be the last game. I was in the slightly better position from the word go and elected to take a chance before I had to but at a stage where it could possibly have been retrieved if he hit me. It was a calculated gamble and it came off. He missed the shot which was a three and, barring flukes, I was high and dry.

Barclay sportingly conceded with about three throws to go, standing up and shaking my hand. The match had been played in good spirit throughout. When we counted there twelve empty champagne glasses lined up by my elbow.

The winning cheque was £10,000, a much-needed cash injection for me and my bookmakers. For, needless to day, I was going through one of my periodical lean spells on the Turf. I also won another £3,000 for owning one-fifth of myself in the auction pool but I had paid out this amount in insurance money to my last three opponents, normal practice when the stakes are high.

The *Daily Express* carried the story on the front page with a rather blurry picture of Charlotte watching me playing and accompanied by a story by none other than Clement Freud. It was very fairly written too. Spurred on by the complaints about the food, the catering officer had gone ashore when the liner docked at Cherbourg and brought aboard special French food for a farewell dinner for us. Then it was the short hop across to Southampton where Victor Lownes had obtained special dispensation for him and us to nip ashore early. We were met in a large Rolls by his then girl-friend and now wife, Marilyn Cole, a former Playboy 'Playmate of the Year' and we drove up to London to celebrate. The first port of call was Annabel's where we were politely told that the club was closed for a private party given by Lord Portman and organized by our mutual friend Graham Hill. I left a cheeky message for Graham saying that he had turned away the world backgammon champion and we went on instead to my other favourite club, Tramp in Jermyn Street.

We got the right reception there from the patron, Johnny Gold, a great friend and racing-fan who has performed an amazing feat in keeping his club at the very top for some twenty years in a dangerously volatile field of entertainment. Johnny led us to his own table inside the restaurant section and had to leave us for a moment to break up a fight. We heard a high-pitched screaming noise and saw Johnny deftly lift young Spiros Niarchos, middle of the three sons of Stavros, from some unfortunate victim whom he was attempting to beat up. This was not the first time I had seen Spiros attack someone in Tramp. Previously I had been at the next table inside the night-club when he had flown at Ryan O'Neil, who was actually in his party but who had shown the temerity to dance with the little Greek boy's girl-friend.

While we were relaxing over several bottles of champagne, there was a telephone call for me. It was Graham Hill from Annabel's. 'What on earth are you doing?' he asked, 'get over here at once.' So we ended up celebrating with Graham at Eddy Portman's party.

Later that year I represented Britain in a backgammon international against America and thereafter I played in several open world championships, first in Nassau and then in Monte Carlo.

I usually justified my seeding position though I never got close to winning. The nearest was in Nassau when Bobby Lorenz had to throw a 4–3 to beat me in the final game of our quarter-final contest and did so, a 17–1 shot. I was also on the committee at these championships which meant, when I was not actually playing, I could be called upon to adjudicate in the case of disputes, which were fairly frequent. I could not believe some of the strokes that players tried to pull, and I became quite angry when I dismissed some of the more outrageous plays.

I also had the board thrown in my face by one of the reputedly better types of American after I had hammered him by an enormous margin in one of the Nassau championships. Even old Oswald Jacoby, a tough-nut often rated the best in the world in his time, who was playing at the next table, apologized to me on behalf of his countryman.

In the end I could stand it no more. With money getting near to the million-dollar mark spread around these tournaments the worst human elements were attracted and seductive though the surroundings are in

115

Monte Carlo, the people spoil the scenery. I prefer to take my holidays elsewhere without the aggravation and a lot of others took the same view, including former world champion Joe Dwek.

I have been lucky in other tournaments in more attractive surroundings though. I have done consistently well in Aspinall's tournaments, winning one worth £24,000 about six years ago at the small club off Sloane Street. I also won the Turf Club tournament the night I first met up with my second wife. But that is another story.

The Ghastly Murder
Of My Brother's Wife

Soon after my divorce my brother Jonathan became engaged to Gail Plugge and I was both pleased and amused. Pleased because Gail was a bright, lively, intelligent, dark-haired girl who never wore nor needed much make-up, and amused because I knew her father, Capt. Leonard Plugge, a somewhat eccentric inventor, business man and a former Conservative MP. I also remembered her elder brother, Frank, though with some embarrassment since I had banned him from visiting my house at school for some reason I can't recall when I was captain of the house in 1953.

Gail's wedding took place in Chester Square and there was a grand reception in Lowndes Square. Leonard Plugge, a small, bald, rather owlish-looking man with a twinkle behind his glasses, had always lived in great style. At one time, he had occupied that magnificent building between Hamilton Place and Park Lane which was formerly the home of the Rothschilds and later for some time the well-known club Les Ambassadeurs.

So they got off to a flying start but, with my brother often away on film assignments and their hopes for a family thwarted by a miscarriage, they drifted apart. I learnt of this when I was on holiday in the south of France with my long-standing girl-friend of that era, Sue Aylwyn. We were sitting in a restaurant in Cannes when Gail came up to us. 'I've just left Jonathan,' she said. 'I hope you don't mind and we can remain friends. He and I are still friends too.' Later she and Jonathan made another go of it for a while, but then she met the man who was to change the course of her life – and ultimately terminate it.

His name was Hakim Jamal. He was black, well over six feet tall and undeniably strikingly good-looking, a point of which he was well aware.

He had the 'gift of the gab' and the combination of his presence, looks, and non-stop flow of rhetoric totally mesmerized Gail, and she started to follow him wherever he went – America (he came from Boston), Europe, and especially North Africa.

He believed he was some sort of Messiah and claimed to be a cousin of the assassinated American black rights leader Malcolm X. This claim was only partially true as he appears to have been married to a cousin of Malcolm X. But Malcolm X was his number-one man and he was keen to follow in his footsteps but with much more consideration for personal reward both for his pocket and his ego.

One sunny Sunday in the spring of 1971, Gail rang me at my flat in Lowndes Street. 'Can I bring Hakim round to see you?' she asked me. 'He has something he wants to show you.' I suggested they came round at midday. The door-bell rang, rather late, and there they were standing together in the hallway.

Before I had a chance to speak, Hakim addressed me. 'Do you believe in God?' he boomed. Somewhat taken aback I mumbled to the effect that I did not but it was nothing personal. 'You should, because you are looking at him,' he announced, staring me straight in the eye.

At least we knew where we stood. I was in the presence of God or, perhaps God was in the presence of me. Gail nodded enthusiastically, a serene smile on her face. He was certainly impressive, standing there in long, flowing robes with a fez on his head. He looked like a dignified Nigerian chieftain, but as we walked through to my large, bright and airy drawing-room, he quickly created a very different impression. Speaking non-stop, he indulged in what was basically an extended anti-white sermon, though somewhat illogically he made constant laudatory references to his own, non-Negroid features. 'Look at my nose,' he commanded, pointing at his undeniably straight and well-moulded proboscis, 'nothing like a nigger. Look at my lips, not fat or rubbery, are they?' Then he flubbered his finger between his lips in what I took to be an imitation of a black man. Then he went, 'You white men brought all the disease into the world. You contaminated the black men in Africa when you colonized them.'

I listened impassively to this diatribe but could not fail to observe the approving smile on the face of Gail, sitting at his feet – he was in an armchair by now – gazing adoringly at him while noting down his every word in a book clearly filled with the wit and wisdom of Hakim. It took some time for the tempest to die down but when the torrent of words began to abate I managed to slip in my first question. 'What exactly do

118

you want of me?' I enquired. He did not answer but Gail glanced down at a thick manuscript which she was clutching.

Then I decided to be a little more provocative. 'If you despise white men so much, why have you come to see me?'

This time Gail spoke. 'Hakim has written this wonderful book. You must read it. It's all about his great cousin Malcolm X and you must do something with it.'

'I don't want any favours,' interjected Hakim, but he quickly changed the tack of the conversation and started extolling the virtues of Malcolm X and black rights generally. It was boring to be harangued in this way, but on the other hand I had to admit that he was a fluent and persuasive speaker and I could see that he might well be quite an orator. If it hadn't been for the fact that he seemed so arrogant and such a bully, I could have understood Gail's being fascinated by him.

Then they mentioned that I was a friend of the Aga Khan. 'You know him well,' pleaded Gail, 'please read the manuscript, then show it to him. I'm sure he will want to help.' Once again Hakim interrupted with all his arrogance and conceit, 'We don't need any help. We are just giving you the chance to be in on something big.'

It was obvious that this was the reason for the visit, even though he wouldn't have admitted it. I had grave doubts whether I wanted to involve the Aga and these doubts soon crystallized into outright rejection of the idea. However, I was spared from having to hedge or express any doubts as I was clearly not required to speak.

Hakim changed the subject and began, much more interestingly, to reminisce about the thrills and dangers of his past. Whether what he told me was true or not, it was fascinating stuff. He had apparently survived no less than five assassination attempts. In one of them, he had been hijacked into a car by four men, driven out into the Nevada desert, and shot five times in the body before being shovelled out and left for dead by the roadside. He head clearly been involved in gangland feuds involving a mixture of drugs, religion, and black rights. He had played a dangerous game in a dangerous area and in view of his subsequent fate, much of what he said may well have been true.

Hakim and Gail were with me for two hours, finally leaving the manuscript with me. I had absolutely no temptation to show it to the Aga Khan, whom I knew would have rejected it out of hand.

'Isn't he wonderful,' Gail whispered in my ear as she went out, 'you must admit that he is brilliant.' Not the first time that day, I was able to mumble something non-commital without either commenting on the

119

utter conceit of the man or admitting that there was something of interest about him. I looked out of the window a minute or so later and saw them walking slowly towards Sloane Street. He was still talking, looking straight ahead, as Gail clung to his arm, smiling, and looking up at him with admiration. The memory hurts me still when I recall her subsequent disillusionment and then, more terrible, her demise.

They travelled the world as he sought recognition as the Messiah, but gradually even his arrogance and self-confidence began to evaporate, and they met up in North Africa with friends or followers of Michael X, an altogether tatty and tawdry imitation of Malcolm X. Whatever may be said about the politics and beliefs of the latter, there is no denying that he had considerable style and charisma as well as an honest belief in his cause and that of his people. And there is no doubt he died for that belief. Michael X had no such dignity and the nearest he ever got to his namesake was the name itself which he had taken on deliberately. Basically a half-cast pimp and small-time gangster, he made his tatty name as a collector for Rachman, the notorious London rent-fixer and racketeer.

After several brushes with the law, Michael X fled the country and eventually set up a small commune of hoodlums in Trinidad. It was at this commune that Gail and Hakim eventually arrived, disillusioned and broke. For Hakim it must have been a terrible blow to his pride to have to bow allegiance to Michael X, a man whom he could physically and intellectually have overwhelmed.

Gail still maintained her simple faith in Hakim, whom she pathetically believed would re-emerge as the natural leader, and she was at first taken in by the absurd pretensions of Michael X and his bogus objectives. For behind a veil of moral fervour, Michael X was still just a hoodlum and con-man. Gradually Gail's eyes were opened. She realized that she was becoming part of a criminal conspiracy, finding evidence to support her view each day.

One evening she was caught going through files in Michael X's office. Soon afterwards, Hakim was taken aside by one of the Michael X's associates and advised that if he knew what was good for him he would leave the island soon and stay in Boston for a while fund raising.

At 6 o'clock the following morning, while Hakim deliberately slept on, Gail was woken up and invited to go and look at something. She was taken to some earthworks and – probably as she realized that she was looking at her open grave – she was set upon by the men around her, beaten and bludgeoned with picks and shovels and a cutlass and hurled, half-dead, into the grave and buried alive. The manner of her dying came out later when the coroner's court was told that she had earth and sand in her lungs, indicating that she was still alive when buried. Nor was she the only one murdered during that purge.

News of Gail's disappearance leaked out to the authorities in Trinidad and Michael X fled to Guyana. Amazingly, and to the credit of the authorities in both Guyana and Trinidad, an exhausted Michael X was later picked up on the run in the hinterland of Guyana and extradited to face trial in Trinidad. He had tried to disguise himself when escaping by shaving off his beard and altering his hair style. At his trial, many of the gruesome details of the tragedy came to light. Despite his odious denials, he was found guilty and subsequently hanged some three years later.

Before his execution, an unbelievable campaign in his favour was waged by liberals around the world, claiming that he was a victim of racial and political persecution and should be reprieved. I was particularly incensed that John Lennon was one of the most prominent members of this misguided campaign and I never forgave him. Many of the campaigns waged by trendy liberal factions are innocuous enough even in one disagrees with them. But this was a particularly vicious attempt to miscarry justice on behalf of a man who had spent his entire adult life conniving, stealing, distorting, extorting, and finally murdering.

The story did not end with the death of Gail and the arrest of her murderers. Her twin brother Greville determined to uncover all the facts behind the story and find out if there were other guilty parties who had escaped. He kept in touch with my brother during the following months and one evening rang in some excitement from Tunisia. 'I think I'm on to something, I'll let you know very shortly,' he declared. A day or so later he was killed in a car accident while the other three occupants were completely unscathed. This extraordinary accident was never explained. Across the Atlantic also a few months later Hakim Jamal was gunned down and murdered in Boston.

Motor Racing:
Graham Hill and Jackie Stewart

IT was Graham Hill who principally caused my involvement in motor-racing from about 1966 to 1978. The death of Graham in 1975 and the retirement of Jackie Stewart, followed by James Hunt, took a lot of the fun out of it and while I seldom miss a chance to watch a Grand Prix on television, and particularly admire the skills of Alain Prost, Nigel Mansell and Nelson Piquet, it doesn't seem to me the same any more.

But during those years it was Graham and Jackie who gave me most enjoyment. Graham and I became very close friends for no other reason as far as I can see than our similar sense of humour. My friendship with Jackie also blossomed on a different basis and we remain in touch today, though, with his constant travelling Jackie is a hard man to nail down.

The highlight of the motor-racing year, certainly in Europe, was and still is, the Monte Carlo Grand Prix which is the number-one social weekend there. For a variety of reasons, I do not think that I am being personally bitter in saying that it is not the same these days. The drivers keep themselves to themselves much more and concentrate only on the mechanics of their cars while the so-called beautiful people who stay in the hotels and aboard yachts moored in the harbour are, for the most part, quite appalling.

Graham and Jackie, though great friends, were also rivals in several areas, notably among royalty, the former being a special friend of Prince Charles and loved to take him to race tracks on non-racing days and let him loose in a car, the latter equally friendly with Princess Anne and would provide similar facilities for her and Mark Phillips.

This royal rivalry occasionally produced amusing incidents. Both were deferential to their royal friends but Graham had the more flamboyant nature and might occasionally have allowed Prince Charles

122

rather more rope than he should have to an amateur. Once, at Donnington I believe it was, Graham let Prince Charles go off on his own in a car before he realized that there had been a rainstorm on the far side of the track which had not affected the home straight. 'Strewth,' shouted Graham, as he recalled the drama to me later, 'what have I done?' He lept into another car and set off at break-neck speed to try and flag down Prince Charles but he was too late. He roared round a corner to face a patch of damp road and there off the track and in a ditch, but smiling broadly and unscathed, was the future king of England. Jackie was always very shocked by this story. 'Grandad should have been more careful particularly with the future king.' Jackie could wax quite eloquent in his famous Scottish tenor brogue and this was the sort of thing that he reacted to.

Graham nearly did the same to me one day at Brand's Hatch, one of England's two Formula One Championship tracks, Silverstone being the other. I had gone down for the day with with Graham and Bette to watch practice and Graham had promised to drive me round in a sports saloon. Despite the fact that I knew I was being driven by a world champion I was creasing my pants in terror as the G-forces tugged my ample frame hither and thither round the bends. Only my pride, plus the inner knowledge that this was a top professional driving, prevented me from calling to Graham to slow down. Then it happened. Somewhere far out on the far side of the track, Graham lost it and we went into a long, hair-raising slide turning round a couple of times.

Graham was more upset than I was. For me it was all over in a few seconds and I still have faith that Graham knew what he was doing. But he was acutely embarrassed even though it had only happened with a close friend, since he knew the other drivers would be pulling his leg. Not least of them, of course, was Jackie, delighted with 'grandad's' discomfort. Jackie always called Graham 'grandad', a nickname which was not wholly appreciated.

However, even Jackie nearly had blood on his hands some time later when, during the course of two of his splendidly organized days at Silverstone for his friends, he watched in horror as first myself and then, more importantly for Jackie, Mark Phillips were involved in horrific crunches both writing off the car. More of that later.

Graham was a man of enormous courage and it was his utter determination that enabled him to be world champion twice and win Monte Carlo no less than five times. His stubbornness against adversity and sheer bravery was never better advertised than in his fight against

123

the crippling and separate injuries sustained to both his legs. The worst of these was suffered in Indianapolis. Few doctors gave him any chance of ever walking again, let alone driving, but he exercised through excruciating pain with his usual determination and left his hospital bed on sticks when most of us would have been lying groaning for pain-killers. It was under this incredible handicap – his legs bowed like two sides of an orange – that he took up golf and became a fanatic. Because he concentrated so fiercely, and tried so hard, a round of golf with him could be a slow business but I was still always happy to play with him as the jokes and the competiveness made it all worth while.

Graham was much in demand as an after-dinner speaker and he practically never turned down an invitation. He was incredibly free with his time and travelled miles to make people laugh at endless dinners and functions. He had an endless fund of jokes and the Guild of Toast-masters voted him speaker of the year at least once.

Graham was a good old Londoner who had once served in the navy and who exercised with the London Rowing Club, hence his use of their colours on his racing helmet. His most famous partnership was with Colin Chapman and Lotus, and it was during this association that he won the world championship in 1962 and 1968. He never had the natural skill and flair of either Jim Clark or Jackie Stewart but he was a hard man to beat.

To accommodate his ever-increasing social round of engagements, he used my flat to bath and change more and more during the last five or six years of his life. The porter had instructions to let him in if I was not there and in the end I gave him a key. So, often he rushed in for the lightning change, sometimes from racing overalls to dinner-jacket and black tie and then, later on, he would appear almost automatically at Annabel's for one drink. He knew we were always likely to be there and it was almost a ritual before he drove home to Bette. Whoever I was with, even if it was a new girl-friend on the first date, I was always delighted to see Graham but, in the end, it did lead to some problems with Bette who, not unnaturally, looked for someone to blame for Graham's late arrival back home.

One day he was invited to visit the London Rubber Company where, condoms, colloquially known as French letters were produced. In this modern Aids-fearing world, they must be doing well. On the night of his visit back in 1974, Graham was using my flat to change for dinner afterwards and I returned home after he had left. As I opened the front door, there seemed to be a change in the décor. On the telephone in front of me was fitted a rubber French letter, from all the door handles dangled others. On the taps in the kitchen were suspended yet more, and every protrusion in the drawing-room was similarly decorated. By the time I got to the two bedrooms and the bathroom I could scarcely count the total product of this virile English company. Graham had certainly used up his complimentary supply on interior decoration!

He could hardly wait to catch up with me in Annabel's later that night to see how the joke had gone down. 'Bloody 'ell,' he chortled, 'you should have been there. There were all these little old ladies trying them out on a bloody great steel spike. It made me feel very inadequate.'

About six weeks before he died, Graham brought Bette to a very small dinner-party of eight people at the Clermont Club on my birthday. I must have been having a bad run that year as I normally have a large party of people on 23 October, usually through the generosity of John Aspinall. But this year there were only eight of us and one of the other guests had given me one of those smart Cartier address books in dark maroon. Graham grabbed it and wrote his name and address under the letter H adding the old legend, 'by hook or by crook I'll be first in this book', and signed it. I kept the book with just this written in it for some years before my wife found it and, without realizing, filled it in with many other names and addresses. We still use it, complete with the Hill memorial.

It was in Monte Carlo that Graham really came into his own and he was literally mobbed, much more than any other driver, during that week. I still remember with some embarrassment being invited by him, together with my girl-friend, to the Grand Prix dinner and ball held at the Hotel de Paris after the race one year. It must have been sometime ago because one of his other guests was the brilliant young Swedish driver Ronnie Peterson, who was only in his first year of Formula One racing. The embarrassment was caused by the fact that I remember being boringly drunk and making crass conversation with poor Peterson, who must have wondered how someone as amusing as Graham had lumbered him with such a bore. Graham thought it very funny.

Graham became much the oldest driver on the tour and, partly because of his cars, but also, I must admit, because of his age and the fact that his many injuries were catching up with him, he did not achieve much in his last few years. All of us including Bette and myself, and even Jackie for the best of reasons, hoped he would give up while the fans remembered him as a champion. Also, of course, there was the always present risk of further injury or even death. But this was a tricky subject even for me who had the closest of relationships with him. Bette, sensibly, did not pressure him since she knew his stubbornness better than anyone and also knew that he took no notice of her whatsoever. But it was a little sad for all of us who loved him to see him struggling to qualify for even a place at the back of the grid.

I had always been particularly careful not to intrude on Graham or my other friends during the day or days before a race for obvious reasons. Graham was, of course, aware of this. So I was amazed when Graham said to me the night before the race in 1975, 'Come up to my room at about 9 o'clock in the morning.' 'You don't want me up there before the race. I'll only make you cut yourself shaving,' I said. 'No, I mean it, just come up and chat,' was his reply. I looked across at Bette who could hear all this and she gave me a little nod.

The next morning at 9 o'clock sharp, I knocked on the door of their suite in the Hotel de Paris and was let in by Graham. There was a barely touched breakfast-trolley in the sitting-room and he did indeed invite me to come in and talk with him while he shaved. I would not pretend that our conversation was quite as light and superficial as usual and it was very noticeable that the tension built up as race time drew nearer. Bette was not much in evidence as she was busy getting together bits and pieces which were put in a bag to be taken down to the pits when they walked down the course. Finally I felt my time had come and I left to get to my viewing position on our balcony in the Hermitage Hotel next door.

Graham knew where we were and gave us a big wave as he walked down. This routine, unique to the Monte Carlo race, is, for me, the most moving tradition in all sport and the reception given to Graham even in these later days was greater than that accorded to any other driver, even Jackie or any French or Italian drivers. We had agreed to meet up later that night and make Graham's traditional visit to a little bar 200 yards down from the casino square, the Tip Top. Graham knew the owner well and it was a tradition for him to go there for a plate of spaghetti just before sun-up. We decided to make the pilgrimage at 3 o'clock in the morning and Graham, Bette and myself walked down from the hotel. A friend of mine had been past the bar an hour earlier and it was half empty. By the time we reached it, with Graham being patted on the back and waved to as we wandered down the street, the bar was packed and the only words you could hear were 'Graham 'Ill, Graham 'Ill', as every fan in the bar turned to stare at him, smile and

126

wave. Graham loved it and the proprietor burst through the mob to embrace him and lead us to the one little table against the wall, marked 'reserved'. We sat down having ordered the traditional spaghetti with either beer or wine and, for once, Bette seemed a bit more relaxed as we chatted and joked for a few minutes.

Then a young English boy came over and said to Graham, 'I'm a sailor and our ship is moored in Villefranche. You were a sailor, weren't you? Some of the lads are over here and they would like to meet you.' Graham's face lit up as if he had been asked to dinner with Princess Grace or Raquel Welch. 'Of course, delighted,' he said, rising to his feet and disappearing into the mob. 'Won't be a mo,' he shouted over his shoulder to us.

I knew what Bette was thinking as I tried to chat cheerfully. I was right. 'Can't they ever leave him alone?' she said, with a look of abject defeat on her face. 'Can't he ever say no?' I tried to comfort her but I knew Graham and I knew Bette. I did my best to explain. 'That's Graham. You and I can't change him and you must admit he does enjoy the adulation, particularly down here. Let him enjoy it. He won't be at it much longer.' It was true, but poor consolation for his wife, as I well knew. The spaghetti came and we ate ours and his got cold. He came back to the table sooner or later and carried on as if nothing had happened. We laughed and joked and eventually walked back up the hill as the sun rose.

'By the way,' said Graham to Bette on the steps of the Hotel de Paris as I was about to move on next door, 'I've said we'll go and visit that ship in Villefranche at 10.30 in the morning.' It was now 6.0 a.m. and I glanced across at Bette. She rolled her eyes skywards. By the time I woke up next morning, Graham and Bette were gone as they had to move on by lunch-time to their next port of call, wherever it was. But I learnt later that Graham did indeed make his appointment on the ship in Villefranche, giving great pleasure to the entire crew and signing countless autographs. That was the man. To our intense relief he retired at the end of the season. Then, weeks later, he was dead.

The poignancy of the tragedy reminded me of the equally sad fate of Mike Hawthorn, the other prototype English world motor-racing champion in 1958. Mike was tall, blond, attractive and dashing, the sort of man who less than two decades earlier would have been a Battle of Britain pilot. He won the championship and retired, again to the relief of friends and fans alike. Again, not much more than weeks later he was killed in a car crash.

The manner of his death was even more unnecessary. He was driving towards London approaching the Guildford bypass where the road joins the Hog's Back, and spotted his friend and rival Rob Walker in a Mercedes. Mike was driving his Jaguar and as an almost over-patriotic Englishman disliked German cars. Signs were made between the two indicating a playful challenge and Mike sped on down the slightly curving road. He lost it on a minor bend near the garage owned by another of his friends, Noddy Coombs, skidded past the central bollard, narrowly avoiding an oncoming lorry and crashed into a tree on the other side of the road. He was killed instantly.

Why do I remember this so well? Because I was driving up to London myself not far behind him having just left my first wife's family home near Witley a few miles back. I saw the wreckage of the car and winced. There was a long double black skid-mark snaking back to the point that I passed and his car was virtually unrecognizable. Only the back seat and the boot or trunk of the car bore any of the original shape.

The deaths of motor-sport champions like Graham and Mike seem all the more poignant and unnecessary after they had successfully survived the terrible risks of their chosen careers and the same remark applies also to the racing and motor-cycling champion Mike Hailwood, who was killed more recently together with his little son, in an ordinary road accident for which a lorry-driver was convicted.

The risks taken by racing-drivers in the normal course of their chosen profession have to be considered more acceptable, since they know of the hazards involved and accept them. On the rare occasions when I have discussed this distasteful subject with my friends, they have all admitted that they take the attitude adopted by soldiers during the two great wars, 'It can't happen to me.'

Yet, during the time that I followed motor-racing closely, more were killed than survived. Three of the best died in one terrible year including a friend, Piers Courage, and that season's champion, who was awarded the crown posthumously, Jochen Rindt. I was also personally saddened by the terrible death of the charming, tall young Frenchman, François Cevert, during practice for the Canadian Grand Prix. He was Jackie Stewart's team-mate and Jackie was due to retire after the race, leaving the number-one spot to François, a brilliant driver who had never once complained or tried to upstage Jackie even though he could have been top man in almost any other team.

Probably the biggest names whose deaths while driving most shocked the public were the legendary Jim Clark in a Formula Two event in

Hockenheim in Germany and Bruce McClaren practising at Goodwood.

During the first Grand Prix I ever attended, at Monte Carlo in 1965, I watched from the harbour aboard the yacht *Sea Huntress* of my host Lord Beatty and we stood horrified as the Italian driver Lorenzo Bandini, in his bright-red Ferrari, crashed at the chicane not far away and burnt to death as the car burst into flames. Bandini did not actually die until he reached hospital but eye-witnesses reported that his body had literally shrivelled by the time he was taken out of the burnt-out shell.

It was no coincidence that Jackie Stewart became a great champion. Unlike Graham who succeeded through grit, determination and self-made skill, Jackie had an inborn feel for the wheel of a racing-car plus a great eye. That eye enabled him to be a champion rifle-shot before he became a champion driver, and it was only the bad luck of suffering the only off-day of his competitive shooting career which prevented him from representing Great Britain in the 1964 Olympics.

Jackie harnessed his inherent skills to Hill-like determination but, even more, a total professionalism that had traditionally been lacking in many of his colleagues and predecessors. He was also a persistent advocate of increased safety standards in both cars and tracks and, incredibly, he faced massive opposition to his many suggestions from either circuit-owners seeking to tighten their purse-strings, drivers who irresponsibly considered that extra risk was part of the act, and bloodthirsty fans and writers who actually believed that the death factor was an important and necessary part of the excitement of the sport.

Jackie thought otherwise. He believed that the fans looked for skill and excitement, daring but not death, and I would agree with him. So, happily, did the majority of people who counted in the sport as they responded to Jackie's continuous urging and nagging. It was fortunate that Jackie was three times world champion and breaker of the record for most Grand Prix victories. He had the clout and people listened to him more than to any other driver. To his further credit he still uses his considerable influence to promote safety, long after his retirement, so that ludicrous accusations of self-interest cannot possibly be levelled at him.

Jackie is the opposite of Graham in many ways, particularly in his pragmatic attitude to his work and his earning capacity. But I have never found anything remotely offensive in this even though, by chance, it has not necessarily matched up to my own policies.

Jackie has a talent, he used it to the full, reached the very top of his

129

chosen profession and capitalized accordingly. But on the track, and then and now in business, he always gave full value. His earnings were and are vast and he has kept his money. He deserves every penny and he is not a mean man. I have seen him pick up many a bill which is not always a common practice among well-known sportsmen and show-business personalities.

Jackie is an able after-dinner speaker, as good in his way as was Graham. In fact, the most memorable of my many birthday parties was at the Clermont one October. I think it was 1973, when Graham and Jackie vied to outdo each other as after-dinner speakers. As always, my party was an informal affair but one of them – I think it was Graham – jumped to his feet to make one of his hilarious speeches, during which the main targets were myself and Jackie. Naturally Jackie responded. Then I had a go followed by another well-known speaker, Winston Churchill's grandson Nicholas Soames, now an MP.

John Aspinall has never been backward in coming forward on such occasions as these and for the first time in his life he found himself batting number five, lashing out as usual at anyone in the room and in the worst but funniest possible taste. There may have been one or two other notable speakers as well before Jackie and Graham both jumped for a second innings and, by coincidence, this was the start of a double act that they subsequently went public with both on television and on stage until Graham's death. It may sound a lot of speeches but I have never seen or heard a dinner-party enjoy anything so much and it was talked about for years by those who were there.

Some of our best times with Jackie were spent at the Monte Carlo weekend. Jackie won the race three times and I was there on each occasion. I well remember celebrating one of these victories on a glorious sunny Monday when Jackie hosted a fabulous lunch at the famous Colombe d'Or in St Paul de Vence. We ate surrounded by paintings by most of the world's greatest Impressionists, many of whom had eaten there free in their struggling days and repaid the proprietor with their works.

But it was in another restaurant in Monte Carlo, on the eve of the race, that I perpetrated a joke in the worst possible taste. I must explain that one of Jackie's little foibles is that he could be incredibly busy and inaccessible to his friends at Monte Carlo when he was dancing attendance on the stars, notably Prince Rainier and Princess Grace and Elizabeth Taylor, whom he had minded in a previous year.

This particular year he was lionizing two most unusual 'stars', two of the surviving members of a Uruguayan rugby team who had crashed in the Andes about a year previously. The reason for the celebrity or notoriety of this duo is that they and a handful of others from a group some twenty-five strong had survived by eating flesh from the dead bodies of their colleagues. This in itself was a horrific but fascinating story and the two men in Monte Carlo has shown incredible resilience and bravery to help themselves and the other survivors to safety. The whole saga was very ably portrayed by Piers Paul Reed in his gripping book *Alive*.

One of the two had made it known to Jackie that he wanted to become a racing-driver and, on this somewhat tenuous link, Jackie invited them as his guests to spend Grand Prix weekend in Monte Carlo with him and his wife Helen. I was staying that year with my old London flat-mate, Phillip Martyn and his wife Nina, who was the widow of world champion Jochen Rindt. They were closer friends of Jackie and Helen than I was, living as they did as near neighbours in Geneva. And Nina was particularly close to Helen, a bond forged when they were both racing-drivers' wives.

Nina, like many Scandinavians – cool, blonde and beautiful and with a very strong mind of her own – had been particularly incensed that weekend by Jackie and Helen's devotion to the two Uruguayans to the exclusion of the three of us. Phillip and I were not so worried but thought it was rather curious.

Where Jackie and I differed, though we never discussed this, was that I felt his lionization of the two cannibals was carried to extremes. I respected their courage in adversity but felt that to gain the sympathy of the world they should hardly be flaunting themselves around at one of the most glamorous and fun-filled weekends in the world. If they chose the glamour course, they were entitled to the same treatment and the same jokes as the rest of us. That was my point of view and Phillip and Nina agreed. Maybe we were being pompous. Maybe Jackie was.

Meanwhile that Thursday morning, Mick Jagger had rung me from London to say that he and Bianca were flying down that day to join us and could I fix him a room. Of course, all the rooms in the Hotel de Paris, the Hermitage where Phillip and Nina put me up in their corner suite, and any other hotel within miles had been fully booked for months if not years. But we pulled a few strings and, with the help of Mick's name, the management of the Hotel de Paris magically discovered one last suite. So Mick and Bianca joined Phillip, Nina and me for dinner in Rompoldi's, only a few yards from our hotel just by the

131

casino square. As we walked in we saw Helen and the two Uruguayans sitting at a table for four on the right of the entrance. We exchanged pleasantries with Helen who explained that Jackie was busy up at the palace with Prince Rainier and Princess Grace but would try and join them later. We looked at each other and shrugged. Typical Jackie.

We sat further down the restaurant to the left and could thus see Helen and her two escorts clearly. The subject of Jackie's behaviour came up once more, raised by Nina, and as we knocked back a glass or two of wine, we became more critical. I was flanked by Nina and Bianca, and Bianca and I had chosen to share a T-bone steak. As the waiter showed us the steak and prepared to cut off the meat from the bone and divide it between us, I conceived my appalling plan. 'Shall I teach Jackie's cannibals a lesson and send them this bone?' I asked. Bianca did not fully understand the loading of the question but Nina was delighted and egged me on, dispelling any doubts or decency that I might have harboured. So I asked the waiter to put the bone on his tray and offer it to my friends over there.

The waiter thought it was a huge joke and carried out his part almost too well, continuously thrusting the gory bone towards the two protesting Uruguayans. They looked across at us and saw the roars of laughter and recognized the source of this lamentable joke.

The evening then progressed normally until Jackie arrived to join them and we saw them explaining the situation, looking angrily in our direction and pointing from time to time. Jackie was furious but said nothing and that was that for the moment.

I have lost count in life of the amount of times that there have been inquests the day after a drama the previous night, whether it be funny or just a disaster. Usually it concerns somebody's bad behaviour and this was no exception. It was race day but by mid-morning the story had circulated and it was also known that Jackie was, not surprisingly, pretty angry.

Our problem was that the three of us, Phillip, Nina and myself, were scheduled to drive up the next day, Monday, to Geneva and for me to stay with them for a couple of days. Jackie and Helen were very much part of this plan and lunches, dinners plus golf and tennis had already been arranged. So how were we going to smooth over the situation in such a short time? Nina was the most militant and would hear no part of the suggestion that one or all of us should write a letter of apology and beg forgiveness. 'Jackie had it coming to him,' she said defiantly. I kept fairly quiet through most of the debate in true heroic fashion even

132

though I had been the perpetrator of the deed. My part in the ghastly joke seemed to have been set aside and the matter appeared to resolve itself between the Martyns and the Stewarts.

Eventually, Phillip, not normally a man to waver, did the sensible thing and wrote a note to Jackie and Helen acknowledging our stupidity and, I believe some time later, Nina did the same under pressure from Phillip. And so, when we got to Geneva the matter was dropped and we had a pleasant two days.

It was Jackie who had the last laugh. Two months later, he had his private day at Silverstone in which, with the help of Ford Motors, he invited various members of the royal family, stars of stage and screen, and a few lucky friends like Phillip and myself. He had asked us all to bring a prize appertaining to ourselves which he would gather up on arrival and then distribute at the end of the day. Being heavily involved in horse-racing, I brought the current copy of *Timeform Annual,* the professional racing-man's bible which details in words, figures and pictures every horse who has run in Britain the previous year.

Among those at the outing was the motor-racing Uruguayan. At the prize-giving ceremony at the end of the day, when my name was called, I was presented by Jackie and the Uruguayan, both wearing broad grins with a copy of *Alive* signed by themselves and the author. Game, set and match.

Those Silverstone days of Jackie's were sheer magic, particularly for Walter Mitty characters like myself. The order of the day after we gathered near the grandstand, usually about twelve or fifteen of us, was for Jackie to give a brief talk and outline the day's activities. The first entertainment was Jackie himself driving one, two or even three of us in a souped-up Ford saloon, for a few laps of the circuit and this in itself was pretty exciting and nerve-racking even though to him it was like driving at 70 mph down the motorway. He also asked one or two of his world-class colleagues to help him with this and I remember being driven by both Denny Hulme and poor François Cevert, who was killed later that year.

Then we all stationed ourselves at vantage-points while Jackie lapped the course about a dozen times in his Formula One Tyrrell, the car in which he was winning or had won the world championship. To indicate the type of entertainment that he put on I remember him either equalling or beating the lap record, unofficially.

Then we had lunch after which, having been sternly lectured by Jackie on technique and safety procedure, we were let loose on the track in cars provided by Ford. Those of us who felt up to it or had some experience were even allowed to have a go in a Formula Ford racing-car.

I was not one of those brave or foolish enough to try out the racing-car since I could hardly fit into it anyway but I remember the courageous Lord Patrick Beresford, an SAS officer who was Sheikh Yamani's bodyguard, growing over confident, giving a little wave to Jackie as he passed the pits and wobbling all over the track before regaining control in the nick of time.

Captain Mark Phillips was not so fortunate a year or so later and he had an almighty crunch from which he escaped unscathed to the greater relief of Jackie even than Princess Anne.

My own adventure was even more ludicrous. Although we had been explicitly warned not to race, Phillip Martyn and myself, with rivalry built up from having lived under the same roof for seven or eight years, challenged each other. We both got into the same car, one as driver with the passenger holding a stop-watch. The driver had three laps, one to build up speed, the second the timed flying-lap from the bridge over the start of the straight, and the third to slow down again and come to a halt. Phillip completed his timed lap, quite pleased with himself, and handed over to me a couple of minutes later.

All went well in my warming-up lap and I was becoming extremely confident as I neared the end of my timed lap and went into the last bend at Woodcote. Then it happened. My wheels just clipped the grass on the inside of the bend and the car, running at something over 100 mph, went into a skid. I had remembered Jackie's advice on all the bends referring to the speeds and gears used by real drivers and Woodcote was 'flat right' which meant that you could stay in top gear, flat-out, right-handed.

Such advice was not meant to be taken seriously by inexperienced amateurs though, and there I was careering all over the track with Phillip shouting, 'You've lost it, you bloody fool,' and me replying at intervals 'No problem. No problem.'

I was wrong. There was a problem. The car skidded back on against the pits wall and then bounced straight across the track head on into the grandstand. Phillip and I sat there heavily strapped in and helmeted, completely unhurt and giggling idiotically as he berated me.

A very worried Jackie and the others rushed across the track and were most relieved to see how lucky we had been. We were also surrounded and helped out by marshals – the track was fully marshalled with typical

Jackie efficiency – and I felt very foolish.

That was the end of my day and, even years later, Jackie still tells Mark Phillips and me that we were the cause of him discontinuing this day. He is too frightened of a repetition with worse results. In retrospect, I think that for once Jackie fell into the same trap as Graham Hill with Prince Charles. He had not thought the whole thing through. Both accidents had taken place after lunch and in my case he had underestimated the greed and intemperance of some of his friends when faced with delicious claret and Dom Perignon champagne.

The Aga Khan:
A Racing Dynasty Revived

AT the time I moved into Bolebec House I was seeing a good deal of Sally. With her perfect bone structure, she had become a much-in-demand photographic model and was soon to be seen in the pages of *Vogue* and *Harpers and Queen*, often on the front page.

It was noticeable that, unlike most of her colleagues who thought of little else but their modelling and earning-capacity, Sal picked and chose her assignments and was nobody's slave.

She was also extremely independent and set herself up in her own flat, first in Eaton Place and then in Eaton Square. But she was in low spirits when she decided to go to stay in the Palace Hotel, St Moritz for the New Year's celebration 1969. She knew that there were several old friends who would help to look after her, including the dependable Janni Zographos. Janni was the sort of man whom anyone could fall back on and be sure of a helping hand or shoulder to cry on. It was at the Palace at the New Year's celebrations that Sal met the Aga Khan. He was immediately smitten by her, and they saw each other, as much as his many duties would permit for the next two or three months during which Sal arranged for us all to meet up for dinner and get to know each other.

The fateful evening took place at Annabel's and, while Sal and I did much of the talking, the Aga was extremely pleasant. K – the first initial of his first name Karim – as he insisted I should call him, was noticeably polite. He was particularly complimentary about the quality and variety of the menu. He certainly appreciates his food, the more so as he never touches alcohol.

It soon became obvious during the year that the relationship between Sal and Karim was a serious one and both of them had to decide whether various obstacles could, or should be overcome.

The question of her previous marriage was one problem but this was annulled in the eyes of the Roman Catholic Church and therefore could hardly exist in the Ismaili faith. The question of Sal's having been a model, albeit an extremely respectable and upmarket one, also arose but K was adamant that they were big enough to override that – the professional should hardly bear a stigma in this modern world.

So greater thought had to be given by Sal to the question of whether she was prepared to give up certain freedoms and take on the heavy responsibilities involved in being the wife of the Imam, his Begum. She readily decided that this would be no problem and, having accepted K's proposal, went through an intensive course on the Ismaili faith and culture. The Aga Khan is spiritual leader of the Ismaili Muslims and his work as leader of such a scattered community is extensive and time-consuming.

So, for the first time, I went down to Sardinia in the middle of July to stay in Porto Cervo, the centre of K's imaginative and rapidly expanding holiday development, the Costa Smeralda. It was the first of thirteen consecutive years that I was lucky enough to be invited down there and I watched the continuous expansion of the resort with admiration and enjoyment. First the tennis-club, followed by the golf club and then the new yacht marina and yacht-club sprung up during those years to add to the facilities of his three hotels, the Cervo, Cala di Volpe, and the Pitrizza.

I stayed in their modest house overlooking the harbour. There I met K's pretty young half-sister, Yasmin, whose mother Rita Hayworth had not yet succumbed to the fearful disease which afflicted her and incapacitated her during the later years, leading to her death in 1987. One particular memory of that first trip was of us all huddled together in a stuffy little office on the quay, the harbour master's office, watching the first moon landing on an old, blurry black-and-white television set. As usual the Italian TV commentator got it wrong and announced that Neil Armstrong had made his first historic step on the moon's surface, whereupon everyone in the room cheered and clapped. We could not quite make out what was going on such was the chaos, but it became clear that the commentator had to apologize and we all had to wait for the second landing!

K had always been boat-minded and we went out each day on *Amaloun*, which could accommodate about eight people with full facilities or up to 20 or more for day outings, swimming, lunching, and drinking.

Although I was much too old for her at the age of thirty-three – she was only about seventeen – I was the only game in town as far as Yasmin was concerned and we went dancing every night after dinner at the local night-club while the old folks, who were both, in fact, younger than me, stayed at home. Going out meant a walk of only a hundred yards or so from house to piazza, very pleasant in the balmy atmosphere and very necessary for me after the heat generated by long sessions of intensive dancing. Yasmin, like her mother before her, was a wonderful and enthusiastic dancer and I gave it my all.

It was during this holiday that I first got to know Henry Ford II, whom I had previously only seen and nodded to in the Clermont Club. He had chartered a vast yacht and we all craned our necks to see who was on board as she hove towards the harbour. I think she was too big to moor alongside the other boats but she may have just fitted, dwarfing the rest near the entrance. On board was the jovial Henry with his second wife Christina and two daughters, Charlotte and Ann. Also in tow was a slightly lost-looking Italian, Count Giovanni Volpi, who sat around looking bored most of the time.

As I later discovered incoming visitors quickly made their presence known to Sal and K and we all met up for various meals, either lunch or dinner. One evening, emboldened by the consumption of wine, I am rather embarrassed to recall joking to Christina in front of Henry: 'What on earth,' I asked her 'is an attractive girl like you doing with old Henry when there are young single men like me around?' Luckily Henry roared with laughter at this impertinent remark.

The two girls were either between or before marriages and I got on fine with the whole family which led to the greatest ego boost I have ever had, one which I feel almost too embarrassed to recount. The Khan group went out on a day trip with a number of extra guests on board and we anchored some way out in the clear blue sea for swimming. About a dozen of the guests were splashing about in the water while Sal and I lay chatting on the sun-deck when a helicopter flew from the direction of the land towards us and, amidst some excitement, stopped, hovering, a few yards to starboard and only 50 feet up. The pilot leaned out and threw a bottle into the water. All the swimmers raced to be the first to reach it and whoever grabbed it handed it up to a crewman who handed it to Sal.

I had been taking no more than an academic interest in the whole thing so I was genuinely amazed when Sal handed the bottle to me and said, 'It's for you. Go on open it. Don't hang about.' The message in the bottle read, 'We leave Cervo this evening for a week in Monte Carlo. We need you. Please come. Let the pilot know yes or no. Love Christina, Charlotte and Ann.'

What an invitation! And what a dramatic and head-swelling delivery! However, it did not take me more than a second or two to make up my mind that I was the guest of Sal and K and should stay where I was. So, though Sal, having read the note over my shoulder at the same time, quickly said, 'Go if you want to. See if I care,' I looked across and up at the pilot, who was still hovering and peering towards me, grinning, and gave him a thumbs down. He acknowledged the message and swung away back to port.

The engagement of Sal and K had to be kept a secret for some time, while she prepared herself for her new role and then K had to make sure that he told the leaders of his community. Eventually the announcement was made and they were married in Paris at the end of October in both civil and religious ceremonies. Many people came over on the day, particularly from England, for the reception party which was held in their Paris house overlooking the Seine on the Ile de la Cité, close to Notre Dame.

Princess Margaret was there, representing the Royal Family – she and Lord Snowdon were regular visitors to Sardinia when they were together – while Mark Birley, a good friend who was also proprietor of Annabel's, rather touchingly brought over the head-waiter, Louis, and the much-loved cloakroom attendant Mabel, both of them legendary figures in their own way. And, not to be outdone, Doris, Mabel's counterpart in the Clermont upstairs, was also there as was, of course, John Aspinall.

The Aga Khans started off living most of the time either in their Paris house or at Green Lodge with adjoining racing-stables in Chantilly. They also had the Porto Cervo house for the summer and tended to rent a house in St Moritz in the winter. But nicest of all was the tiny cottage at Saint Crespin in Normandy in the middle of his main stud. This and Green Lodge were K's father Aly Khan's favourites and it was easy to see why. Aly Khan had been tragically killed in a needless car crash in the suburbs of Paris in 1959, an accident from which his companion Bettina and his chauffeur, Lucien, escaped relatively unharmed.

We often used to meet Bettina in later years both in Paris and Sardinia. She had a house in each place. The chauffeur Lucien continued to work for K, who like his father, preferred to drive himself with the chauffeur either by his side or in the back to take over the car for parking or other chores.

I was often driven by Lucien, usually rushing to Le Bourget for Charles de Gaulle airport from Paris or, more often, Chantilly and he was a very fast, though expert driver.

Incredibly and sadly, he was also killed when driving himself off duty.

From those early days of our friendship, K had two main dreams: to build a bigger and more effective family house on his own private bay on the Costa Smeralda and, more urgently, build a complex of house, offices, and stables in Chantilly. Though many times we pored over the impressive plans for the Sardinian house, which included a swimming-pool and an elegant guest-house, which appealed to me, this was always put off. Mañana, was the order of the day on that one, but the Chantilly dream gradually became reality. A large plot of land was purchased at Aiglemont by the outskirts of Chantilly and close to the famous gallops 'Les Aigles'. Magnificent stables in the shape of American-style barns were erected, complete with every modern equine convenience and these stables bear favourable comparison with anything else in the world even ten years later.

A modern office building was constructed which became the head-quarters of K's many enterprises world-wide, and finally the château was built as his main dwelling. These three complexes, though no more than a few hundred yards apart, are invisible from one another by a carefully planned screen of trees and shrub.

One of the more important items in the main thoroughbred office, where the secretaries and managers of his bloodstock empire are based, is a computer which stores the racing record and pedigree of all the horses – running into many thousands – K has ever owned.

The Aga Khan's life is divided into three clear categories, each of them enough to keep one normal man occupied full time. First, there is his religious responsibility as Imam to his millions of followers. This is a demanding enough role and he could double or treble his commitments there if he acceded to all the requests and demands of his people.

Then there is his business life. The best-known manifestation of this is the Sardinian development, the Costa Smeralda, though he owns hotels and other businesses all over the world. For instance, he recently acquired the Ciga chain of hotels in Italy. His several schools and hospitals come somewhere under both of these categories, mostly the first. His multi-million dollar Karachi hospital development, which has long been opened but continues to expand, is easily the largest operation of its kind in Pakistan.

Finally, there is the administration of his racing and breeding empire and this is something that brings him enormous pleasure due in no small measure to the incredible success he has enjoyed.

When his father died and left him the horses, together with those of his grandfather, the previous Aga Khan, K was not much interested. His mind hankered after more mechanical things. He still retains his mechanical leanings – he owns many fast cars, boats and planes – but he grew to appreciate the fascination of a properly administered racing and breeding programme.

Unlike some major owner-breeders in recent years, he was not content to rest on the laurels of the fabulous Aga Khan bloodlines and he bought up lock, stock and barrel, first the entire breeding empire of Madame Anna Dupré, widow of the hotel magnate, François Dupré, and then in a controversial deal, the racing and breeding interests of Marcel Boussac.

There was no hitch in the take-over of the Dupré horses, best known of which, the 1963 English Derby winner, Relko, was not part of the deal since he was at stud under separate ownership, but there was plenty of trouble with the Boussac consignment.

Marcel Boussac, who ran a vast textile empire in France, had been the main factor in French racing and breeding for something like 50 years, interrupted only by the war. Soon after the war, he sent his horses over from France to England for a series of successful raids on our Classics, so much so that there was considerable muttering and agitation in England that some of them were being helped by advanced medication.

The Boussac bloodstock fortunes began to decline in the 1960s and 1970s, mainly due to the old man's stubbornness in refusing to diversify. Much the same thing was happening in his business empire and his fortunes deteriorated to such an extent that his business was declared bankrupt in May 1978. There was little doubt that his personal bankruptcy would follow as he was too old and infirm to do anything to halt the downward slide. But many breeders eyed his bloodstock empire hungrily. With good management and diversification, there were plenty of valuable bloodlines there.

Among those considering making an offer for the whole consignment was K himself and also important French breeders like Alec Head and Roland de Chambure. But these three, and others interested, knew the ethics of French law. As far as the French were concerned, this was what, roughly translated, is known as the suspect period, the time

141

between the bankruptcy of a business and a man's personal bankruptcy.

Two Americans, the Murty brothers, who prided themselves on their sharpness and speed of action, observed no such niceties. In mid-June, acting through Boussac's secretary, they purchased about 50 of the choicest items from the whole empire, paying a ridiculous price well below market value. They paid half the money down. Soon afterwards, in early July, Boussac's personal bankruptcy was declared and the trustees were furious when they heard about the Murty deal and declared it void. The Murtys in turn thought they could outsmart the trustees and other prospective purchasers by paying the other half of their money into the bankruptcy funds. However the French racing and breeding authorities backed the trustees' decision to void the Murty deal and held a private auction to include all the Boussac horses, including those claimed by the Murtys as well as Acamas, recent winner of the French Derby.

The Aga's bid valued the Murty consignment at a much higher price but the brothers held many of the horses' passports and refused to return them or acknowledge the validity of the Aga Khan deal. There followed a whole series of law cases all over the world. The Murtys brought case after case in France, all of which they lost and even tried to writ the British Jockey Club. They also took to employing bailiffs to slap writs on the Aga when he visited America. One of them was served in the United Nations, which created some sort of scandal, and one in or just outside the Carlyle Hotel in Madison Avenue. Although none of these legal darts affected the outcome and must, indeed, have cost the Murtys millions of dollars, there is equally little doubt that they had a measure of support among the uninformed. And this harassment was inconvenient for the Aga, particularly where travelling his horses was involved.

It took years for the Murtys to finally run out of steam but the deal has benefited K and made the hassle worth while since he has successfully integrated the Boussac bloodlines with the Dupré strain and, of course, his own.

He allowed Acamas to run in Boussac's name and colours in the big race at Ascot at the end of July, the King George VI and the Queen Elizabeth Diamond Stakes even though the overall deal had already been ratified in France. It was probably just as well that he made this gesture since Acamas after finishing second failed his dope test and was disqualified, forfeiting all prize money. The trainer carried the can for this and whether as a result of illicit medicines administered up until then in his racing career, Acamas proved impotent at stud, was sold for a song and I last saw him trailing pathetically in the rear of the field in a race at Longchamp at the age of nine.

The Aga came in for quite a bit of flak from people highly placed in racing circles from both sides of the Atlantic and I was able to put many of them right since I firmly believed that he had behaved correctly and the Murtys deceitfully. Their rage was intensified when, whilst one half of their money was returned, the other half, paid before Boussac's personal bankruptcy had been filed, was swallowed up and could presumably only be paid back at the same rate received by other creditors. The Aga's enthusiasm for his horses reached its peak during the 1970s when he enjoyed continuing success in the French Classics with the likes of Kalamoun, Nishapour, Blushing Groom, and Top Ville. Kalamoun was a brilliant grey colt who dominated the milers of his year in France and it was a pity that he did not try his luck in England as a three-year-old. He died prematurely after a promising start to his stud career and the Aga named his superb new yacht, built in Bremen, after him, taking the place of *Amaloun*.

Blushing Groom won all the four group I races in France for two-year-olds in 1976, putting the top English trained two-year-old, J. O. Tobin in his place on the last occasion. He continued where he left off in 1977 and, having proved himself outstandingly the best horse in France, was made hot favourite for the Derby at Epsom.

He had been ridden in all his races so far by the French stable jockey, Henri Samani, but pressure was now placed on K to replace him round the tricky Epsom course with its bends and gradients, by Lester Piggott, the undisputed champion of the world's premier Classic. Piggott's great friend was journalist Peter O'Sullevan, my colleague at that time on the *Daily Express*. At that time K was none too fond of Peter and there was little love lost between them, but O'Sullevan insisted on ringing up K at least once to try and persuade him to offer the ride to Piggott. This was clearly an unwise move because of the feelings between them and I remember being in the Paris house when O'Sullevan rang to bring up the subject. K with a grin on his face, beckoned me over to listen to the conversation, though I had no intention of eavesdropping. This was sheer bad thinking by Piggott and O'Sullevan, neither of whom were giving away many secrets to me in those days. The obvious pragmatic thing for Peter to have done would have been to ask me to do the job since he knew full well at the time that K and I were on the best of terms. Curiously enough, K very correctly stayed loyal to Samani so the whole thing worked out well for Piggott and my friend Robert Sangster, whose horse, The Minstrel, won that year.

K invited me over to France to witness Blushing Groom's final gallop about a week before the Derby, which was a great journalistic coup for me. Sal, K and I were up at the crack of dawn and, in conditions of great secrecy, met up with the jockey and the great trainer François Mathet in the saddling-boxes at Chantilly racecourse. Samani and the other jockeys taking part in the gallop were all meticulously weighed under Mathet's watchful eye while the horses circled peacefully in the early morning light. They galloped past the stands going away from us the wrong way round the racecourse, simulating Epsom's left-hand bends, and then as they raced back the reverse way along the back straight, passing the famous château, Blushing Groom, despite only minimal encouragement from his jockey, drew right away from his rivals to finish, hard held many lengths in front. It was a dazzling performance and convinced me that Blushing Groom would stay the Derby distance and win the following Wednesday. Our mutual confidence was enhanced by the knowledge that one of the horses left struggling in his wake was Exceller, one of the best four-year-olds in Europe and soon to become champion in the USA.

There was some debate about how soon before the Derby Blushing Groom was to travel over. In the end, Mathet made his decision and as far as I remember he chose Monday. In the race, Blushing Groom ran well enough and no blame could be attached to his jockey but he could never quite go with the two leaders in the last quarter mile and finished an honourable third. The race was won by Lester Piggott on Robert Sangster's, The Minstrel.

Those who had forecast that Blushing Groom would not stay the Derby trip – he was by the sprinting stallion, Red God – were jubilant and I had to face a lot of 'I told you so's'. But K told me sometime later that, although he refused to make an excuse in public or even in private at the time, Blushing Groom had not seemed one-hundred-per-cent himself on the morning of the race, though he was not below par enough to justify withdrawal. So the smart alecs were not necessarily right about his stamina and we will never know the true answer. Perhaps he was just off-colour that day. Either way, Blushing Groom still ran a fine race and was a great horse, one of the best I ever saw. The Aga had already agreed to sell him before the race to go to stud in Lexington, Kentucky at the Gainseway Stud owned by the resourceful breeding entrepreneur John Gaines. He was to stay in Europe until the end of the season and

144

race in K's colours but he only had one more run and was unluckily beaten in a farcical, muddling race back at a mile in Deauville in August.

Sally quickly got into the swing of life as the Begum Aga Khan and soon proved her worth to the community, as I knew she would. She looked good in anything, she has always been a superb dresser, but she never looked better than when wearing a sari. She gave birth to a daughter, Zahrah, in September 1970 and their elder son, Rahim, a year later. Hussain was born some two and a half years later, an ideal-sized family. She devoted a huge amount of her time to her duties as a mother though she was still keen to accompany K to the races whenever possible.

Her love of racing caused us both a problem in June 1970 during Royal Ascot. The first day of the meeting, K allowed her to go without him, somewhat against his own better judgement, but he knew she would be tightly chaperoned by both her mother and myself. She spent a blameless, racing enthusiast's day with us, meeting only ultra-respectable and mainly older friends for conversation and tea. Imagine her and my horror next day when a completely fabricated story about her being in the stands with the people she had not even spoken to all day appeared in the gossip column, William Hickey in my own paper, the *Daily Express*.

This sort of publicity, though not of great account to the average person, was very damaging for Sal since everything about her or K in the English papers was liable to be picked up and reprinted, out of context, in papers around the world read by their community. K was predictably angry and Sal rang me in desperation. Their lawyer would seek an immediate retraction but the *Daily Express* refused point-blank, believing their gossip reporters. So Sal rang me back to see if I would file an affidavit which I was pleased to do, even though it meant flogging up to a lawyer's office somewhere towards the City before going racing.

Luckily for us, Nigel Dempster, who was one of the three men who had concocted the story, knew nothing of the drama unfolding and came up to me in the press room at Ascot to say mockingly, 'Ha, ha, ha we took a dig at your friend.' I asked him how he came across such rubbish and he admitted then that he had not seen the incident which he had described, nor had his informant, but that a third party had thought he had seen it. It was fortunate for me that I now knew how the story had been concocted. Very fortunate since the following day, by now Friday and the last day of the Royal Meeting, I received an urgent call from the

145

office telling me to be in the editor's room immediately after racing.

I drove back to London and straight to Fleet Street where I faced up to the editor at about 6.30 p.m. He was sweating and was redfaced with fury. 'I am so angry with you that I don't trust myself with what I may say or do. You are a traitor. See me here on Monday morning at midday. You are suspended until then. Get out.' I did not get a chance to say a word during this outburst and strode out. The editor Derek Marks, was a huge, fat man with one leg, formerly the political correspondent. Some people swore by him but I never thought much of him as an editor and even less now.

I was quite relaxed about the whole thing and, as a matter of fact, the suspension suited me quite well as, by pure coincidence, Sal, K and I were due to go down to Warwick Castle for a short weekend with Lord Brooke, now Earl of Warwick.

Brookie and I, as I mentioned earlier, had shared his flat in London for a couple of years when we were both separating and being divorced from our respective wives back in 1964 and 1965 so we knew each other extremely well. Brookie liked nothing better than a bit of drama and gossip and he enjoyed the situation enormously though even he did not make too many jokes about it in front of K, who was still livid with the *Express*. Meanwhile I enjoyed the weekend despite being woken up by the piercing screams of the spectacular peacocks, whose cries echoed within the historic castle walls. Brookie proved himself a dab-hand at making Pimms, a refreshing summer drink, and I dubbed him Warwick the Pimm maker.

I was able to relax through not having to write my column but on Monday morning my sports editor, who had much more responsibility for me than the editor himself, rang me to say, 'What on earth have you done to me now?' His name was John Morgan and we got on well so he believed me when I told him what had taken place and he instructed me to go to his office at once. 'You must tell this to the office lawyer,' he added. So I went through the whole story with the lawyer, Andrew Edwards, who said, 'Right. Leave this to me.'

At midday Andrew and John escorted me into the editor's office; it was rather like a court-martial. The editor was sitting there glaring at us, but before even he could open his mouth, the lawyer said, 'I'm afraid there has been some mistake here. Benson has only told the truth here and it is our own William Hickey reporters who are in the wrong.' He then told the rest of the story to the still-fuming editor. At the end of his statement the editor turned to me with a look of loathing on his face,

146

'Well,' he said, 'you seem to have got away with it and I must reinstate you. But I want you to know that, as far as I am concerned, I despise you for what you have done. I care nothing for you and I care nothing for the Aga Khan.' And he turned away in a fury. I marched out, hearing his shout, as I left his office, 'Send for that little toad Dempster.'

And when Nigel came clean, it was he who was in the doghouse for a while and the apology was duly printed.

The postscript to this drama came exactly 16 years later to the day. After I had retired from the *Daily Express* I did occasional articles for the *Sporting Life* and *The Times* and Monty Court, editor of the *Life*, asked me to do a piece on my Royal Ascot memoirs to be printed on Royal Hunt Cup day. I thought that the suspension story would make one appropriate memoir and wrote it in much reduced terms. After all, it was a dramatic Ascot-time story.

Sally was none too sure that I was well advised to resurrect this incident, but K himself was friendly and chatty when we met at the races subsequently. Only a fortnight beforehand, I had organized successful parties for them at the private room in Annabel's. The first was the night before the Derby, with Sal presiding since K was working. The second, at his request after Shahrastani's thrilling defeat of Dancing Brave at the big race.

I took a variety of girl-friends down for those idyllic summer holidays in Sardinia until my second wife, Carolyn, claimed the position as her own from 1976 onwards. I was not always accompanied, as in that first year, 1969, and the one who probably made the most impact with the locals was the blonde Lady Charlotte Curzon. She didn't talk very much, hence her ironic nickname 'Lady Chatty' but she looked quite magnificent in her favoured position right at the very front of the boat, whether it was the large and stylish *Kalamoun* or the brilliant speed-boat. With her blonde hair flowing behind her and her chin thrust forward to combat the wind and waves, she looked for all the world like a figurehead on a galleon of old. I was usually lucky enough to stay on board *Kalamoun* in air-conditioned comfort, taking breakfast on deck while awaiting news from the house of the day's outing. Occasionally it was too windy to go out in which case we would have lunch at the sheltered golf club or in other people's houses.

My other obsession during my visits to Sardinia was tennis, and each year I joined up with a circle of keen players for an evening game at the excellent tennis-club. I often had to run already changed from the boat as we reached harbour to join up in time and we would play, usually for

147

two or three hours before a quick shower and change for dinner.

K himself was a useful tennis-player when I first knew him with a very good, well-coached style. He was a more than useful athlete, being an Olympic skier and a very high-class water-skier. For the first two or three years that I was there, he would entertain us with his water-skiing and he and I would also play tennis. But he could never quite beat me, though this was hardly surprising since he had so little practice and played much less than me, apart from working hard sometimes late at night. For these were our holidays, not really his, though he did snatch the odd day on the boat and otherwise would usually join us on board just for lunch, coming by speed-boat driven by himself.

He did try and put one across me the first evening he had put flood-lights in at the courts. 'Come and try out the lights with me after dinner,' he cunningly suggested. I should have smelt a rat when he jumped up in the middle of dinner – he loved his food, remember – and said, 'I must go on ahead and do a few things. See you on the court in 25 minutes.' I finished my dinner, changed and walked down to the club, where he was already standing on one side of the net chatting to some friends and relations of his who were sitting by the side. He strode purposefully to the back of the court, leaving me with no choice of ends, and said briskly, 'Right, let's start.' This was also odd since it was very much the custom among the French and Italians to have long knock-ups before a game and in these matters K conformed with the Continentals rather than the British.

I was soon in terrible trouble, four games to love down in about ten minutes, flailing wildly and often missing the ball altogether. I could not see a thing as the lights, certainly down my end, were wrongly adjusted. As K won point after point, his little fan-club roared and screamed their enthusiasm. I became quite irritated at this. I gritted my teeth and managed to get the hang of the conditions enough to take a couple of games before losing the set 6–2.

'That was great Charlie,' grinned K, 'let's go and have a drink.' 'Oh no we don't,' I replied, 'that was much too quick. Let's change ends and have another set.'

So we changed ends and the lights were much easier for me this time. I tried my hardest and beat him just as easily as he had humiliated me in the first set. Honours were even at one set all, and this time I agreed to call it a day, or rather a night.

In July 1979, we had a wonderful week when a friend, John Bowes-Lyon, and I organized for four world-class players to come

148

down, partly for a holiday and partly to put on two exhibitions. John and I were both friendly at the time with Vitas Gerulaitis, and Vitas gathered the other three who were John McEnroe, Peter Fleming, and Ilie Nastase. K sent his plane to collect them and they arrived late one evening and came straight to the house for some food and to meet Sal and K. Robert and Susan Sangster were staying with us, too, but they were due to leave the next day and were not over impressed by the demeanour of the players, who fell upon the food and didn't waste much time on small talk. I quite understood the players' attitude. They were tired and hungry and it was late. So, unfortunately, the Sangsters missed the fun by leaving next morning as Robert had to go to the sales in Kentucky.

Vitas stayed on board K's number-two boat, which was moored alongside us on *Kalamoun*, and he impressed us when he emerged each morning and asked for a dozen scrambled eggs for breakfast. The other three players stayed at the Cala di Volpe and some days they played golf. The course there is notoriously difficult and they took great delight in counting who lost the most balls rather than who took the least shots. McEnroe was the winner one day with the staggering loss of twenty-four balls. Most of the days they all came out with us on the boat and enjoyed trips on the speed-boat. I never saw McEnroe so relaxed again.

The exhibitions were a huge success with the players giving great value for money both singles and doubles. Incidentally they were there only for expenses, waiving their normal fee in favour of charity. They played hard but with plenty of laughs and some amazing, spectacular shots which I, a veteran spectator at Wimbledon for nearly 30 years, had never seen before.

In the evenings we sometimes went to the local night-club and Nastase grew very attached to an extremely attractive French-based Swiss lady who was staying with us. As we left the night-club they were walking beside me, hand in hand and seemingly very close. I could not help overhearing the following dialogue which she confirmed to us the following day.

Nastase, 'Let's go to bed.'

Pretty Swiss lady, 'We can't. I'm married.'

Nastase, 'That doesn't matter. So am I.'

It seemed to me that the Aga's work load became ever and ever more onerous, and he never went anywhere without armfuls of files. He literally had offices full of files needing his attention wherever he went and anyone who thinks he leads a glamorous and indolent life could not

149

be further away from the truth. Though he may fly in his comfortable and speedy jet, a Grumman Gulfstream III – it was a G II in those days – to watch one of his horses running at, say, Newmarket in England and then return to Sardinia, nearly two hours flying time away, he is working flat out every minute on that plane, usually with a secretary sitting opposite him.

This was never so much in evidence as when I went on two trips around the United States with K and Sal in 1974 and 1976. For the long trip across the Atlantic, sometimes landing at Shannon or Gander to refuel, he hardly looked up from his papers while Sal and I played cut-throat games of gin rummy or backgammon. The first of these trips was primarily to pick up hints at yacht marinas around the States before he built his new harbour in Porto Cervo. We went to places like Fort Lauderdale and St Petersburg, and to Carolina to see the Grumman factory, and stayed at a fabulous holiday development, Sea Pines. We flew to Dallas and then Fort Worth to visit the Bell helicopter plant and arrange for the delivery and décor of his new Long Ranger.

We also visited New York and Lexington to tour the four great studs there, seeing legendary stallions like Nijinsky, Sir Ivor, Vaguely Noble, Secretariat, and some of the old-timers like Nashua and Round Table.

America is the land of the private jet and the moment we arrived anywhere, there were cars by the side of the tarmac as we left the plane and we were whisked like lightning to our lodgings. But every minute we were on board, K was working, working, working and he is no different today.

During the 1980s, K's racing programme has gone from strength to strength and he has won two English Derbys, three French Derbys, and the Arc de Triomphe as well as innumerable important races world-wide, including the $2,000,000 mile-and-a-quarter turf race at the inaugural Breeders' Cup at Hollywood Park, Los Angeles in 1984.

It is only K's resources and his determination, which few other owners would have been able to match, that have enabled him to get extremely embarrassing injustices to him and, more particularly his trainers, put right.

One of them concerned Lashkari, who had won in the Los Angeles race, when involved in an extraordinary incident after finishing fourth in the same Breeders' Cup race at Aquaduct in New York the following year. Some time after the race, it was claimed that Lashkari's after-race dope test had proved positive to an almost lethal drug colloquially known as 'Elephant Juice'. The New York Racing Association sus-

150

pended K's French trainer, Alain de Royer Dupré, without a hearing and an international row ensued.

However, it was subsequently discovered that separate tests on Lashkari did not tally and the experts began to disagree. There was also some mysterious security lapse on the day of the race when the security men suddenly went off duty. K fought the case hard and the New York Racing Association was forced to climb down and reinstate the trainer. But there was no official apology.

The other case was in 1981 when the Aga's horse, Vayrann, won the Champion Stakes at Newmarket in mid-October. K was in China visiting one of the farthest outposts of his followers, but Sally, my wife, and I, were staying at Stanley House, Newmarket with Lord and Lady Derby for the three-day meeting.

We were amused to have to accept reversed charge calls from K in China since even for him, they would not allow a direct call. So we were thrilled to be able to give him the good news of Vayrann's victory, particularly as I had tipped the horse to my readers in my column and, just as important, had backed him at odds of 10–1. But again something showed in the post-race test and weeks later it was announced that Vayrann showed an infinitesimal positive reading and an inquiry would be held. Again, following the assurances of veteran trainer, François Mathet, K took up the cudgels and, with the aid of forensic evidence, was able to prove that certain colts produce naturally the same substance that had been found. Mathet was finally cleared and this normally crusty old veteran was so overjoyed as I gave him a lift to Victoria Station from the hearing at Jockey Club headquarters in Portman Square, London, that he chattered and laughed with me all the way – almost unheared of for him. In French, of course, which made it hard work for me.

The greatest drama and sadness for Sally and K was, of course, the kidnapping and almost certain killing of Shergar, their great 1981 Derby winner. This extraordinary crime, perpetrated by the IRA, affected Sally so much that she lost much of her erstwhile enthusiasm for racing, hardly attending a single meeting the year it happened. Nor does she go racing today nearly as much as she used to.

K decided in the mid-1970s to abandon his practice of having all his horses trained in France and send thirty or so a year to each of two English trainers, Michael Stoute and Fulke Johnson Houghton. This figure has increased recently and he has also taken on the Italian, Luca Cumani, at Newmarket to give him three strings to his bow. By April

1981, the system was going well, and it was obvious to Stoute that Shergar was a very good horse indeed. On Easter Monday, I had a bet on him to win the Derby, eight weeks hence, at odds of 25–1. I had £200 each way, which landed me a win of £6,250, less four per cent tax, when Shergar came home alone by a record margin of 10 lengths at Epsom on the first Wednesday in June.

What a great horse he was! He then went over to Ireland to win the Irish Derby equally impressively though not by quite such a wide margin. Lester Piggott rode him in Ireland as his Derby-winning regular jockey, Walter Swinburn, was suspended after an incident at Royal Ascot and he had eased Shergar down to a canter well before the winning-post.

On the Thursday of the Newmarket July meeting, K announced the syndication terms for Shergar's stud career to commence the following year and he and Sal gave my wife and me a lift down to Sardinia for our annual holiday. This lasted exactly a fortnight: we all had to return together on the Friday for different reasons and then Shergar was due to run at the big race at Ascot on the Saturday.

So the syndication had to be completed by the day before the Ascot race and all the shareholders notified. The terms were £250,000 down for a share – one fortieth – or £280,000 spread over three payments and over two years. By keeping the horse in Europe to stand at his stud in Ireland, K was valuing him at £10,000,000. Each day of that fortnight in Sardinia, he showed me the list of offers made for the horse from all over the world, mainly America, as well as the daily list of applicants for shares.

Even though it would have made him a great deal more money, he refused all offers for complete purchase of the horse. One of them, for more than $25,000,000 would only have involved the lease of the horse for five years before he reverted back to the entrepreneur who suggested the move.

I was able to advise him on the many applicants for shares, which far exceeded the quota. I was particularly pleased to be able to recommend the Maktoums, ruling family of Dubai, whom K knew nothing about in racing terms. But I had heard some good and interesting things about them, especially Sheikh Mohammed and, even though they did not get the full allocation applied for, they did get one. Now, of course, they are easily the biggest factor in European and particularly British racing and will probably be the most influential owners in the world, overtaking K himself and Robert Sangster.

152

With the syndication completed, Shergar duly won the Ascot race against older rivals, proving himself the all-age champion of Europe. After the race, Sal and K were summoned to go to the Royal Box to accept the Queen's congratulations and were told to bring any friends with them. They brought us along as well as Gerard and Sylvia de Waldner, who had travelled back from Sardinia with us all to see the race and we all had lunch together with the sponsors, De Beers.

My wife and I had dinner with her parents the night before when I had been able to tell the Queen the details of the syndication of Shergar, as well as Robert Sangster's simultaneous 28-million dollar deal with Storm Bird, so she was fully briefed.

Then came the anticlimax at Doncaster in September when Shergar ran in the St Leger, his last race. Running him in the race was a surprise to many people and his participation was in doubt for some weeks preceding the event. It had rained heavily at Doncaster and Shergar seemed out of sorts in the race, eventually beaten into a moderate fourth place to the amazement and dismay of the crowd. Michael Stoute could never really find a reason for such a poor showing but the horse did not seem himself at home afterwards and was retired to stud forthwith. K took the defeat incredibly well – he has always been a good loser and gave interviews to the press when many others in the same position might have removed themselves from the firing-line.

But the final part of the Shergar story was yet to be enacted. He did one full season at stud in 1982 and then, only days before the new covering season was due to begin, he was abducted by an armed and masked gang from the stud just outside the Curragh, along with the stud groom who was quickly released. Some strange negotiations ensued but it seems almost certain that the gang had completely misjudged and bungled the situation, did not understand syndication, panicked, and shot the great stallion. The kidnappers' calls to Paris stopped and no more was heard of Shergar. Police who had a shoot-out with an IRA gang sometime later during an attempted kidnapping are confident that they were the same men who had abducted and killed Shergar.

Why did the IRA not claim 'credit' for the abduction? Because even the men who proudly admit to wholesale murder of human beings realized that they had hit at the very heart of Ireland itself and jeopardized the whole breeding industry there.

My regular visits to Sardinia ended after 1981 and we have varied our summer holidays since then, being particularly spoilt in 1986 when we went on two cruises of the Greek Islands and Turkey, one of them Vivien Duffield's seven-day cruise with no less than 114 friends on the superb *Sea Goddess II*, and the second with Henry Ford and his wife Kathy on their yacht. We went on from that to Jordan for the third consecutive year to stay with Princess Firyal at her superb house just outside Amman. She even put up with our daughter for the second time.

Jordan is an amazingly varied country and the ancient city of Petra, generally regarded now as one of the wonders of the world, fascinated and enthralled even a hardened heathen like myself. We are pampered and guarded there, where another highlight is a trip to the Dead Sea in which I was able to lie, floating and reading a paper. We took Honor on this outing and we misjudged the strength and potency of the incredible salt water. We knew that it is imperative not to get water in the eyes or anywhere above the neck but we overlooked the fact that a small child is always covered in little abrasions and she was stung severely when she went in the water. Luckily we were close to a sweet-water stream with rock pools creating floating areas and we were able to rush her to this, which she quickly came to enjoy.

Princess Firyal, former sister-in-law of the King, is a popular hostess out there, particularly among the young members of the Royal Family and there is a non-stop stream of visitors, especially when her two grown-up sons, Tallal and Ghazi, both educated at Harrow, are in residence.

We have become somewhat Middle-East minded and have close friends in both Oman and Dubai, instigated by horse-racing connections. In March 1985, together with Robert Sangster, John Magnier and Vincent O'Brien with their wives, we were guests of Sheikh Mohammed in Dubai. This was an eye-opener. Apart from two visits to the palace, including a sumptuous lunch, our host took us to both his private zoo and aviary, also to the vast camel-racing track with its picturesque grandstand and the Sheikh's pavilion behind. Most fascinating of all, though, was when Sheikh Mohammed took us out to the desert to see his camels and then watch him work his falcons. We happened to be in the Range Rover with the keeper and were therefore nearest to the 'kill' after Sheikh Mohammed had released his colourful falcon. I use the word kill figuratively since the Sheikh is an animal- and bird-lover and conservationist and the falcon only stuns its prey, a sort of buzzard, and is taken off before inflicting any structural damage. The prey always come in pairs and both are caught and usually taken to the aviary.

The Sheikhs have become the greatest collective owners of both racing and breeding bloodstock in the world and, together with Prince Khaled Abdulla, are likely to dominate British racing for years to come.

Robert Sangster, an Influential Friend

My close friendship with Robert Sangster since 1973 is based on a mutual sense of humour. It was the same basis as my earlier friendship with Sally Aga Khan.

I knew Robert casually on the racecourse for some years before this as he dabbled quite successfully in ownership in a small way though it was not until 1975 that he formed the syndicate which was to change the face of European and world-wide racing. Robert's father, Vernon, who died just before Christmas 1986, built up Vernon's pools founded by his father in Liverpool in the 1920s, much the same time as the Moores family founded Littlewoods. Vernon Sangster devised the idea of giving employment to Roman Catholics in an area where a good job was always a luxury and their inspiration helped Vernons go stride for stride with Littlewoods in the flourishing football-pool business. Vernons was the basis of Robert's own fortune but his foresight and business acumen enabled him to multiply his original stake in the bloodstock world.

I first stayed with Robert for Chester races early in May 1974, just after I had won the backgammon championship aboard the QE2. I remember organizing an in-house backgammon tournament and Robert being delighted to beat me. I also remember that Chester meeting for one of the worst decisions ever made by the stewards when Robert's filly Shellshock was not awarded the race after being carried and intimidated half-way across the track by her much bigger opponent. It turned out later that the winner had cracked a bone in his foreleg which explained his behaviour, but in no way nullified the clear responsibility of the stewards to do their duty.

Robert and I have mainly similar interests but contrasting personalities which are complementary to each other. For all his great success in

156

life, he is a shy man and particularly dislikes public speaking. I am more extrovert and have grown used to speech-making, informal as well as formal. So, as a team, we work perfectly, particularly in Australia, where they love speeches. Robert gets me to speak for him and I need little coaching since I know pretty well how his mind works. He laughs louder than anyone when I tease him on these occasions though, particularly in Australia, audiences who do not know us and understand our relationship are sometimes quite shocked. This amuses Robert even more.

That stay during Chester race week was the only time I visited Swettenham Hall under Robert's auspices, though I stayed there many times later with Bobby McAlpine, as, soon afterwards, he left the country for tax reasons. He then tried Marbella and Normandy as possible new bases, going as far as to buy a house and estate in France. He rejected the Channel Islands but his essential Englishness led him back to the Isle of Man where he bought a large, slightly run-down house and estate, The Nunnery, just outside Douglas. This suited him perfectly since he was only about twelve minutes from the airport and the flight in one of his Kingair or Queenair planes to Liverpool was less than half an hour. He was also about the same time away from Dublin in the other direction, which, bearing in mind the rapid growth of his Irish bloodstock interests, was equally important.

It was at about this time that his marriage to his first wife, Christine, by whom he had three sons and a daughter, crumbled. Susan Peacock, wife of the then Australian Foreign Minister, Andrew Peacock, later leader of the Liberal Opposition over there, flew to Europe to move in with him and they married in March 1978. Just to set the record straight, Robert and Susan were divorced in August 1985 and he married his third and I am sure last wife – the extremely pretty and nice Sue – shortly afterwards.

In 1975, Robert finalized his plan to rationalize the owning and breeding of top-class bloodstock and he formed a syndicate, the basis of which was himself and the master Irish trainer Vincent O'Brien with his son-in-law John Magnier, who would mastermind the breeding empire. Vincent trained at the already famous Ballydoyle, from where he had already sent out scores of big-race winners, originally jumpers, but in the previous fourteen years, flat-racers. Magnier, married to Vincent's middle daughter Sue, lived near by at Coolmore stud and already the two establishments were regarded as the finest in County Tipperary and, indeed, all Ireland. The basic trio took in other partners including

157

Simon Fraser and David Aykroyd, though these two pulled out some years later to pursue their own interests.

Armed with ammunition raised from the banks, the syndicate moved in on the Keeneland sales in Lexington, Kentucky in July 1975 and came away with their first batch of expensive yearlings. They also raided other yearling sales later on in the States, England, France and Ireland. They struck gold with their very first crop for the following year one of their horses (nearly all of which carried Robert's famous green, blue and white colours) won the Dewhurst Stakes at Newmarket in October and was confirmed top horse of his generation in the British Isles. This was The Minstrel. Only Blushing Groom in France was rated above him in Europe.

The following year, Be My Guest proved himself a highly successful three-year-old just below classic standard and subsequently became a top stallion. But it was The Minstrel who was the stable star. Things did not start off too well, though. The Minstrel won his preparatory race at Ascot but, starting hot favourite, could finish only a disappointing third in the first colts' Classic, the Two Thousand Guineas at Newmarket. Worse was to follow when he was again beaten in the Irish Guineas against slightly weaker opposition. Even Robert and Vincent were disappointed in him.

It was Lester Piggott who saved the day. He had been trying desperately to book himself for Blushing Groom in the Derby but the Aga Khan wasn't having any, and stuck to his stable jockey Henri Samani. This may have influenced Lester's attitude but it was he who said to Vincent and Robert 'Don't worry about The Minstrel. I'll ride him in the Derby and he'll win.' Reassured by this advice and delighted with Lester's confidence, Vincent trained The Minstrel for Epsom where the presence of Piggott in the saddle was a distinct advantage.

Blushing Groom, however, remained firm favourite in the Derby betting but The Minstrel became second favourite partly on the strength of the reputation of O'Brien and Piggott. Robert was hopeful but no more and I freely admit that I favoured Blushing Groom and advised my readers accordingly.

About a week before the race, Robert, the Aga Khan and myself agreed that whatever happened, we would have a dinner-party in the private room at Annabel's on the night of the race. If either of them won the Derby, the party would be on the successful owner, otherwise expenses would be shared between the three of us. This was the true arrangement although, knowing the other two as well as I do, I think

158

that the Dutch plan would have been high unlikely to have taken place and it would have been a race between the other two quietly to advise head-waiter Louis that the party was on them.

Ever since, an apocryphal story has gone round – I have heard it hundreds of times – that I had been so confident of the result that I had arranged for the room to be decorated in the Aga's colours and had made a frantic call to Louis from the racecourse to change the décor when The Minstrel won. The only truth in this was that I did, indeed, make most of the arrangements, but there was nothing so vulgar as winner's colours draped around in Annabel's. I did make a telephone call to Louis from the press room after the race to confirm the menu, discuss numbers and warn him that it would be Mr Sangster's bill!

For The Minstrel justified Lester's optimism by winning in a frantic finish with Hot Grove, Blushing Groom being a well-beaten but respectable third. Two factors contributed to The Minstrel's win in the last few strides, his own indomitable courage which he was to show again in his two subsequent races and Lester's unequalled riding skill and strength. So it was Robert who was invited up to meet the Queen though there was some comment when Susan, who was nine months short of being married to him, went along too.

The party in Annabel's, with the Derby trophy, small and elegant, and the only visible fruits of victory, was a huge success and no one enjoyed himself more than Lester. He tucked into a man-sized meal of caviare, lamb and a delicious dessert. So no one was more surprised than he to read an exclusive front-page story in the *Daily Mail* the next morning reporting that he had gone straight back to his Newmarket home after the race and had celebrated as usual in frugal style with little more than a salad for dinner. I retell this story not so much to take a dig at the opposition but to give just one minor example of the hit-or-miss tactics of so many journalists, particularly those working for tabloids. It is similar to their tipping on the racing pages. Their successes are trumpeted and their failures, which inevitably are considerably more, are not mentioned. So the ludicrous invention about Lester's frugal evening went uncorrected and presumably even sold papers. I can honestly say that the policy of the *Daily Express* concerning myself, certainly in the last fifteen years was to only 'blurb' – the word used to describe those boasts on either the racing or back pages and occasionally even the front page – when I truly deserved it and was in a genuine winning run. I did have a tipping record to match up to the best during my near twelve years as the 'Scout', winning the *Sporting Life* naps table

– the tipsters' championship – by a clear margin in 1977, being pipped for the same title in the final two days a couple of years later, and frequently finishing with a profit and up with the leaders. I also established a record as far as the *Sporting Life* is concerned by napping thirteen consecutive winners in July 1985, finally breaking the run with the photo-finish defeat of the great filly, Oh So Sharp, at the hands of Petoski in the big race at Ascot. The Sports Editor's reluctance to boost my achievements can be gauged from the fact that this run was not even mentioned until it had reached something like seven or eight winners on the trot which deprived the paper of a good deal of ongoing publicity and, therefore, increased sales.

Most of the other tabloids scream and shout about nearly every winner tipped and since they all have six, seven, or even eight different prognosticators including representatives from the different training-centres, this means that there is something in practically every day. This is based on the principle that every now and then a blind sow treads on an acorn.

For his own professional reasons, Peter O'Sullevan demanded a blurb or mention for practically every winner he ever tipped even when, as was often the case, the horse started at odds-on. Peter believed in his own particular brand of statistics and in his earlier days he had a wonderful record. He understands betting and is a very shrewd punter, probably the best around. But during his last ten years on the *Express*, he and I profoundly disagreed on the service to be provided for our readers. His statistical obsession was for mere numbers of winners, normally at very short odds, which I believed was doing the readers no favours. Sometimes, particularly when his selections were showing a loss on a season, he would make what I considered to be useful and informative selections based on his great knowledge and experience. Incidentally, there was no rancour in our disagreement on this subject and, who knows, maybe he was right, maybe I was. But one thing I do know: the 'blurbing' policy of most of the tabloids now is blatantly dishonest.

On the topic of newspapers and tipping, my close friendship with Robert was of enormous professional use to me. Robert had virtually no secrets from me and almost every day we discussed the racing both appertaining to the day's card and also to the future. I could not always print everything he told me or tip every horse he gave me, but I still had an enormous advantage over my rivals in this department. When Robert became the top man in racing, I co-ordinated much of the information

160

for him and did a great deal of his betting. So trainers, jockeys, owners and bloodstock agents from all over the world would speak freely to me, many of them with messages to be passed on.

From the Derby onwards, 1977 was a year of almost unbroken success for Robert. The Minstrel went on to win the Irish Derby and then the King George VI and Queen Elizabeth Diamond Stakes at Ascot in July. This latter was another Piggott triumph, The Minstrel winning by a short head after a thrilling finish. He was then retired to stud and left for Maryland in the autumn. But this left Robert's challenge on the big end-of-the-season prizes unaffected since he now had possibly an even better deputy, also trained by Vincent – Alleged.

Alleged had been bought as a two-year-old in the March sales in LA, and was so backward that he only ran once that year. He had been purchased on Robert's instructions by the Irish agent Billy McDonald mainly for himself and Bob Fluor, the Californian industrialist as well as other partners. As a three-year-old Alleged was unbeaten and his potential was untapped until he ran in the St Leger, the last Classic of the season. He started favourite but Lester did not ride one of his best races, going to the front much too far out and was worried out of it by the Queen's filly Dunfermline who had won the Oaks. Although Alleged started favourite, this was an immensely popular victory since the Yorkshire crowd at Doncaster love a royal victory. And this was the year of the Silver Jubilee.

The defeat of Alleged turned out to be beneficial to Robert as Bob Fluor and one of his main partners, Shirley Taylor, were so disappointed that they sold their shares in the horse to Robert. Up till then Alleged had run in Fluor's colours. But it was Robert's green, blue and white colours that Lester wore in the Arc, possibly Europe's most prestigious race, on the first Sunday in October and they made all the running to gain a famous victory. Although Piggott was praised to the skies for winning, as is the fashion with the racing press, it is worth putting on record that Vincent was highly critical of his tactics both then and to this very day. He did not want Alleged to make the running and Piggott rode a very different race the following year, pleasing Vincent immensely, when coming from behind to complete a very rare double.

Nor was the O'Brien–Sangster–Piggott combination finished for the year since they again won the season's top two-year-old prize, the Dewhurst Stakes, with Try My Best so things looked rosy for 1978.

The six-month period from mid-September to mid-March 1978 saw a rash of marriages among our group. First to fall was trainer Barry Hills who married his wife Penny during St Leger week. We took the vows the following month, then Nick Robinson, publisher and co-owner with Robert of the glossy racing magazine *Pacemaker*, followed with his extremely attractive wife Jane, and finally Robert and Susan were married early in March.

Sangster's wedding to Susan took place in the little chapel adjoining The Nunnery and a whole series of celebrations followed for the international group of guests. I made a speech or two as usual, and this time only one man took exception, an inebriated Kentucky breeder Arthur Hancock, who misunderstood one of my jokes about the much-married Battle of Britain fighter-pilot and war-hero Tim Bigors who was also among the guests. Arthur had a wicked thirst and had once walked straight into the Aga Khan's bedroom looking for me in the middle of the night at the Hilton Hotel in Lexington when we were on our whirlwind tour of the USA.

He was also the central figure of one of the great anecdotes of our era. He was courting a lady who refused to accede to his main and insistent requests. She had a little dog whom she preferred in her bed. Eventually, repulsed yet again in her hotel room on the twenty-sixth floor, Arthur grabbed the dog, strode over, opened the window and held the dog out at arm's length, intoning the immortal words 'All right Lady. Take your choice. Dog or dick.'

Arthur was the breeder and part owner of Hawaiian Sound, trained by Barry Hills for Robert. Ridden by Bill Shoemaker, he was caught and beaten virtually on the line by Shirley Heights in the Derby that year. 1978 was not quite such a brilliant year for Robert but he still had his share of success and was now established as the top man in British racing circles. Hawaiian Sound gained his reward for several near misses in the highest class by winning the valuable Benson and Hedges Gold Cup at York in August, ridden this time by Lester Piggott.

That October, Robert invited us to accompany him to Australia via California, which we regarded as our belated honeymoon. This was the first and only time I ever went to Australia travelling westwards. We went from LA to stay at Palm Springs for a few days with Danny and Natalie Schwartz and Danny took us all to Las Vegas for the evening to celebrate my birthday on 23 October. Or was it our wedding anniversary three days later? Either way it was a less than satisfactory evening. We flew in Danny's Falcon jet and went straight to the MGM casino where we sat down and Danny, very much Mr Big, ordered champagne. 'Dom Perignon for my friends,' he instructed the scantily clad waitress. She reappeared a few minutes later without the champagne and whispered quite audibly to all of us in Danny's ear, 'Do you realize that Dom Perignon is eighty bucks a bottle?' Danny exploded with rage at this extremely gauche remark. He was not used, as a very rich man, to being asked such questions and was in any case a very big punter, well known to the management.

So the evening had started badly and deteriorated. Danny, mortally offended, contacted a friend who either owned or ran another casino, the Aladdin's Cave, and we moved there to drink and await dinner while Danny and Robert paid a preprandial visit to the gaming-tables. This proved disastrous and we waited and waited while Danny lost more and more though Robert managed to hold his own or perhaps lose just a little and stop. Eventually we were invited by the management to order our dinner and Danny arrived in a thoroughly bad mood having lost $300,000. Earlier in the day we had been asked to select which of the many cabarets we would like to see and had chosen Don Rickles, the acerbic comedian whom I was sure would be right up my street. Frank Sinatra's great friend and warm-up act, another funny man Pat Henry, had pulled all the Sinatra strings to get us a table since the show was fully booked. But Danny wasn't having any. At 11 o'clock when the show began he said, 'You don't want to go and watch that. Come and see me get my money back.' Danny's reluctance to face Rickles could be explained by the fact that the comedian always made outrageous jokes about Danny and Natalie when they were in the audience, particularly if they arrived late.

In fairness to Danny, I should mention that he generously gave $2,000 to my wife as an anniversary present to gamble with, but we sat for hours at the baccarat table while Danny struggled, muttering and swearing to recover his money. There were arguments with the management about limits and they kept him to a tight maximum which made his recovery more difficult. Eventually it was Phonsie O'Brien, brother of Vincent, formerly a great amateur steeplechase jockey and a considerable character, who saved him. To beat the limits applied to him, Danny made Phonsie sit down and play for him, staking the maximum. The bank went to Phonsie and he ran it thirteen times before losing, extricating our host from the mire.

Luckily Robert won as well and, at about 5 a.m. we left for the short jet ride back to Palm Springs. As we drank champagne on the plane, Danny all smiles by now, said 'Wasn't that great? Didn't you enjoy seeing me get my money back?' As a gambler myself, I had indeed been mildly interested and we were all pleased to see him out of trouble. But the evening could hardly have been described as a success particularly for my wife and Susan Sangster. Otherwise the Schwartzes were generous hosts as always and we enjoyed living in the lap of luxury with tennis and swimming during the day in what I regard as the best weather conditions in the world.

We returned to LA and went racing before attending a party to kill time while we waited to board the late night plane for Sydney and Melbourne. I was witness to a near drama in the kitchen at the party.

Vincent O'Brien's son David, now a successful Derby-winning trainer himself, was out there learning the business and that evening he was becoming extremely friendly with Linda Pincay wife of the great jockey Lafitt Pincay. Lafitt, who comes from Latin America, has a volatile temperament and became more and more agitated as David pushed his luck. Eventually, as the couple were chatting and laughing in the corner of the kitchen, Lafitt strode in and grabbed a large knife, striding purposefully towards David. Nothing serious was going on and I am sure that Lafitt would not have used the knife but it was a nasty moment and he was speedily disarmed before there was any serious trouble. It was time for us to leave.

My wife, never a light traveller, had excelled herself on this trip and she knew there would be a heavy social itinerary in Australia. It is true that the ladies do dress up for the races during Melbourne Cup week and also that the weather can be variable. But this was ridiculous. She had a vast suitcase, more like an elongated crate, which rejoiced in the name of 'Globetrotter'. It was certainly that and we received many complaints and threats from porters at airports during our travels. Apart from my own complaints, which were justified, as I also had to carry masses of hand-luggage including hat-boxes, the other girls who either travelled with us or met up with us in Melbourne also joined in the general mocking. But my wife had the last laugh, for there was a steady stream of ladies coming to our room to borrow umbrellas and various items of apparel which she had in duplicate and triplicate.

It was a wonderful experience which confirmed, for me, that Australia was the place to go again and again. The party split up then and we went on to Johannesburg to stay with Nicky and Strilly Oppenheimer, but we left rather promptly as we wanted to be back in London in time for Prince Charles's thirtieth birthday ball at Buckingham Palace. Nicky is the son of the legendary Harry Oppenheimer, South Africa's most influential business man, and his regal and splendid wife Bridget, whom we also saw. We were only there a few days but were able to go racing and also pay a visit to their most productive diamond mine, the Premier Mine in Pretoria, for which we had to don overalls and a helmet as we were transported thousands of feet underground.

There was no denying the glamour of Prince Charles's party as we first sat through a splendid cabaret given by the host's favourite singing group, The Three Degrees, and then danced and drank and were fed in one of the state apartments. I found myself having a long chat with Susan George, the actress, who told me that I was one of the only two civilized people there. We could never make out who the other one was. She had been sitting with the lovable Harry Secombe and we debated whether she was referring to him or Prince Charles himself. Perhaps she did not include Prince Charles in the assessment.

Robert built up his racing and breeding stock in Australia and his name is a household word out there. He is treated almost like royalty on his many visits. Apart from Melbourne Cup time, he always goes down there on one or two other occasions each year, notably for the Sydney Easter Racing Festival. Unfortunately I was unable to go with him in November 1981, when he won the Melbourne Cup with Beldale Ball, a grey, American-bred horse by the stallion Nashua which he had bought in England after Royal Ascot the previous year. Robert had two runners in the Cup that year, both with good chances but Beldale Ball came out well on top.

1981 was an unparalleled year for Robert since he also won the Derby with the brilliant, unbeaten Golden Fleece, who then had to retire due to recurrent lameness. He also took the Arc with a filly, Detroit who was trained in France by the then little-known Olivier Douieb. Both Golden Fleece, one of the easiest Derby winners I have ever seen, and Detroit were ridden by Pat Eddery, who had taken Lester Piggott's place as the Vincent O'Brien stable jockey in a much publicized transfer the previous year.

Great jockey though he was – and there was never a better at Epsom in particular – Lester was an appalling work-rider since he only suited himself and spent his entire career disobeying trainers' instructions to find out things for himself. This would drive Vincent mad. He knew exactly how he wanted his horses to work at home and he had a set of extremely talented work-riders to carry out his instructions. In fact, Vincent would do everything in his power to prevent Lester from coming over to Ballydoyle, though this made no difference to Piggott

165

who would just turn up, particularly if he was going over to ride in Ireland anyway.

So the relationship was strained, and worsened after Piggott won the Dewhurst again on Robert's Monteverdi. The colt hung towards his left after hitting the front and Piggott struck him two or three blows across the side of his face, probably flicking his left eye, with his whip. It was an extraordinary thing to do and Vincent was incensed, the more so since Monteverdi did not achieve much as a three-year-old, showing signs of temperament. Vincent, probably rightly, blamed Piggott for this and the opportunity to entice Eddery at the end of his contract with the Lambourn trainer Peter Walwyn was irresistible.

There was a general jockeys merry-go-round at this juncture and Joe Mercer took Eddery's place with Peter Walwyn while Lester moved to Henry Cecil and became champion again after a lapse of some years.

Robert only had Detroit – who showed great bravery allied to Eddery's strength when winning the Arc – with Olivier Douieb because of a tragedy which affected us both. Douieb had taken over the stable of our very special friend Miguel Clement after Miguel had been killed in a car crash returning from Deauville to Chantilly at the end of August 1978.

Miguel was a one-off, a French Basque who had been a cavalry officer and who had learnt his trade as an assistant to François Mathet. He was a successful trainer himself with a French Derby winner to his credit but horses and training were not everything to him and he lived a full life. He was known and loved in most of the leading night-clubs and restaurants in Paris and was also a regular visitor to the best places in London.

He had three sons, all of whom worshipped him. The eldest one, Marc, was with him in the car when they crashed and was badly injured, but, happily, recovered. The accident was no fault of Mig's. He was driving his Jaguar on the straight road near Chantilly when a huge lorry pulled straight out from a car park, making a U-turn in the dark. Miguel went straight under. I had just enjoyed the happiest two weeks ever in Deauville with him. He had rented a house a few yards from the Hotel Royale, perfectly situated and with a garden in which he often cooked delicious barbecued lunches and dinners. Another of his guests from London, Anthony Speelman, and I, both of us food fans particularly enjoyed his barbecued sweetbreads and English sausages, which we bought over for him and which he considered a great delicacy. Both Robert and Jimmy Goldsmith were among his owners.

166

I was much affected by his death and I have cut back my visits to France ever since, particularly to Deauville which has never been the same for me. Several of us went over for his funeral in Chantilly which was a very moving occasion with his elderly mother and his sister shaking hands with every one of the packed congregation. So much loved was he on both sides of the Channel that my suggestion that we should hold a memorial dinner late in September, particularly for those who were unable to make the funeral, was enthusiastically supported.

Anthony Speelman, Mickey Suffolk and I were hosts at the inaugural dinner which was held in the private room upstairs at Langan's, just off Piccadilly. Among those there, and the most enthusiastic supporters, were Peter O'Sullevan, Robert Sangster and Gordon White while from France came the great trainers François Boutin, Miguel's 'copin' (French for mate), Alec Head, the greatest French jockey Yves St-Martin, and the leading breeder over there, Comte Roland de Chambure.

Subsequently, all of these plus Jeremy Hindley, Barry Hills, John Aspinall and Jimmy Goldsmith have hosted either singly or collectively the dinner which was held each year alternately on either side of the Channel. Sadly, because of date problems, there has been a lapse but it will be resumed, I am sure.

The intention ultimately was for Miguel's own racing and horse-mad younger sons, Nicolas and Christophe, to take over when they were old enough. Meanwhile, Alec Head the busiest of men but a true friend, held the fort till the end of the year while the situation with the owners was sorted out and then Douieb took a lease on the house and stables. Hence Robert and Detroit.

Apart from his three major racing victories on 1981, Robert had another important engagement in June, the christening of my daughter, Honor. This turned out to be quite an event due to a combination of circumstances. First of all we appointed no less than nine god-parents since we had agreed that Honor would be our only child for a variety of common-sense reasons – finance, space and age (mine) the main ones. We argued long and hard about whom to ask – particularly difficult as we both had lots of friends. The trickiest part in several cases was to decide between a husband or a wife and to a certain extent these choices fell automatically into place. Everyone was very kind and diplomatic about it.

All the nine approached generously and flatteringly accepted; they were, in no order of merit or protocol, Robert Sangster, Jeremy

167

Hindley, Peter Halifax, Richard Hambro and Archie Stirling as god-fathers, and Camilla Parker-Bowles, Jane Spencer-Churchill, Philippa Courtauld and Sally Aga Khan as godmothers. Sally, who was also godmother to my younger son, Edward, all those years ago, demanded to be included and I was hardly likely to refuse her.

Through the influence of my father-in-law, we were allowed to use the Guards' Chapel just down the road from Buckingham Palace. He obtained this privilege from his former position as Colonel of the Life Guards and Commanding Officer of the Household Cavalry during which he was Silver Stick-in-Waiting to the Queen and subsequently a gentleman usher, whose duties included helping to run investitures and playing important roles on state occasions. He was a key-figure at the wedding of Prince Charles and Lady Diana Spencer, for instance.

What we lacked was someone to perform the ceremony. The resident chaplain of the Guards' Chapel was on holiday. A friend of mine, John Santer, who had formerly worked with me on the *Daily Express* and was then doing public relations for William Hill suggested his brother who had just been ordained as Bishop of Kensington and Chelsea. This seemed a brilliant idea as we were within his diocese. Unfortunately, he refused the job and I think he was reluctant to become involved in what he saw as a social bun-fight.

Then, between us, we had a brain wave. We all knew an extremely jovial character, the Vicar of Chaddleworth, not far from Wantage and, therefore, Lambourn. The Reverend Bob as we all knew him had a prodigious thirst for a man of the cloth and was also a fanatical horseman, with a great interest in racing. He had previously mentioned to Barry Hills that he would love an ex-racehorse needing a good home as a hack and when Robert heard of this, he gave him one of his horses which was still in training and had originally cost more than 50,000 guineas. The Reverend Bob had gone to Lambourn to collect his horse and had ridden him home, some eight or ten miles. The problem with Bob was to keep him in reasonable shape for the ceremony so he was carefully guarded until 3.30 p.m., the time for the off. He did a wonderful job and conducted both a correct but attractive ceremony, the highlight of which was when he lined up the godparents all of whom were there and made a few comments about each of them.

For example: 'Lord Halifax. Knew your father. Good to have a look at you.' 'Richard Hambro. I do my life insurance with you.' 'Jeremy Hindley. I have to keep in with you. Your father-in-law, Sidney Smart owns my living.' 'Robert Sangster. You gave me my horse and I'm most grateful.' 'Mrs Courtauld. I expect you are a member of the textile family.' 'Begum Aga Khan. I've heard a lot about and you don't let me down. I've never had a Muslim godmother before but I don't expect God will mind.' He was right there. Incidentally I have learnt quite a bit about the Ismaili religion since and have been most impressed by the balanced way in which they accept that there are other gods than their own.

The Reverend Bob had the congregation in fits of laughter, amazing several of our foreign friends who happened to be in London and who had asked to be included. So the ceremony was a very happy one which is as it should be.

We had the reception afterwards at our new house in Trevor Square which included limitless champagne supplied at competitive rates by my wicked young wine-merchant Andrew Brudenell-Bruce and also some whisky on which the Reverend Bob assuaged his thirst.

My trips with Robert to Australia resumed in 1982 and I have been back every year since. The pattern now is always the same. I follow him out a week or so after he goes out there; then a few days in Sydney where I have many sporting friends like Kerry Packer, Ian Chappell and John Alexander; and then the whole of the build-up to the Melbourne Cup carnival and the race week itself, which runs Saturday to Saturday inclusive and has four actual days racing.

The Melbourne Cup is celebrated by a full day's holiday in Victoria while the nation comes to a halt for the television or radio commentary of the actual race. It has been a lucky event for me and I backed the winner at good odds in 1983 (Kiwi), 1984 (Black Knight) and 1986 (At Talaq). Furthermore, as a visitor believed to have some racing knowledge in England and also as a known associate of Robert's, I seem to be invited to appear on various television programmes, usually 'Good Morning Australia', and tipped the winner on these three occasions. One year there was a theatrical gala on the eve of the Cup, made up of normal cabaret-style entertainment in the second part, preceded by a series of talks and interviews connected with the Cup. Robert was too shy to appear but Susan needed no second bidding and I was asked to deputize for him. A jockey, trainer, commentator and presenter, most of whom I knew, made up the group. Later we retired back-stage and after a couple of drinks, Susan and I drove off to the restaurant where we were all due to meet. The others who had been in the audience were stuck for the whole show and thus we were alone in the restaurant for about an hour. Susan and Robert had not been getting on well and I knew, both from Robert and from my own observation, the things which we causing him most embarrassment and, sometimes, anger. Gently, I took the opportunity to discuss the incompatibility which was causing the problem and gave her examples and the best advice I could. I freely admit that I sometimes found Susan, or 'The Sheila' as I christened her and which became her widely used nickname, extremely irritating. Her exhibitionism and taste were lamentable on occasions as when she deliberately danced alone on the floor with her former husband Andrew Peacock surrounded by cameras at the Derby eve ball at Melbourne leaving Robert and the rest of us writhing with embarrassment. She also insisted on leading in even the most minor of his winners, which caused much adverse comment in England particularly.

Once, after a filly of Robert's called Orange Leaf had won the last race of the day on the Friday of Epsom week, a maiden race of no significance or value except to the participants, she was with me near the winner's circle and said to me, 'I'm going to lead her in.'

I turned to her. 'Susan, I beg of you not to. Nobody does that here and it will embarrass Robert dreadfully.' She heard me but took no notice, turned on her heel and was back minutes later hauling in the horse with Robert trying to look the other way. And, except when he had plenty to drink and was past caring he did not particularly relish her flashing her bosom in public dancing on the table, or the perpetual rendering of 'Waltzing Matilda'. The tradition in England, by the way, is for the owner to lead in only winners of Classic races or very important, usually group-1 events plus such national institutions as the Grand National, the Cheltenham Gold Cup or the Champion Hurdle. Prince Khaled Abdulla, the distinguished Saudi Arabian owner, who has been so successful notably with Known Fact, Rainbow Quest and Dancing Brave, once dressed down his nephew, Prince Ahmed Salman for leading in his colt Lear Fan after winning the Craven Stakes at Newmarket, a group-3 event. 'We do not do this sort of thing in England and I don't want to see you doing it again,' he stated quietly but emphatically.

Anyway, I gently pointed these things out to Susan that night in Melbourne and she seemed to appreciate what I was saying. The next day I asked her if there was anything more worth discussing and she replied, 'I can't remember a word you said last night,' and carried on in exactly the same way until Robert left her.

There was another sticky year for me in Australia. I had arranged to

170

go to Sydney as usual a week or two after the others and stay with them in their house, 'Toison d'Or' with its fabulous view over Sydney harbour. But Robert decided to break the sad news to Susan that he wanted to split and, together, he and I decided that it would be a good thing and helpful to all if I stuck to my plan to stay with Susan in the house for a few days, even though Robert was moving out and staying in a hotel in Melbourne.

I readily agreed to this both for his sake and also for Susan's. I felt desperately sorry for her. She was distraught and could not understand his decision. So I stayed with her for a few days and did my best to console her. We had long talks and I took particular care to be as helpful and attentive as possible when we moved on to the Hilton Hotel in Melbourne as usual for race week. She had been particularly anxious that we should all behave as normally as usual as she did not want the news to leak out at that time on her own ground, with the press concentrating on them so much. The Duke of Roxburgh was also out there for business reasons and, as an old friend, joined our group, staying in the next room to me. Robert's youngest son Adam was also there so there was plenty of padding, so to speak. Incidentally, Robert has three of the nicest sons I have ever met, Guy, Ben and Adam. They all went to Harrow and I hate to say this as an old Etonian but they are a credit to our rival school. Their young sister Kate is full of character, too.

So we got through that Melbourne Cup week, 1984, and my wife and I saw quite a bit of Susan in London in November and December when we had all returned home. Then, shortly before Christmas, when she was due to return to Australia she was taken ill. She went back to the Isle of Man instead and became for a while a virtual recluse. We rang several times to see how she was, particularly at Christmas on my insistence but the calls were usually taken by her eldest daughter, Caroline Peacock.

I was disappointed though not particularly surprised to hear that she and the daughters had subsequently told friends that I had been particularly heartless and was the partial cause of many of the problems.

Robert's party for Susan in happier days for her back in 1982 was one of the most enjoyable ever. But the party he and Sue gave for his fiftieth birthday in May 1986 beat everything. More than 500 people came from all over the world, particularly from Australia. There was a seated dinner for all in a fabulously decorated marquee, a cabaret given by Paul Anka (best known for writing 'My Way') superbly and professionally presented with a backing group of more than twenty musicians like him from America, two bands plus the band of the Royal Marines and a firework display. The latter caused many complaints from some of the spoil-sport locals including an MP who appeared at the gates in his pyjamas. Most of us went to bed at about 6 a.m. and were up again for day two of the celebrations which included a lunch for all at the golf club, another party at the local hotel and night-club afterwards, and, in between, the Isle of Man races including the Manx Derby, which Robert won. We had a special tent and the only misfortune was when, after the Sangsters and ourselves had left just before the sixth race, the portly comedian Mel Smith, a friend of mine who had spent most of the afternoon with me, was beaten up by some local yobs, jealous of the privileged ones allowed in the private tent.

Apart from many of the most notable figures in world racing, such stars as Albert Finney, Diana Rigg who is married to Archie Stirling, and David Frost were there. It was a particularly good effort of two of the top Australian trainers, Colin Hayes and Bart Cummings, to make the effort to travel all that way, as well as Keith Miller and the attractive Kerry-Anne Kennerley, who presents 'Good Morning Australia' and has at different times interviewed Robert and Sue, and my wife and me for good measure.

Apart from all our jaunts to the Isle of Man, Australia and race-courses everywhere, Robert and Sue provide us with our holiday of the year these days in their house in Barbados, 'Jane's Harbour', bang next door to Sandy Lane. The highlight of the holiday for the men at least, though even the girls seem to enjoy it, is the pro-am golf tournament put on since 1981 by Robert and John Magnier plus Trusthouse Forte, who own both the course and the hotel.

The tournament has grown and grown as more people hear of it and ask for an invitation, and the pros are just as keen. We have many of the great names in British and Irish golf each year including up to ten members of Ryder Cup teams. Sam Torrance is a regular and enters into the spirit particularly well. So too are such stars as John O'Leary, Christie O'Connor Jr, Eamon Darcy, Michael King and Billy Longmuir, who has twice led the British Open Championship and who is a natural holiday-maker. Others who have played there in their time include Ian Woosnam, Paul Way, Brian Barnes and Tony Jacklin.

In 1987, we were up to 51 amateurs and 17 pros, making 17 teams of four each day. The auction at the pre-tournament lunch at Sandy Lane the day before play starts is one of the most popular features. It is a tough job for me to sell off 51 players and make jokes about all of them and it took an hour and three-quarters this time. But we raised just over £100,000 which was the highest ever until we topped it by £2,000 in 1988.

The worst aspect of it all from Robert and Sue's point of view is that, having had a house full for a fortnight with up to seventeen people for each meal plus outside guests, they need a holiday to recover.

The Disappearance of Lord Lucan

THE disappearance of Lord Lucan in 1974, with all the attendant gruesome details, was probably the most traumatic event in my life. The murder two years earlier of my sister-in-law Gail Benson was bad enough, but this was right on my own doorstep and concerned a close friend whom I saw practically every day that I was in London.

I had known Lucky, as we usually called him, for twenty-six years. When we first met we were at Eton together, he a few months older than me and then called Lord Bingham. He inherited the title, Earl of Lucan, after he left school on the death of his father.

At school he was conspicuous for his ordinariness. He was an adequate scholar and not a notable games player though he had some musical aptitude. He was very upright and had a deceptive sense of humour which he hid behind a bland exterior. After school he went into the Army for a short while and then became a brave and successful winter sportsman, notably at St Moritz on the dangerous bobsleigh run.

But it was our mutual love of gambling which brought us back together in the early 1960s. We were both founder-members of John Aspinall's Clermont Club and both, in those early days, became addicted to the French card game chemin de fer, popularly known as 'chemmy'.

Lucky, and to a lesser extent myself, had already played the game in French casinos, in particular at Deauville and Le Touquet, but we could be found on the first floor at the Clermont night after night shovelling out the cards and uttering the magic words 'Banco' and 'Suivi'. Extremely expensive words they often were too, with the former indicating our willingness to bet against the banker and the latter stressing our right to follow up that bet. Without going into too many details the way to win at chemmy is to run a bank, while the way to lose the maximum is for a player to bet and 'Suivi' against a running bank.

In the stylish days of Aspinall at the Clermont, chemmy was very much the popular game and there were many dramatic and amusing incidents which I have chronicled elsewhere. But John Lucan was the most regular player of them all, sometimes playing for himself alone and sometimes fronting partnerships which could well include Aspinall himself. In those days it was perfectly legal for a casino proprietor to participate in gaming himself or even be a silent partner.

From the spring of 1964 when I was separated from my first wife (and later that year divorced), it would be a rare day that Lucky and I did not have either lunch or dinner together when I was in London. In particular, I always lunched or dined with him the moment I returned from my many holidays or trips abroad. The reason was simple. He was always there. He hardly ever went away. He liked to hear what I had been up to and tease me about my foreign friends. 'International white trash,' he would growl.

We dubbed him with a variety of nicknames. When he was plain Lord Bingham he seemed only to be called by his Christian name, John. But later, mainly due to his slightly tongue-in-cheek reactionary insistence on making himself out older than he really was and maintaining dated virtues and some vices as well, he was variously known as 'The Fossil', 'The Relic', and 'The Old Timer'. But the name which stuck was 'Lucky' which he acquired during a winning spell in the Deauville casino and which fitted nicely and alliteratively with his title Lucan. I think Aspinall gets the credit for that one and the newspapers picked it up when he achieved his subsequent notoriety.

Basically Lucky's daily pattern during the 1960s was to lunch at either the Clermont or the Mirabelle and dine at either the Mirabelle or the Clermont. Occasionally the Guinea was thrown in for variety. His choice of menu was equally adventurous: smoked salmon to start with and lamb cutlets to follow was his staple diet. Between lunch and dinner, he played backgammon in his own distinctive style. He wasn't bad but stubbornly adhered to one or two basic, nursery plays which none of us who achieved somewhat more advanced status could dissuade him from maintaining. 'The dice can only see two men,' he would growl, a cliché coined by himself which I never fully understood. He would leave the game and slump down on a sofa or armchair for an hour's snooze around tea-time before embarking on another evening at the backgammon board accompanied by a steady flow of cocktails, usually based on vodka.

Lucky was the ultimate conservative, ironic since his parents had, surprisingly, been ardent and practising socialists. He had reacted as far as possible from his parents' political philosophy though he certainly played it up to the full and enjoyed shocking the occasional liberal who showed the temerity to take him seriously and challenge him. Lucky might well have coined the current political insult 'wets' in referring to lukewarm conservatives while he frequently used and enjoyed the insulting 'champagne pinkies' with reference to socialists who lived an opulent life-style.

Lucky's other diversions were bridge and golf. Almost every Friday unless I was away on the racecourse we would go down to either Sunningdale or Wentworth and play with the eccentric Ian Maxwell-Scott, Aspinall's right-hand man in a job at the Clermont which could only be described as a sinecure. Maxwell was unique, an opinionated and fearless gambler on the horses, much given to backing no-hopers at odds of 33–1 or more. He also helped himself liberally to the cash-float which was available to him and other employees at the Clermont in the careless 1960s.

So Lucky referred to our Friday morning golf game as 'a little redistribution of wealth'. He and I played against each other for a small stake, with neither of us much caring who won while we each played against Maxwell for considerably more. This system was eagerly encouraged by Maxwell who had a high opinion of his appalling golf and who, anyway, would never dream of doing or playing anything for less than a substantial stake.

Lucky was very much the ring-master on these little jaunts and it was he who would calculate just how much we should try and take off Maxwell. He had an uncanny knack of discovering the size of the float that had been filched. 'He's got two grand today so we should go for about £300 each which will leave £1,400 for the local Uckfield bookmaker and Susie and the housekeeping if they are lucky.' Lucan was of the opinion that Maxwell went down to his bookmaker's office every Saturday morning and blew the remaining cash-float, regardless of the fate and the stomachs of his wife, Susie, and an ever-increasing string of daughters. Occasionally, of course, Maxwell had a win and the family could eat while Lucky and I would aim a little higher on the following week's golf match.

They really were quite ridiculous games. None of us was particularly good. I was a reasonably steady and authentic sixteen handicapper at

176

Sunningdale and could look after myself. Lucky had a fine, old-fashioned upright swing. He hit the ball a long way but not always in the right direction. But Maxwell was dreadful and so the result was nearly always as anticipated. The caddies could hardly restrain their mirth, particularly at Maxwell's antics and Lucky's brusque, sometimes quite fierce, though tongue-in-cheek manner. Anyway the caddies enjoyed it since Maxwell was a liberal tipper and so too was Lucky, particularly when he had his Dobermann pinscher dog with him. The caddy was paid extra to drag round, or more often be dragged, by Otto, the aptly named German hunting-dog. Lucky was very proud of Otto's strength. When we were well out of sight and earshot of the clubhouse, he would instruct the caddy to release Otto, who being London-based would career around the course, totally out of control and ignore his owner's increasingly loud and angry commands and protests.

Otto lasted for a few years before Lucky's wife, Veronica, won a domestic power struggle and forced Otto's return to his breeder. The crunch came in the bedroom where Lucky insisted that Otto slept on the end of their double bed. Otto developed an even more frequent tendency to fart during the night which Lucky regarded as manly and professed to enjoy, while Veronica became increasingly disgusted. On this matter Veronica was the winner and my sentiments were all with her.

During the 1960s John and Veronica produced two daughters but the great moment of Lucky's life was when Veronica gave birth on 21 September 1967 to their first and only son, George, Lord Bingham and thus the male heir to the line. That night Lucky and I went on the town together to celebrate, just the two of us. It was Lucky's idea at the time more than mine. We dined at the Mirabelle where we ordered two bottles of particularly fine red burgundy.

His favourite tipple was burgundy and he knew a good deal more about it than I did. Most Englishmen, including myself, tend to prefer claret, the wine of Bordeaux. We then walked back to the Clermont to try our luck there and then Lucky had his brainwave. 'Before we go to Annabel's we'll pay a visit to the White Elephant and teach Mancini a lesson.' The White Elephant was actually a restaurant club in Curzon Street, still in existence and much favoured by members of the film and show-business world. But in those days there was a small casino above it, presided over by the considerable character Tony Mancini, actually officially called the AM Casino but known to all of us at the White Elephant.

177

It was the second-string casino to most of Aspinall's clients because of the sporting atmosphere generated by Tony himself, a gambler as sick as the rest of us.

Tony greeted us particularly warmly that night – he could see a couple of mugs coming from many miles away. Unfortunately, I had £5,000 or £6,000 in bookmaker's cheques on me, much needed for other commitments while Lucky had limitless credit. The end-result was inevitable. I lost my all and Lucky blew about twelve grand. Neither of us minded as much as we should and we still had time to nip back to Annabel's for a late-night snifter, often, and probably in this case, that rather potent and strong German beer, Löwenbrau.

On these late-night gambling binges, Lucky would become rather pale and sweaty, a fairly general reaction, but he always remained stiff-backed and upright and maintained a commanding presence. He only normally lost his cool if a dealer did not carry out his clear request, or more particularly, if the overseer who was to bring him more money or chips was slow. Late at night, his signature was no more than an 'L' with a straight line. It was his commanding bearing and bristling moustache at the gambling tables of Europe that caused him to be offered two film contracts both of them from Italian film producers. I think they were Carlo Ponti, the husband of Sophia Loren, and Vittorio de Sica. John politely declined one of them which was made in the Clermont, but went for a screen-test in Paris after the other request, I think from de Sica, for a film called *Woman Times Seven*.

John did not enjoy the test which was for a part as an English lord in a film about seven different characters in the life of one woman.

'Stupid bloody fools,' expostulated John on his return from Paris, 'they expected me to smile and prance in front of coloured boards. Can you imagine me laughing at nothing with a lot of idiots standing around moving pieces of cardboard.' I am sure that he was a thoroughly difficult customer and, in fairness, he had told the producer that he would be no good, but he had finally given in under persuasion.

About a week later John brought in a letter from the producer and showed it to me while we were lunching at the Clermont. He thought it hugely amusing. 'Told the bloody fool but he wouldn't listen,' he said handing over what, when I read it, I thought a rather charming message.

'Dear John,' it read, 'I have received the results of your film test. As you warned me you do find it hard to smile and unbend in front of the cameras. You did look handsome but I agree that you are perhaps not ready for such a part. Perhaps we can try again some other time.' The producer then signed off in cordial terms and that was the end of Lucky's screen career and the unlikely possibility of his being embroiled in a screen kiss with Shirley MacLaine.

By the late 1960s and early 1970s relations between John and Veronica had become more strained and she, in particular, was increasingly eccentric. She has many times been quoted, or journalists have taken it upon themselves to suggest, that Lucky's friends cold-shouldered her and treated her like an outcast. Since these friends referred to could only have been myself and three or four others, all of whom I knew well, I can refute that criticism. I cannot count the number of times that I had dinner with Veronica, whether I was on my own or with a girl-friend, and I always did my best to be chatty and friendly and help to make the evening enjoyable. It was John's arrangement with her that she should turn up for dinner each evening and not lunch and this was an arrangement between them alone. But she was not always easy and I often had to correct her as gently as possible when she expounded some of her more violent flights of fancy. She basically hated a lot of women and would loudly accuse perfectly decent and normal women of being whores. 'She's a whore,' she would shout, pointing at some perfectly innocent lady at a nearby table. 'She's jealous of me because I'm the Countess of Lucan and she's not even married,' she would say of another. 'She hates me because I've got a son and she hasn't,' was another favourite and completely groundless accusation.

'You can't say that,' I would quietly answer, 'she's a perfectly nice woman and that simply isn't true. You mustn't go around saying these things.' I would protest, quietly and gently trying to calm her down. Lucky would cringe with embarrassment and seethe with inward rage which no doubt exploded when they got home later. So in fact my own chiding would probably save Veronica from a worse scene later provided it had the desired effect and quietened her down.

One of the worst and most physical explosions took place in the Clermont one evening. The main downstairs room of the club was a sort of drawing-room with two backgammon tables, two sofas and some armchairs where members and guests sat or stood drinking before dinner. There was also a television set in the corner which was normally only used for watching racing and other sport in the afternoons. That evening it happened to be still on. There was also a lot more people there than usual and Veronica slipped in to join up with Lucky and stood, half chatting with us and half watching the television screen. Inadvertently, a tall, attractive blonde girl, Billy Buckley, the wife of

Michael Buckley, a successful racehorse-owning member moved between Veronica and the television. Before anyone could move, Veronica stepped forward and hurled the contents of her glass, red wine, all over Billy and her white dress. 'We don't want the likes of you here,' shouted Veronica as she stepped back triumphantly from the fracas. Billy behaved magnificently and left in a most dignified fashion to be mopped down by the legendary Doris in the ladies' cloakroom. John was overcome with embarrassment, particularly as he knew the Buckleys, and was temporarily at a loss to know what to do. Thanks to the adult behaviour of Billy Buckley, a major crisis was averted and she felt almost as sorry for John as she did for herself.

But it was incidents like this which led to Lucky's fears for the safety of his children and which caused him to have recourse to the courts for possession of the three children and separation from Veronica.

He moved out of the family home, 46 Lower Belgrave Street, a few yards from Eaton Square, and moved into an apartment only a few hundred yards away. On 23 March 1973, he obtained a High Court order from Mr Justice Arnold granting him custody of the children and we all saw much less of him as he devoted more time to them. He showed me messages from their teachers saying how much happier they seemed at school and this certainly seemed the case to me when I visited the apartment and saw them all.

However, Veronica prepared a counter-punch as she was legally entitled to do and some months later there began a much bigger, longer, and more acrimonious court case. This time a lot more mud was thrown at John and some doctors or psychiatrists on whose evidence he depended either changed their tune or failed to appear. John, who was fast running out of money as the legal bills mounted, was forced to withdraw from the case and the children, in floods of tears, were returned to their mother and 46 Lower Belgrave Street.

John's character changed from that day. He felt let down by the lawyers, the judge, and particularly the medical profession. He feared for the safety of his children and he became embittered. He particularly felt that Veronica had deliberately extended and increased the costs of the case and resented paying her lawyers' bills. He was financially stretched to the limit even though he had various trusts and properties scattered around which meant that he was not technically broke.

But he was forced to borrow money from several friends and began drinking much more heavily as he brooded for retribution and revenge. I reproach myself for not seeing the violence of his ultimate reaction. I knew he was not himself and he was not such good company as he had been. His gambling was idiotic and he did not·take kindly even to gentle advice from myself, Aspinall and other close friends to take it easy, even though he must have known in his heart of hearts that we were right. Few of us were speaking from a position of strength, anyway, since most of us had been in similar positions ourselves though without the extenuating domestic circumstances.

Lucky's change of attitude was clear to me just over a week before the tragic events of the night of 7 November 1974.

Back in April, I had won the Dunhill International backgammon tournament aboard the liner QE2, known that year as the World Championship. I was thus selected to represent Great Britain against the United States in a five-a-side international contest which we played in the last week of October.

I had beaten the American captain Barclay Cooke in the final of the QE2 championship, 29–28 in the final game after four and a half gruelling hours. So the return contest between us in the international, which was played at the Clermont, had more than the usual element of needle. The British side were very much underdogs in this contest but I had managed to win two of my three matches on previous days, one of them by an easy margin over Barclay's son Walter Cooke who was widely regarded as the world's most brilliant player. Add to this the fact that Barclay had written a much acclaimed backgammon book *The Cruellest Game*, and it can be seen that he badly needed his revenge.

The matches in this competition were played after dinner each evening at about 9.30 or 10.00 and, by chance, Barclay had been dining with Lucky at the Mirabelle beforehand. Barclay was never a drinker so he turned up sprightly and punctual for our contest. As on the QE2 six months earlier it was cut and thrust all the way with never more than a point or two between us. After about two hours Lucky lumbered in very drunk and sweating profusely and plonked himself down between us, half leaning across the board. The rules and ethics of competitive backgammon are very clear and very correct. No spectator may comment or advise on any play. The same common-sense rule would apply to almost any other competitive game such as bridge, chess, or even golf. But Lucky immediately began pointing out the plays he would make as we each rolled the dice, behaviour of which he would normally have been most critical in another. Because of our special relationship and friendship with him, I never complained or chided Lucky though Barclay, in the nicest possible way did occasionally try to

181

quieten him. 'Aw John,' complained Barclay from time to time in his gentlemanly Boston drawl, 'give us a break.' Luckily Barclay and I were also good friends and we managed to finish a thrilling match after three and a half hours with him the winner on the last game, this time by 26–25. We were thus 54 points all after eight hours of intensive international backgammon for the year, and honours were even.

As an aside, I must add that I was delighted that honours were even but finances were strongly in my favour since the Dunhill event was worth £10,000 to the winner, a lot of money and much needed by me then as always, whereas the international was for the love and the reputation of our countries. So I most certainly won the right match.

Lucky's behaviour that night did not worry me from my point of view – we were too good friends for that and he had helped me on many occasions previously – but I was sad since he was letting himself down. Only afterwards, with the benefit of hindsight, did I realize that he was probably living off his nerves, planning a means of rescuing his children. He was reading scores of detective stories and obviously preparing for what he must have perceived as a sort of SAS venture.

The following week I agreed to go across to the Isle of Man at the invitation of Robert Sangster to speak in favour of a legalized change in the Betting Act there. I was to stay a couple of nights and various other functions had been arranged.

Robert arranged to send his plane to London airport to pick me up on Tuesday afternoon at about 5 p.m. There were two or three others flying out, including Britain's most brilliant sports writer Hugh McIlvanney, who was spending three days with me to research an article on my life-style for the glossy horseracing magazine *Pacemaker*. So Hugh had chosen this week to do the job, commissioned by *Pacemaker's* publisher Nick Robinson because I had recently inherited the top racing job on the London *Daily Express* writing under the nom-de-plume the 'Scout', succeeding the great Clive Graham.

I was enjoying entertaining Hugh, a great character as well as a wonderful writer. It amused me to introduce him with his broad Scots accent to a rather genteel debby cocktail party at the old St James's Club and follow up with the Clermont and Annabel's. My girl-friend then was the beautiful but demure Lady Charlotte Curzon who found Hugh's accent a little hard to fathom and who was particularly baffled when Hugh slipped several slices of beetroot into her evening handbag during dinner. She opened the bag in Annabel's and found herself with a handful of beetroot which hardly improved the interior of her bag

182

and purse.

'He's rather strange, your friend,' she whispered to me through pursed lips, 'he's put a lot of beetroot in my handbag.' 'Don't worry,' I replied, 'he always does that sort of thing. He comes from Glasgow and he's worried that he might starve one day.' 'Poor thing,' she whispered, totally satisfied with my ludicrous explanation.

So Hugh, Charlotte and I had lunch together at the Clermont on Tuesday and I mentioned to Lucky, who joined us, that we had to be at London airport at 4.30 p.m. Lucky knew that my car was in dock and said 'Borrow my Mercedes to take you to the airport. Charlotte can drive you and bring it back.'

This was typically generous and thoughtful of Lucky who had a very warm heart behind his slightly forbidding exterior. Few of his good deeds were recorded though he helped me out on numerous occasions and every doorman and waiter associated with the clubs and restaurants that he frequented were loyal to him to a man.

As one other example of his kindness, he bought a couple of horses in France which he subsequently brought over to race here. He sent them to be trained at Newmarket by Arthur Freeman, a fine and brave ex-steeplechase jockey who was struggling to be a trainer. John did not know Freeman from Adam but was persuaded by a mutual friend – stockbroker Stephen Raphael – that he would be doing a good turn to support a struggling man. So Freeman trained the two horses, one of whom, Le Merveilleux II, had quite a bit of ability.

Sadly Freeman did not do particularly well with them but John stuck by him and even gave him a brand-new Rover car as a present. It was only when Freeman had to give up training with financial and alcohol problems that the horses were switched to another local trainer, Thomson Jones, who won several races for Lucky with Le Merveilleux.

So Charlotte drove us to London airport in Lucky's car which was going perfectly well and that was the last that I ever saw of him. For I didn't return until Thursday evening and, hardly surprising, didn't know where he was. I knew nothing about the events of that evening and night until 8.30 the next morning, Friday, when Stephen Raphael rang me.

'Bens, something's happened to Lucky. Raymond Clifford-Turner lives in Hobart Place opposite the mews behind Lucky's old house and he says police have been swarming about there all night. You are the sort of bloke who can ring around and find out what's happened and what we can do.'

I rang up Gerald Road police station, explained that I was a close

183

friend of Lucky's and lived in the same area. There was a long pause at the other end and then the officer said, 'I think you had better ring Inspector Gerring on this number.' I rang Gerring on the number that he gave me, gave him my qualifications as a close friend, and volunteered my assistance. He decided to tell me the story as he knew it so far which was that a man had got into Veronica Lucan's house, 46 Lower Belgrave Street and at about 9 p.m. the previous evening, had battered the children's nanny to death in the basement and also tried to batter and strangle Veronica when she had come down some minutes later. Veronica, injured and badly shaken, had managed to escape and had named Lucky as her attacker.

I gave my name and telephone number to Gerring and asked if I should stick around rather than go down to stay in Gloucestershire for Cheltenham races that weekend. He told me to go ahead with my plans and he would see me some time the following week. There was no great urgency in his attitude and it is significant that the same attitude prevailed with other officers on the case who did not see fit to alert ports and airports until later that day.

I rang Stephen back, put him in the picture, and he agreed that I should contact Lucky's closest friends with a view to meeting and discussing what we should do for him. I alerted John Aspinall, Dominick Elwes, Dan Meinertzhagen, and Lucky's brother-in-law Bill Shand-Kydd. Some of them, particularly Bill, knew more than me. We agreed to meet for lunch, the first suggestion being at the Mirabelle, but then it was agreed that this would be too conspicuous, so Aspinall invited the party to convene at his London house, 1 Lyall Street.

We sat round drinking rather ordinary white wine and eating cold meat and cheese from the refrigerator plus some small portions of smoked salmon. I can't remember who had what but it was a frugal meal. I mention it in detail, like one or two other incidents, because of subsequent ill-informed and misleading criticism.

For instance, when he heard a garbled version of this lunch a few days later rabid left-winger Clive Jenkins, leader of one of the clerical unions, sought to make a name for himself by issuing a statement deploring Lucky's privileged friends quaffing expensive wines and guzzling smoked salmon and other rich foods. It was typical of several other cheap political attacks that we had to endure. Another was a question posed to the Home Secretary in the House of Commons under privilege by the ridiculous Labour MP Marcus Lipton who demanded to know if the Government was doing anything about this privileged gang of

Lucan's friends obstructing the police. I wrote a letter to *The Times* about that one, which was printed, merely asking Lipton for any evidence or foundation to back his complaints. Needless to say he had none and did not have the guts to reply.

Meanwhile, back at the lunch everyone had a say. While all six of us were doing our best to help Lucky, the whole thing was hypothetical because none of us knew where he was. Bill knew most as he had been alerted by the police during the night and was about to be the recipient of two of Lucky's farewell letters.

Aspinall, ever the orator, indulged a little rhetoric and presuming Lucky's guilt declaimed dramatically: 'He must fall on his sword. That's the only course left open for him.' Elwes, an artist and of a more nervous and dramatic disposition than the rest of us, devised elaborate schemes for Lucky to be smuggled on to a cargo ship to South America. The others, including myself, were more pragmatic and I observed that it was futile to speculate until we had further news, but that I would help in any way possible and he would be welcome if he turned up at my flat.

This was a point that I reiterated when I finally was allowed to make my police statement the following Wednesday, even though I was warned that if I did harbour him, it would be a grave breach of the law. Several of us, notably Elwes and Meinertzhagen, were round at the police station nearly every day, trying to glean information and offer assistance.

And Dominick went off to visit Veronica in St George's Hospital off Hyde Park Corner to comfort her. He did this on his own initiative and received a nasty shock. When Dominick, an attractive fellow with lots of charm, reached Veronica's bedside and started muttering words of sympathy to her, she hauled herself up and looked at him with a glint of triumph in her eyes. 'Who's the mad one now?' she hissed, a none too subtle reference to past court cases. So much for sympathy. Dominick was much shaken and chastened by the experience when he reported back to me.

Yet again this humane gesture was subsequently misreported. It was quite wrongly suggested that we had jointly sent Dominick round as the man most likely to be able to persuade her not to incriminate Lucky.

Gradually the story came to our ears. The murderer had waited in the basement having taken the light-bulb from the socket. He had an American mailbag to dispose of the body and lead piping wrapped in the middle with Elastoplast for grip. It was the evening off for Sandra Rivett, the nanny, and Lucky not only knew this but had checked that

185

morning with his elder daughter Frances that this was still the case. Lucky had his own latchkey. Unfortunately for the wretched girl, her date that night fell through during the day and she decided to cancel her night off. She sat watching television upstairs with Veronica and at about 9 o'clock went down to the basement to make them both a cup of tea. She was hit violent blows on the head and died almost instantly.

Minutes later Veronica herself went down to find out what the delay was and was herself attacked and also half strangled. She said to police and later at the coroner's court that it was Lucky, and she explained how she had just managed to resist him in his weakened state and persuade him to come upstairs to the bedroom. Frances was sent to bed while Lucky and Veronica talked. Veronica said that she would say nothing about him to the police and they would try to start off again. Lulled by this, Lucky volunteered to go to the bathroom to get a sponge and towel to clean her bleeding head. But as he left the room, she slipped quietly down the stairs, rushed out into the street and ran into the Plumber's Arms pub in Belgravia screaming, 'Murder, murder!' She also added that her husband had tried to kill her. By the time the police reached the house, Lucky was gone. But it seems certain that he visited an older and trusted lady friend, Madeleine Florman, who lived not far away around the corner and rang urgently on the doorbell of her flat. She heard the bell but was unwilling to open the door at that time of night. Later blood was found on the doorstep.

Sometime later but before midnight, Lucky arrived at the door of the Maxwell-Scott house in Uckfield, half-way between London and the South coast.

He was dishevelled, there was a dark wet mark on his trousers, and he was sweating and distraught. Susie Maxwell-Scott let him in and, being as unemotional as her husband Ian, who was out, was remarkably unphased either by his appearance or his demeanour. She poured him at his request two or three large whiskies which he gulped down. He then asked for writing-paper and envelopes and wrote two letters. It also transpired that he had already phoned his mother saying, without full explanation, 'There's been a terrible accident at the house. Go round and collect the children.'

After he had been at the Maxwell-Scott house for some while, he instructed Susie to post the letters, both of them to Bill Shand-Kydd, and left. Curiously, at some stage he also wrote a third one to Michael Stoop. He was driving a nondescript, oldish Ford Corsair which he had borrowed from Stoop, an old friend of his, two weeks earlier. The police seemed to be under the impression that his Mercedes was being repaired, the same car that had taken me to London airport on Tuesday.

The trail ended next morning at Newhaven on the Channel coast where the car was found empty close to the sea. And that was the last that anyone saw of Lucky. Susie Maxwell-Scott thought so little of the fact that he had called at the house that she forgot to tell Ian until the next day when he commented on a television news-flash about the whole affair.

Most of Lucky's closest friends were ignored all weekend by the police even though all were available. None of us was interviewed until the following week. A series of ludicrous police gaffes followed. For instance, police rang John Aspinall's home, Howlett's, in Kent where he kept his famous private zoo, to make an appointment to visit the place the following morning and search for Lucky. They wanted to look in the tigers' and gorillas' cages. And later it was decided that a squad of detectives should make a secret visit to Annabel's to mingle with what they believed to be the so-called Lucan set and elicit information by eavesdropping on idle gossipers. All that happened was that one of them got so drunk that he had to be carried out by his embarrassed colleagues.

It was in the light of the lack of urgency shown by the police and these examples of utter incompetence that we became so enraged by stories of the Lucan set closing ranks and obstructing the police. The truth was the opposite. In fact, Elwes in particular, and the rest of us to a great extent, were constantly in touch with the police and would answer any questions they asked. But Detective Chief Superintendent Roy Ranson, a decent enough fellow who led the inquiry from Gerald Road, began to realize that he was hopelessly out of his depth. He also realized that he knew nothing of the life-styles and attitudes of the people he was dealing with and that he was reaching a dead-end, not because of obstruction but because the trail was dry. None of us knew where Lucky was.

So the dirty tricks came into play. Leaks were arranged to pressmen hungry for news to the effect that the police were being obstructed by this privileged group. And the newspapers, particularly the tabloids, were only too pleased to believe and print this rubbish while the police were creating an alibi for their own lack of progress.

Then came the sightings. Lucky was spotted in Australia, South Africa, Brazil, and just about everywhere else, often on the same day. The police believed many of these reports and once again made fools of themselves by launching a raid, at great expense to the taxpayer, on

187

St Malo in France.

The most ironic mistake led to a notable arrest. Police in Australia suspected that a mystery Englishman who had just arrived there was Lucan. They set out to arrest him and found out that they had landed John Stonehouse, a Labour cabinet minister who had misappropriated charity money and who had faked his drowning from a beach at the other side of the world while slipping off to Australia. He was extradited and was sentenced to a five-year stretch in England.

Now, some fourteen years later, no one is any the wiser. The key officers in the case have retired. The police have stopped blaming the so-called Lucan set. Sadly, Veronica became a virtual recluse and has been in and out of various sanatoriums. But the children have grown up remarkably, as attractive, well-brought-up young adults showing no sign of the ordeal that they suffered. Credit for this must go to Bill Shand-Kydd and his wife Christina, who is Veronica's sister.

I have no personal doubt that Lucky is dead and that he killed himself the following day when he realized the enormity of the error that he had made. That error ruined his life and to a certain extent those of the rest of his family. Equally I have no doubt that he did plan to murder Veronica for the sake of his children. He feared for their safety and resorted to the horrific and misguided plan as his mind became distorted by the many injustices he suffered at the hands of doctors, psychiatrists, and lawyers.

What the world failed to recognize was that none of us condoned the murder or the plan that led to it. But Lucky was a very special friend and I find it absurd to hear suggestions that we should have abandoned him. I stand by my immediate reaction that I would then (or now) have harboured Lucky until I found out when he wanted to do. I would then (and still would now) have tried to persuade him to turn himself in because I believe that a fair trial would have taken note of extenuating circumstances. He was found guilty in his absence by the coroner's court though there was no evidence put forward on his behalf. The whole charade was fairly pointless since he would still be tried if he turned up now.

I believe he planned it, did it, and killed himself. I don't know where or why or how he hid his body but I believe that he did to himself what he intended to do to the body of his victim. I still think about him often and dream of meeting up with him. There is so much to tell him.

A Traumatic Year

1974 was a tragic year for the Lucans and traumatic for their friends. It was to be followed by a year in which, including Lucky himself, I lost three of my closest friends.

First, the Lucan affair had the most disturbing effect on the volatile temperament of Dominick Elwes, and he could not leave the subject alone. He was always round at the police station in Gerald Road seeking evidence and he was frequently pathetically upset.

Dominick was a good artist, the son of the portrait painter Simon Elwes, but it seems that he allowed his talents to founder at a crucial stage of his life. Fair-haired, good-looking though inclined to be overweight, Dom was a wonderful mimic and a great raconteur when in the mood. Also, unusually for a funny and attractive man, he was a great audience and always egged me on to do my stuff, laughing the loudest and the longest even at stories and anecdotes which he had heard before.

But, sadly, Dom was given to bouts of depression and more than once in the past we had had fears that he might take his own life.

One evening in May 1975, Dominick rang me to suggest dinner. I had the great racing driver Graham Hill in tow and the three of us decided to go to the Ladbroke Club in Hill Street, around the corner from the Clermont and Annabel's. During dinner Dom told us that he had been approached by a journalist, James Fox, from the *Sunday Times* who was planning to write a serious article about Lucky which he hoped would help to ensure him a fair trial if he ever turned up. Then Dom added the bombshell. 'They've offered me five hundred pounds to create a cartoon of Lucky and all the other leading characters who would normally be having lunch in the Clermont.'

It was Graham who reacted more strongly against the plan. He was always very straightforward and decent. 'Dom, you must not do it,' he said aghast, 'you mustn't risk upsetting your Clermont friends for money.' He turned to me, 'Charlie,' he said, 'you've got more influence over him than I have. Tell him.' I was dubious about the idea but not as strongly opposed to it as Graham. 'If he knows what he's doing he must make his own decision,' I answered, adding, 'after all he is desperately short of money and he is a professional artist.' Graham shook his head and was very unhappy about the whole thing so we changed the subject.

Dominick introduced me to James Fox, who had been at Eton and whose family was vaguely known to me. I gave him certain information about Lucan in the belief that it would help his case in the event of a trial.

When the *Sunday Times* appeared in mid-June, the bombshell fell. The story and pictures were featured in the colour supplement and the story itself, though well enough written, was not at all along the lines that had been promised by Fox but was a straightforward gossipy piece. But this did not cause much offence. It was photographs featured around the article and on the front page of the magazine which upset the key characters. They were private photographs of Lucan with Lady Annabel Birley and others taken on holiday, and the centrefold cartoon by Elwes included Jimmy Goldsmith in a prominent position, drawn without his permission which would not have been granted.

Jimmy was seething since the photographs were of his holiday. He was very close to Annabel then and subsequently married her. Mark Birley was also angry while John Aspinall felt equally strongly that Elwes had forfeited his trust and let down Jimmy as well. There is little doubt that Jimmy and Aspers would have been irritated by the cartoon but it was the photographs which really caused the trouble.

Poor Dom did not know what had hit him. He was blitzed by a three-pronged attack during which he was banned from Annabel's by Birley, was the recipient of furious messages from Goldsmith, and was viewed coldly by Aspinall.

Probably the decisive factor which led to Dominick's mental collapse was the letter he received from young Robin Birley following the publication of the *Sunday Times* article and pictures.

Robin, who survived the terrifying incident with John Aspinall's tiger, wrote a strong letter to Dom accusing him of wrecking his life. 'How could you allow pictures of my mother with a murderer to be printed?' he wrote. Poor Robin was being badly teased by his friends at Eton and reacted accordingly. Dominick was devastated. He showed the letter to me and to his patient girl-friend Melissa. 'I didn't sell or provide those photographs, but they won't believe me,' he wailed.

Annabel Birley, and therefore Mark Birley and Jimmy Goldsmith all reacted as a result of Robin's distress and their strong sanctions against Dom followed, including a writ for a small unpaid Annabel's Club bill.

Dom came round in hysterics to see me, his whole life having collapsed around him. He went to the Clermont and Annabel's practically every day and night of his life and all his friends were there. 'What shall I do? I know nothing about the photographs and James Fox won't return my calls.' He was desperate and I agreed to help. I first tried to telephone Fox myself and left many messages at the *Sunday Times* for him to contact me urgently. To his eternal shame he never did and he has a lot to answer for. It was a cynical and cruel thing to have done to Dominick. I then tried to plead Dom's case to Aspinall and Birley but got short shrift from both of them and Jimmy was inaccessible.

Dom was on the verge of cracking up when he was lent the use of a house in the South of France and went there alone. Nigel Dempster, the *Daily Mail* diarist, was on the plane to Nice and saw Dominick in his deep depression. He helped him to get to his house and visited him several times during the trip, often finding Dominick huddled, staring into space, in a darkened room.

At the end of July I went down to Sardinia to stay with the Aga Khan, and Jimmy was not far away having taken two houses for his family. We met for a drink at the tennis club in Porto Cervo and we paced around the pool discussing the case. But Jimmy was implacable. 'He betrayed my friendship. That's the worst thing that any man can do,' he declared and so we agreed to differ.

That autumn Dominick seemed to cheer up and there was some intimation that with continuing pressure from us, his friends, the bans might be lifted. I was delighted to go to dinner at the house off the Fulham Road of Bill and Bridget Mond one evening and find Dominick there in great form. He, Nicholas Soames, and I, who had sparked each other off on this sort of occasion for many years, laughed and joked and it was just like the old days. When I left the party, I remember saying to my lady companion 'Dom's pulling out of it. That was the old Dom.'

I think he walked home – he lived only a few hundred yards away – and his ever-patient girl-friend Melissa Wyndham last spoke to him in good humour. Next day she found him dead in bed when she went to see him. He had taken an overdose of sleeping-pills and written a bitter, damning note, the contents of which I know but would serve no good purpose in repeating.

Thus Dom was gone. He was one of the brightest, kindest, most attractive friends I ever had, and an asset to any party except when in the depths of gloom. I was very involved with his brother Tim in sorting out his affairs and there was a big memorial service arranged at Farm Street, the Roman Catholic church, ironically just around the corner from the Ladbroke Club and thus not far either from the Clermont and Annabel's. Dom had laid down his own specifications for the service including the request that John Aspinall should make the address. This seemed a slightly unorthodox request in view of their recent disagreements but Aspinall accepted the job.

Aspers is no man but his own – and perhaps Jimmy's – and he made a speech which I thought acceptable and much as I expected. It was not an eulogy though he brought out many of Dom's best characteristics. But he also stressed the wasted talents, which may have been true but many of the congregation thought could have been left out on such an occasion. All in all though, it was quite a clever speech, one which Dominick might well have expected when nominating the speaker.

Unfortunately this cut no ice with Dominick's cousin Tremayne Rodd, a former Scottish international scrum-half. He waited outside the church for Aspers, who was with his mother Lady Osborne, and attacked him, hitting him on the side of his jaw, loosening two teeth. Aspers, a bigger and stronger man, used to wrestling with tigers and gorillas, sensibly did not fight back, merely fending off the blows and Tremayne, now Lord Rennel of Rodd, ran off down the street before any serious damage was done. After that about twenty of us went on to the private room at the Mirabelle for lunch, a sort of wake, where we behaved as Dominick would have liked.

By chance, I sat next to Graham Hill and we recalled that dinner at the Ladbroke Club when, had Dom heeded Graham's advice, the whole disaster might have been averted. We talked together virtually throughout the lunch and I mentioned that I would be shooting in Hertfordshire the following Friday.

'Fine, come and stay the night with me,' said Graham who lived in a rather splendid new house at Shenley, near Elstree. Graham's house was only forty minutes from my flat and was thus about half-way to the shoot but I had nothing on that evening so I was glad to accept. Two days later, I was driving down Park Lane after dinner at about midnight when there was a news flash on the radio. 'A light plane has crashed on the golf-course near Elstree. It is believed to have been piloted by its owner Graham Hill.'

I pulled in and sat for a while deciding where to go. First Lucky then Dominick, now Graham. My first thought was to contact Charlotte Curzon since she of all my friends had been particularly fond of him. She came from a fanatical motor-racing family and her father and grandfather, both Earl Howe, had been racing-drivers themselves, particularly the grandfather in the days of Brooklands race-track before the war. I reached her at her sister's house off Bayswater Road and we sat in depressed silence.

The news was all too true. Graham had been testing, near Marseilles, a car which he now managed, having just retired as a driver to our intense relief. Also in his plane there had been the brilliant and promising young driver Tony Brise as well as the rest of the mechanics and managers involved. Graham had been trying to get into Elstree, his home air-field, on an unpleasant, foggy night though he had been advised that it would be better to divert to Luton, some twenty miles away. What went wrong no one knows for sure but it was either pilot or instrument failure since the plane just flew straight into the golf-course.

The next five days were full of more sadness and horror as I went down to see Bette, Graham's long-suffering wife, on several occasions. Once when I was in the house the pretty young widow of Tony Brise arrived which was extremely harrowing. The funeral took place in St Albans the following Friday, the day I should have been shooting near by after staying the night with Graham and Bette.

That was December and I was glad when 1975 was over.

193

Marriage: A Return to Sanity

In the midst of all this gloom, there was a bright-spot. I met Carolyn Gerard Leigh, who was to become my second wife, when she was sitting on the stairs at the Turf Club in London in July 1975. To be one hundred per cent accurate, I had run into her briefly on several previous occasions like Royal Ascot when she had been with another friend of mine but I had never taken her in or talked to her at any length.

This particular night I was playing in the Turf Club backgammon tournament which I ultimately won at about four in the morning but the memorable encounter took place earlier. For the first time, I thought she looked rather good and turned out to be not as snooty as I thought. Because of the backgammon, I did not have a great amount of time to extend the relationship then and there, but I obtained her telephone number without any difficulty, and we made a date for dinner with John Aspinall the following week. Ironically I was forced to stand her up the first time but we rearranged a romantic twosome on the Friday night instead.

The relationship picked up momentum during the summer though in fits and starts since we each had our separate commitments. She went to Deauville for a few days and was hotly pursued by a very good friend of mine, the French trainer Miguel Clement and she also went for a fortnight to South Hampton on Long Island, the famous American upmarket holiday resort. By then, though, we had a certain commitment to each other though it was not remotely binding on either side. I, or course, had fitted in my annual trip to Sardinia with Sally and K, taking no one with me.

All that autumn I was taking out three girls almost equally, Carolyn – universally known as Chubby from her schooldays but a name that I feel

194

is rather ridiculous and hardly ever use – and two others, Melody and another cruelly nicknamed 'Jaws'. All were most attractive and I had equal though different feelings about each of them. I also had one reserve up my sleeve who very rarely qualified for a hot dinner.

It was an ideal arrangement for a selfish bachelor and they clearly thought that seeing me twice a week, or three times for the lucky one, was quite enough.

Matters came to a head soon after Christmas. All three had known for some time that I had booked my usual holiday in Mustique and had already arranged to share the 'Gingerbread House' again with Bryan and Jerry. I even discussed the question of my companion with them but they were, quite rightly, most diplomatic and passed the buck back to me. So, with only a week to go, the situation was still up for grabs and it was the character of Miss Gerard Leigh which clinched it. We were staying with the Courtaulds near Newbury when she blurted out, in front of them. 'Now stop all this childish messing around about Mustique. I know you are going to take me so you might as well come clean. And I need a week to sort my clothes out.' I was forced into a corner and had to admit, meekly, that she would be the selection. It was a fateful moment as I have no idea what I would have done if one of the others had made the same bold statement.

In the light of my later knowledge of her, it was a miracle that Carolyn was able to get her clothes together in a week even though Mustique is not a very dressy place. Now, she sometimes prepares for months before our foreign trips and in the final week the house resembles the clothes department of Harrods, with dresses hanging from every doorway.

In order to reach Mustique during daylight, we decided to stay over night in Barbados at the famous Sandy Lane Hotel before taking the short hop across in the morning.

I remember being fairly irritated to be presented with a bill for about £100 simply for a bed for the night since the breakfast we had ordered never arrived and we did not get our alarm-call. We also had difficulty in getting our bags taken to the taxi in time so Sandy Lane took some time to live that down. However, the holiday itself was a great success, and Bryan and Jerry admitted that I had made the right selection, though in fact the selection had picked herself.

When we flew back to England, I told my companion that I could not see her for a week or ten days as I had other obligations. I knew that I had bridges to mend since I wanted to pick up the previous three-way arrangement where I had left off.

I knew that the other two were pretty angry at being dropped from the Mustique outing and discovered later that they had met and made a pact for neither of them to see me as *a punishment*. I am glad to say that a few words on the telephone to each of them and a grovelling apology quickly ended that pact and I took the pair of them out in equal proportion for the next ten days before slotting the future wife back into the roster.

All good things come to an end and, by autumn, the other two had quite rightly grown fed up with my behaviour, particularly when Carolyn came on the Sardinian jaunt. In fact, she got a short extra visit to the Costa Smeralda when we had a few days down there in May, together with Bryan and Jerry. I can't think how Sally swung that one but she did. So the die was cast and, from Christmas onwards, the future wife became known, jokingly, as my 'constant companion', a gossip columnist cliché.

For the first time, the winter holiday was spent in Barbados, staying with Jeremy and Sally Hindley in their cleverly situated beach-house, 'Dudley Wood', about ten minutes further down the road from Sandy Lane. We had visited Barbados once or twice before for a day or two, apart from the one night at Sandy Lane, but this was our first full trip and we loved it. So much so that we have been back every year since.

It was either that year or the next that the whole of the Monty Python team had taken the most famous house on the island, 'Heron Bay', built by and lived in for years by Ronald Tree, father of the great racehorse trainer Jeremy, and also of Michael Tree and their half-sister Penelope, then a successful model.

The Pythons were writing and generally conceiving their sacrilegious film *The Life of Brian* and we were invited to a party there and got to know some of them, notably Eric Idle, whom I have run into several times since in London and LA. John Cleese, the best known of them, was surprisingly one of the quietest, though the most introverted of them all at that time was Graham Chapman, who was suffering from an identity crisis.

At the party, I noticed a smallish, long-haired young man who seemed rather out of it and who was walking, very lame, with the aid of a shepherd's crook. I sat down to chat with him and he turned out to be an American by the name of Gary Rossington. He had a horrific story to tell. He was lead guitarist in the very successful heavy-metal rock group Lynyrd Skynyrd and, a few months earlier, he had been flying with the group and other members of the entourage, in a chartered Convair jet to do a concert. Somewhere over Ohio, the pilot had switched on the PA system and said in a fairly matter-of-fact way, 'I'm afraid there has been a terrible mistake and we are running out of gas. It is too late to turn back for the nearest airstrip and I will have to try to crash land. I must tell you that you should make your own arrangements to face up to the next life.'

Gary and the members of the group had been up in the forward compartment and he told me how they had said their last farewells. The full horror of the story was that they had so much time to face the terror ahead, minutes probably as they glided down. He remembered the moment of impact, re-living the staccato cracking of severed trees as they crashed through a wood and then the big bang and unconsciousness. When he came to, one leg was severed at the knee and many bones and limbs were broken. But he was still alive though all his friends in his compartment were dead. There were more survivors from the rear of the plane as well.

He was rushed to hospital and the severed leg sewn on. But he told me, 'I don't think I could ever play the guitar again.' He was a gentle man and we got to like him very much and saw him several times during the holiday. Also out there was the singer and keyboard player Alan Price and he too became a regular friend. He was staying down our end of the beach and was with his regular companion and now wife the actress Jill Townsend, who turned out to be an old friend of Jeremy Hindley.

Julian Wilson, the BBC TV racing correspondent and commentator, was in the next house to us with his group while about four houses down the beach was Lord Hesketh with his extremely attractive wife, one of her sisters and their mother. It was like a village.

Alexander Hesketh, who by then owned his private Formula One racing-team and had given the subsequent world champion James Hunt his break, was an old friend of mine, his mother having bought my London house some fourteen years previously. We got into a fair amount of mischief together as the island's heavyweights and he towed me home in the sea by my big toe one afternoon after I had consumed too much rum punch.

The Heskeths decided to give a party with live music and they booked the island's top band, Ivory. The preparations were most professional with the necessary speakers and electrics installed all day. The party was a huge success in spite of heavy rain. Luckily the band was completely covered so they could continue, despite the electrics, and the racing

197

people in particular kept going, totally ignoring the weather. Even leading trainer Henry Cecil let his hair down. It was then that the drive and aggression of Alan Price, in particular, took a hand.

Alan and I decided that it would be a great idea to try and make Gary Rossington play again, surrounded by his new friends and in a private atmosphere.

Gary repeated his protestation that he could not bring himself to play but he was gently guided to the bandstand. A guitar was planted in his hands by one of the Ivory members, a couple of them stayed on the stand, Alan sat down at the keyboard and the famous Charlie Watts, the Rolling Stones' drummer and another old friend of mine who was staying down the road, took up his position behind the drums. After a few minutes cajolling and bullying from Alan Price, a very determined character, Gary strummed a couple of chords and the impromptu band needed no further encouragement. Soon he was riffing and strumming with the best of them and the session lasted an hour with the whole party remaining, dancing and applauding, to the bitter end, soaked to the skin. It was all very touching and Gary embraced his fellow-musicians before slumping down for a well-earned drink. It broke the ice for him and he later formed his own band and, indeed, reformed Lynyrd Skynyrd a couple of times. The original band had become a cult by then and could hardly be emulated.

I have not at the time of writing seen Gary since then though I saw plenty of Alan Price back home. For a while he combined with another good friend, Georgie Fame, in a brilliant double act. But, despite their vocal and keyboard talents, they were ideologically unsuited, Alan being a life-long socialist and Fame an equally ardent conservative. Luckily their politics have never affected our own friendship, but it made their own double act impossible.

They played together one election night in Annabel's and it must have been during the 1970 election which Edward Heath won. The atmosphere was almost outrageously conservative, with the fat cats of the property world cheering loudest at the announcement of each Tory victory from television sets specially set up. Even I was fairly disgusted by some of the more extreme examples of blatant self-interest and was not surprised when Price jumped to his feet and strode out.

Their partnership dissolved in Annabel's some time later. They had been booked to do their cabaret but, unknown to Fame until the last minute, Price had left on the QE2 for America that very day to publicize *Oh Lucky Man*, directed by Lindsay Anderson, for which he had written, played and sung the music. Fame turned up, not unnaturally in a towering rage, and played just three numbers, ending with the hymm 'For those in peril on the sea' before himself striding out.

I have been to several of their separate concerts since then and was instrumental in booking Fame and his band for Susan Sangster's fortieth birthday party at Newmarket in 1982, at which he played until nearly six in the morning by popular demand.

I also booked Fame and his band for the ball in Chantilly given by the Aga Khan to celebrate his half-sister Yasmin's wedding in July 1985 but this was not an unqualified success. Yasmin wanted a rhythm and blues band as well so Fame secured the outrageous Gino Washington and his Ramjam band. They had never previously played before such an aloof, international gathering and insisted on lacing the music with a certain amount of fairly contentious political chat. Fame had warned me that Gino could be quite controversial and was a little embarrassed but could do nothing to change the act. I loved the music and danced like a dervish myself to both sets of music but I had made a misjudgement and it was the wrong atmosphere. The trouble was that I had been acting under two different sets of instructions. It is impossible to please all the people all of the time, however.

Unlike Lord Howe, William Henry Gerard Leigh and his extremely good-looking wife, Jean, behaved in a gentlemanly fashion towards me from the word go even though I must have been the last thing they wanted on their doorstep. I was a frequent visitor to their house, Bartlets at Holyport near Maidenhead and stayed there for Royal Ascot 1977. They gave lunch-parties each day to which they allowed me to invite many of my racing friends including the Aga Khans, the Sangsters, the Bobby McAlpines, the Jeremy Hindleys and the Barry Hills. These were mixed up with their own, mostly older friends and it all worked very well.

The question of marriage repeatedly cropped up as, for some reason, Carolyn seemed eager to make the arrangement permanent. I used every excuse in the book – lack of money, previous marriage failing, boys at school, irresponsible behaviour, gambling, raffish sporting friends, etcetera – but to no avail. She kept plugging away. After Sardinia again, we were invited once more to stay with the Khans for the Arc weekend and they gave a dinner-party in the Paris house on the eve of the race which included the Sangsters and Vincent O'Brien and his wife Jacqueline. As always in that household, the hospitality was lavish even though the Aga himself never drinks. After dinner, having consumed several very large glasses of brandy, I decided, for no obvious reason, to go and sit on the stone staircase of the extremely old and elegant house. I remember Vincent, very concerned, coming out to see if I was all right. The others were less concerned, knowing me of old.

The next morning I woke up to the sound of breakfast arriving in my bedroom which was very bright with windows down to the floor overlooking the river Seine and the Île St Louis on the other side. I had a steaming and richly deserved hang-over and was so weakened that when the inevitable subject of marriage arose for the umpteenth time, to her utter amazement I announced romantically 'Oh, all right.' It was neither romantic nor gentlemanly but the world is not always as Barbara Cartland sees it.

Carolyn was not one to let the opportunity slip and she could not wait to speed to the connecting door and tell Sally what she believed to be good news. By the time we reached the racecourse, the whole world seemed to know and I could see little escape.

I made one final lame attempt, though. After Robert and Vincent had won the Arc with Alleged, I suggested that the in-laws should be phoned before they heard the bad news second-hand. My future mother-in-law insisted that we should tell the Colonel, universally known as G, and that we should go round for a drink in their London house on our return from Paris the following evening. When the door was opened by the rather grim-looking Colonel, I held my hand up like a policeman stopping traffic. 'Before you say anything,' I intoned, 'I want you to know that anything you can do to prevent this union has my full support.' That did it. We all laughed and the Colonel opened the bottle of champagne which he had been holding rather ominously in his hand when he opened the door.

We arranged the wedding for Wednesday 26 October, three days after my birthday. The banns had to be read three times, which was not that easy to arrange and we booked in at midday at Chelsea register office, opposite the Town Hall in the King's Road. We had a quiet family dinner the night before and my future in-laws insisted that their daughter stayed the night with them on the eve of her wedding. The registrar, a woman, demanded £14 in cash from me, a sensible precaution and performed the brief ceremony in front of a handful of witnesses which included my two sons and Sally.

'You may kiss the bride,' said the registrar before we signed on the dotted line. Never one to miss a cheap shot, I countered 'I've done that already.' The reception lunch was held at Searcy's in Pavilion Road. My old mother was well enough to attend with my two sons, while Sally brought her three children and we posed for photographs by a *Daily Express* cameraman. My wife always complains that it looks as if I married Sally and not her. I sat between Sally and my mother-in-law while my young brother, at another table, with typical Benson manners, had brought a small portable television to watch Ascot races. I stood up to make a brief and what I thought witty speech. One of my bad-taste jokes went along these lines. 'I have good news and bad news for Col. and Mrs Gerard Leigh. First the good news. They always wanted their daughter to marry a man called Charles. Now the bad news – they got the wrong one.' This was a reference to the fact that my wife had been spoken of in the press as a possible future wife to Prince Charles with whom she was on good terms.

After the fourth joke, Sally dragged me down by my jacket tail. 'You've said quite enough,' she hissed. She was quite right and I was deservedly banned from speaking at the larger cocktail reception held at the Turf Club a couple of weeks later.

We had no formal honeymoon but about a week later we went to Iran for a backgammon tournament, very romantic. I was one of two Englishmen invited to play in the tournament, which was due to be held at Ramsar, right on the Caspian. The other Englishman was stockbroker Stephen Raphael, a senior figure in backgammon circles. It was an all-expenses-paid trip for the brand-new bride and myself and the three of us flew out together and stayed in Tehran for a couple of nights before the short hop over the mountains to Ramsar. I thought that Tehran was one of the most unpleasant and dirty cities I had ever seen and the people were frightenly unattractive. Small wonder that there was a revolution within twelve months. I was taken by the General in charge of sports and recreation to see the new racecourse complex just outside the city and nearing completion. It was a most impressive grandstand and track, much along Hong Kong lines, particularly the stabling for the horses which was built in long blocks, one above the other, leaving a gap for the straight sprint track.

We had lunch, with plenty of the local product caviare, with an old friend from schooldays, Philip Harari and his wife Diana, in a house they had rented from one of my London-based Persian friends, Mahmoud Izadi. Philip was working for a bank out there but he is now an art dealer in London as was his father before him. We stayed in Ramsar in the old royal summer palace which had been converted into an upmarket hotel. Members of the Shah's family still used it in the

201

summer. It was extremely comfortable and situated next to the caviare factory. We ate the local product for breakfast and every other meal.

I cruised comfortably through the first three of four rounds of the backgammon even though the locals were extremely suspicious and grew very angry whenever I threw what they considered to be good dice. The fact that I was better than they and had set up my board to allow for several useful combinations never occurred to them.

Unfortunately, Stephen was knocked out fairly early on but I was in the quarter-finals and looking good to reach the final, which would most certainly be against another of my London-based Persian friends, Moise Elghanian. Moise kept an eye on us to see we were being correctly treated. The hotel and casino were run by British management with a well-known figure in London casino circles, Bill Meaden, in charge of the organization.

There was a lot of money at stake, something like £24,000 to the winner, and I started my quarter-final match in a confident mood. Stephen and my wife watched and supported for a while and I quickly went into a clear lead – something like 12 points to 4 in a first-to-18-point match. They then decided that I was safely home and dried and went out to the garden to enjoy the sunshine, take a drink and probably sneak a little caviare. Then everything changed. I was surrounded by a hostile crowd of Iranians who clearly wanted their home man to beat me. I was continuously cheated – there is no other word for it – as they turned my dice over, claimed my opponent had rolled numbers that he had not and gave him constant advice and hints, all illegal.

But what could I do? I could not speak or understand a word of their language and I was an invited guest when all was said and done. I kept looking desperately for one of the organizers or Moise or Stephen and my wife, but they were nowhere to be seen. When I stood up to go and look for someone, I was manhandled down again. It was all very unpleasant and for once in my life I had no control over the situation. In the end I was beaten and when they heard about it, Stephen and my wife could not believe it. I thanked them for their loyal support for had they stayed, they could have gone for help. Moise was very embarrassed when he heard about it but there was nothing to be done. Even so, I ended up with a fair amount of loot. I won a valuable Rolex watch with steel-and-gold bracelet and a battleship-grey face, a silver plate, a portable backgammon board which I still use, some money and plenty of caviare. And all this as a beaten quarter-finalist.

When we returned to London airport on the Sunday evening, I

declared the watch but explained that I had won it and gave the Custom's man a certificate supplied by the organizers to confirm this. He looked at it and said, 'I'll have to take this back to show one of my colleagues. You will have to pay some duty on it, of course.' I waited in trepidation not knowing what to expect but anticipating a levy of a minimum of £100, probably more. Then the officer returned and spoke. 'That will be £5.' I couldn't get the money out of my pocket quickly enough.

My relationship with my in-laws prospered and improved even more with the birth of our daughter, Honor, on New Year's eve 1980. I only half agreed that we should start a family but was happy enough when my wife announced that she was expecting a child and my daughter has certainly transformed my whole life for the better. The whole race-course knew about it when my wife was only about six weeks pregnant so we went through seven and a half months of leg-pulling. There seemed no doubt that we would have a girl, which is what we wanted and I readily agreed to my wife's suggestion that she should be called Honor, provided that if it were a boy, the name would be Swindler. So she was Honor, seven and a half months before birth and this saved a lot of trouble afterwards. My wife had one false start and I had to take her to Welbeck Street at six in the morning, with her mother rushing in excitedly only minutes later. This proved to be a false alarm, and she returned home rather shamefacedly after lunch. However, on New Year's eve, it was the real thing and I went on to lunch with my oldest friend Colin Ingleby-Mackenzie at the Wig and Pen Club opposite the Law Courts, an old haunt of ours and which had been used, on my introduction, by Kerry Packer every day for lunch during his long case against the cricket authorities in 1977.

There was news from Welbeck Street as the afternoon drew on and I got stuck into the vintage port. Luckily I didn't have to work that day. At about 4.30 I got the message that our daughter had been born, weighing just over six pounds. The head-waiter insisted on my leaving my car outside and driving me to the nursing-home and the club sent champagne and flowers which was an extremely thoughtful gesture. When I arrived I was met by my mother-in-law looking a little grave. 'It's all right,' she said ominously, 'but there has been a problem.' Apparently Honor had turned blue for a while soon after birth and had trouble with her breathing. I went and gazed at her in a little glass incubator and tears poured down my cheeks. She seemed all right by then. I went up to see my wife in her room and we rang everyone we

203

could think of all over the world including the Sangsters in Barbados.

When I got home, I started telephoning again many people for the second time including my elder son Harry, the Sangsters and the Hindleys, also in Barbados. I then went out to dinner with Jake and Davina Morley at the Mirabelle but I was too tired and drunk to stay up for the New Year and took myself home in a taxi at 11 o'clock.

Next day I went up to the Law Courts to collect my car and then drove down to Windsor races. My father-in-law was a steward and I had lunch with him and the others in the stewards' room. Near the end of the racing, we got a message that all was not well and we were directed to a hospital just behind Paddington. This time Honor, who had turned blue again, was in an incubator with all sorts of tubes attached to her and her heart-beat registering on a machine but, once again, the young doctor said she was quite all right and tests could find nothing wrong with her. She was discharged and returned to her mother but the same thing happened a third time and the ambulance had to rush her back to the hospital near Paddington where the stayed until Sunday morning.

Once again they could find nothing wrong with her and I had nothing but admiration for the doctors and nurses at the hospital, who worked incredibly long hours. I took them some bottles of champagne.

I'm glad to say that the problem never recurred from then on and we lodged for some months at my in-laws' flat back in good old Cliveden Place, so near my parents' old house. This was because we had sold my flat and had bought the house in Trevor Square which was still a shell awaiting decoration. I had gambled on buying just a two-and-a-half-year lease, knowing that we could not be evicted. The whole square was owned by Trevor Estates and managed by Harrods. We managed to move in during May and the house proved itself perfect for a family of our size plus a nanny.

This led to a great stroke of luck when our lease ran out. Without warning the entire square was bought by a property company controlled by Gerald Leigh, a friend and keen racing man. He was also a very successful breeder in his modest way. I discussed the situation with him and he agreed to sell us the freehold at a reasonable price so, from nothing, we found ourselves with a desirable residence with only a reasonable mortgage. I don't know what we would have done otherwise.

The house has become something of a mecca for sportsmen, particularly Australians. We had one memorable evening when Ian Chappell and Allan Border argued until dawn with Pat Cash and John Fitzgerald, who had just been beaten in a men's doubles final at Wimbledon. Cash excused himself after dinner, though that was 1.30 in the morning, to go and look after his girl-friend. He must have done a good job as little more than nine months later she bore his child.

Cash and Fitzgerald won the Davis Cup final for Australia against Sweden at the very end of 1986.

Another night John McEnroe senior arrived unannounced and joined us as we were finishing dinner. Dennis Lillee and Rodney Marsh were dining and McEnroe hadn't a clue who they were. He started lecturing them on physical fitness and how hard his son worked at his game and condition. Dennis was amused but Rodney Marsh began to get angry and Ross Case, a former Wimbledon doubles champion, also Australian, explained to father McEnroe exactly whom he was lecturing. It made little difference. 'You guys don't have to work hard for that game of yours,' continued the voluble lawyer, which was particularly inappropriate since Dennis probably worked harder to keep fit than any other cricketer. It is easy to see where McEnroe junior gets some of his aggressive nature though I have a soft spot for both of them.

Another great tennis player Vitas Gerulaitis very nearly killed me one November Sunday in London shortly before we moved from the flat to the Trevor Square house. In fact my wife thought she was about to become a widow when I returned from playing tennis with him that afternoon.

It all started innocently enough. Vitas was rated three or four in the world, having reached successive Wimbledon semi-finals and won the Australian open. The first of the semi-finals in 1977 against Björn Borg was the greatest match I ever saw at Wimbledon and I have been going there for thirty-seven years. It was a five-setter nip and tuck and in the final desperate set every point was won. There were just no unforced errors. It was tragic that Vitas lost and there is no doubt that it affected his whole career afterwards. He was a great friend of Borg and they played nearly all their exhibition matches together but he never beat him in a competitive match and it all stemmed from that semi-final.

Vitas was such a good friend and so good natured that he invited me to play with him at dinner on the Saturday night that November. He fixed up a court at the Vanderbilt Club in Shepherd's Bush. We asked my young brother Jonathan, a useful player, along and Vitas asked the club to provide a fourth. The extra player turned out to be an old friend Michel Carvalho who was known as Michael Ray as a young actor and played the part of the boy-friend of Lawrence, played by Omar Sharif,

205

in *Lawrence of Arabia.*

Michel was a good and keen tennis-player but after we had completed just two points, he collapsed with a back or leg injury and had to retire. So the club supplied another player, a stranger to us all. I don't know what I had eaten for lunch but I played the game of my life, helped, of course, by the fact that Vitas put the ball just where I could reach it. Even so, he was quite impressed until I became over-confident and slammed a ball cross court towards the wall of the indoor arena. Vitas moved like lightning – he was one of the fastest players on the circuit – and still had time to shout 'Oh, it's like that is it' as he slammed the ball back past me at an even sharper angle. That put me back in my place and, after three sets, I was dead.

When we got back to the flat, I was grey in the face and the bride was all set to call the doctor until I stopped her but we did not go out that night.

Vitas was a truly outstanding man in those days though the pressure seems to have changed his character though we are still on good terms. During Wimbledon in those days, he had access to grass-court facilities at a club near Kingston but he would still allow my old flat-mate Phillip Martyn and me to go down there with him most mornings. He would practise with his coach, Fred Stolle, himself a great player, a former Wimbledon singles finalist and several times doubles winner. His sister Ruta would also practise while, sometimes, his father, a registered coach in America, would work us out or we played among ourselves. Then Vitas and either Fred or Ruta would make up a four with us, a great privilege. I can't think of many Wimbledon players who would ever have done such a thing during the tournament.

At about this time, Vitas won an amazing bet of $20,000 with one of the members of his tennis-club in New York. The member, a keen club player, bet Vitas that he could return just one service out of thirty over the net and in court against either Vitas himself or any nominated professional. Vitas took the bet and nominated John McEnroe. It was before McEnroe had actually won Wimbledon but all the players agreed that he was already the best server in the game.

The one advantage to the professionals was that faults did not count and therefore they had thirty first services. They won the bet.

Meanwhile, although I had more responsibility and was in a senior position in the *Daily Express,* I became increasingly disenchanted by both the successive editors and the management. I was lied to about a promised wage-increase and I had much more contact with the management in my first fifteen years than I did in the second.

None of this reflects on my sports editor, Ken Lawrence, who was having much the same problems – probably worse – and who supported my promotion to the 'Scout' when poor Clive died of brain cancer in August 1974.

Curiously enough, for a while my relationship with Peter O'Sullevan deteriorated after my promotion and I realized why Clive and he had not always got on well. Peter was a good man to work with when one was a junior and no threat to a sophisticated and amusing dinner companion, but he guarded his own position very jealously and did not appreciate the strength of my French connections which had hitherto been his exclusive province. However, I am glad to say that we came through these problems, and remain on good terms these days. He was shabbily treated by the management when he retired and I was friendly enough with him by then to advise him not to allow himself to become so upset. He would take their every insult to heart while I would ignore them.

So it was not a difficult decision for me to make when the opportunity arrived in March 1986 to apply for voluntary redundancy. The new management, who had succeeded in lowering morale to unprecedented depths, asked for a 2,000 reduction in the work-force of something over 6,000. Some people were surprised by my decision to apply but I was really sweating to get out and was more than relieved when, after a game of cat-and-mouse, the management paid me and the others off on 12 April.

I still have great affection for the *Daily Express*. After all I was with them for just over a month short of thirty years and most of the time I was well treated. Even cursory perusal of these words would indicate that the job was not over arduous but, equally, I believe that I served them well.

Mick Jagger and My Rock 'n' Roll Years

I INHERITED my love of music from my father but I think he would have been somewhat surprised by my involvement in the rock and pop world. As a regular night-clubber during my adult life, I was a close follower and participator in the musical fads of their time.

I was in on the start of rock and roll with the likes of Chubby Checker and Bill Haley and the Comets, and then the twist, ridiculous as it may seem now, was equally popular. Indeed, I can remember well the beginnings of both the Beatles and the Rolling Stones and followed with interest and sympathy the arrest and subsequent prison sentence meted out to Mick Jagger, since the friend arrested with him and given a stiffer sentence was Robert Fraser, who had been at Eton with me and had been my bookmaker. I did not meet and get to know Mick until 1973 and, by a strange fluke, I also met Bryan Ferry at the same time. We were all, independently, on holiday in Mustique in January. My companion was Charlotte Curzon and it was she who recognized Bryan and brought him into our lives. I formed a good friendship with this extremely nice but basically shy man and we started and have remained on the best of terms. Indeed, I am godfather to his elder son Otis, named after Otis Redding.

Otis's full name is Charles Frederick Otis Ferry and, when I first heard this, I misguidedly thought he had been named after me. However I was wrong as the Charles Frederick bit followed the name of Bryan's father, universally known as Fred. Ferry was lead singer, main writer and very much the boss man of the successful group Roxy Music in those days, though he branched out on a solo concert tour and album sometime later before re-forming the group for another successful run. They finally disbanded about two years ago.

208

In those days, while Bryan was unmarried, Mick was married to Bianca and we all met and went on jaunts together.

I went to Mustique for the following three winter holidays, sharing a house with Bryan. On the first of these I was still with Charlotte and Bryan had with him an American actress and model called Barbara Trentham. She had just finished making a film called *Rollerball* with James Caan, in which she played the part of his wife. The way she told it, which was often, made it sound a pretty big part but regrettably most of it must have ended up on the cutting-room floor as there was not much evidence of her in the film when it was released.

We had rented an attractive little house from the island's owner Colin Tennant, now Lord Glenconner, called the 'Gingerbread House' and we had a wonderful cook called Jocelyn. We were very happy except that almost from day one Bryan became irritated by Barbara and could hardly bear to be with her or even speak to her. I think it was basically a culture clash since she had the American actress's habit of talking constantly about herself, which embarrassed the shy and ultra-modest Bryan. Matters came to a head one afternoon when the four of us were sunbathing on the jetty down at Basil's bar, the popular meeting-place on the island. We were all either reading or snoozing and I was only vaguely aware of a small yacht pulling in at a jetty twenty yards away. I was also only vaguely aware of the shadow of a man casting briefly over us and then disappearing up the road towards the middle of the island. But Barbara and Charlotte were electrified and sat up, staring. 'Paul Newman,' they both said to Bryan and me, 'look, he's going up towards our house.' There was nothing that either Bryan or I wanted to do about it but the girls were fully awake by now and very excited.

Barbara could not leave the subject alone, 'I must talk to him. I think I used to know him when I was younger. We all come from Connecticut.'

At about 5 o'clock we drove up to the tennis-court underneath the swimming-pool and bar of the Cotton House, the only hotel on the island. Bryan, Charlotte and I, all reasonable players, leapt out of our moke for our daily game, which had been somewhat spoilt up to then by Barbara's insistence on making up a four even though she was a very poor player. To our surprise on this occasion, she leapt into the driving-seat of the moke and roared off. It did not take us long to work out that she was in hot pursuit of Paul Newman, who had arrived, we now knew, on the boat, with George Roy Hill, director of most of his best movies, and the captain of the yacht.

So we had a better game of tennis that evening and had to walk back to our house, some 1,000 yards, since Barbara still had the moke.

We had planned to eat at home that evening as usual, but when Barbara returned she was keen that we should go to the Cotton House instead. 'Paul Newman has booked in to eat there,' she explained excitedly, while admitting that she had yet to catch up with him. We all refused to change our plans to pursue the wretched Newman, who was probably on the island for peace and quiet, and Barbara went into an extended sulk.

She maintained her icy silence through dinner until finally Bryan and I, as with a single thought, said 'Go on, take the moke and go and see him up at the Cotton House.' She needed no second bidding and shot out of the house, driving furiously down the road and over the hill. Ten minutes later she was back. There was no Paul Newman at the Cotton House and she stormed to her bedroom without a further word. I'm afraid there were a few sniggers.

The next morning Bryan joined Charlotte and me for breakfast as usual, very cheerful, though he said that Barbara had not spoken to him and was still sulking. After breakfast the three of us drove down again to sun ourselves and drink at Basil's bar, leaving Barbara to enjoy her self-pitying lie-in.

The three of us took up our sunning and reading positions on the jetty but I was restless and thirsty and wandered back to the bar for an early beer. I sat on the bar-stool and had just taken my first gulp when Paul Newman appeared around the corner and slipped on to the stool beside me. Modestly he introduced himself, ordered a beer and we started chatting. Principally the conversation concerned our mutual friendship with Graham Hill since Newman is a motor-racing fanatic, a great racing-driver himself and had recently been breaking some world records in Utah with a team he had sponsored and which included Graham and himself. We chatted non-stop for two hours without interruption, trading beers, probably about a dozen. Then he looked at his watch, said that he had to leave, shook hands with me and wandered around the corner back to his little yacht.

Minutes later we all waved as they slid off and when he was about two hundred yards off shore, Barbara arrived at the bar. At first she could not understand the guffaws of laughter which greeted her and when she finally was told the reason and what she had missed she went into a further decline and never recovered for the rest of the holiday. Though she disappeared from our lives, I did see her a couple of times some years later on television in LA where she was reporting for a local station. And more recently, I saw pictures of her in the English newspapers, following her marriage to John Cleese.

On another occasion in Mustique, Bryan and Mick and I decided to pay a day visit to Martinique, about an hour away in a small plane. So six or seven of us filed into the plane including Bianca, who was still with Mick at the time, and we appointed Mick tour leader since he knew the island and also spoke a little French.

Mick did his stuff well and led us to a charming restaurant up in the hills, surrounded by flowers where we had a long and delicious lunch. The cuisine, being French, was a cut above anything available in Mustique and Madame who owned and ran the restaurant knew Mick of old and gave us the treatment, including, from what I can recall, several liqueurs on the house. There was then some debate whether to stay the night or return. Our plane was booked only for the day and had to leave in time to get us back in daylight, before 6 p.m. In the end, some elected to stay including Mick and Bryan while Charlotte and I were among those who returned on schedule.

It can be seen from incidents like this that Mick and Bryan were on the best of terms. They both came to Berkshire to play for me in my annual cricket match against my friend Simon Courtauld's team at his house in August 1974.

Then just before Christmas Bryan met Jerry Hall in the nick of time to take her on the annual jaunt to the 'Gingerbread House' in Mustique in January again. Jerry was wonderful company in those days and she and Bryan got on like a house on fire, though she was much more outgoing than he. She introduced us to the Texas custom of leg-wrestling and she could turn over men twice her size. She had already taught us the art back in England and, in all modesty, I was the only person who ever beat her. This is hardly surprising bearing in mind my size and massive undercarriage. In fairness to Jerry, she did record this in her book *Tall Tales* – one of the truer items.

That year in Mustique we indulged in a bit of leg-wrestling and, to my amazement, Bryan was half able to topple her. 'But only because I let him,' Jerry confided to us later. 'I didn't want to hurt his pride too much.'

The following year I was with my future wife, Carolyn, when we once again shared the 'Gingerbread House' with Bryan and Jerry and all seemed well between them. We saw Mick from time to time and got on

211

as well as ever but Bryan left soon afterwards to live in LA and work there for tax reasons. He did not enjoy it there as his work did not progress as well as he had hoped. Jerry was there much of the time but she travelled on modelling assignments and, unknown to Bryan, or me for that matter, started dating Mick. Unfortunately, though not surprisingly, considering the flamboyance of the two people involved, the story came out and soon the papers were full of it. Poor Bryan's nose was well and truly rubbed in it as Jerry moved in with Mick and he was very cut up though he did not talk about it much.

My sympathies were with Bryan, of course, though the others need no sympathy. I was well aware that these things do happen – we had all been through it in our time – but the publicity made it much harder to bear. I kept in close touch with Bryan even though he was out of the country for some further time and I managed to walk the tightrope by remaining friendly with Mick and Jerry since the actual cause of break-up did not directly concern me. I always made it clear to Bryan that I still saw the other two and he never requested me not to, as one would expect of a very decent man.

Bryan's career continued most successfully in Britain, Europe, Australia, Japan and in many other countries though it never really took off in the USA even though he has a cult following there. He had a number-one album in Britain for some weeks in the summer of 1986 with a collection of Roxy Music hits and his solo career continued. Now married to Lucy Helmore, he has two sons and he went to work in LA during the winter of 1986–7 before continuing his travels.

Bryan hates touring but his concerts are always a sell-out success and his fans clamour for more. His shyness is a handicap – he even feels uneasy in the recording-studio particularly if too many people are watching him, but you would not know it when he prances on stage, rocking and rolling to the shrieks of his legions of fans. I always go to his concerts in England mostly at Wembley but once or twice at the Albert Hall and join in the general enthusiasm.

One year at Wembley I took three or four of the Australian cricketers including Dennis Lillee and Greg Chappell and these hard men were mesmerized by the atmosphere and the music, and tongue-tied when we went down to Bryan's dressing-room afterwards. Unlike most rock stars, Bryan favours an elegant little dinner-party after his concerts. We went to one in a private room at the Savoy recently while he had his birthday party also in a private room in the Ritz. He likes a bit of style unlike most of the other bands whose parties are normally vast, drink-spilling affairs in cavernous clubs full of hangers-on. I must add that Jagger shows similar style and his parties in London are usually at Mark's Club or the private room in Langan's.

Jagger and I were together to witness the greatest upstage of my time. It happened in Mustique in November 1976 when Colin and Anne Tennant gave an amazing week-long party to celebrate an anniversary. The host and hostess invited nearly a hundred friends for the celebrations, including chartering a plane from Gatwick for all of us from England. Everything was on the house. Jagger and wife Bianca came down from the States independently.

Highlight of the week was the Golden Ball, where everyone had to wear something gold. I had borrowed a gold kaftan from William Pigott-Brown. We all had to enter the open-air arena and be led up to Colin and Anne to musical accompaniment, everyone aware that the stars were to arrive last, with Princess Margaret the guest of honour.

There was much speculation as to whether Bianca or Oliver Messel the exotic designer and Lord Snowdon's uncle, would try to upstage Princess Margaret.

I had made my way to the bar and stood watching the arrivals, with a rum punch in my hand. Suddenly, Mick materialized by my side, dressed in a rather bizarre gold tunic looking for all the world like an elfin Robin Hood.

'Get me a drink,' he hissed.

'Where's Bianca?' I enquired, 'Isn't she here yet?'

'Oh, I couldn't wait for her to get ready. She spent hours tarting herself up. That's her scene. This bar is mine.'

So Mick and I tanked up on the cocktails till nearly everyone had arrived with the exception of the three prima donnas.

Then, to the general amazement, Oliver made his entrance in a mind-boggling outfit which could have been designed for the demon king in a pantomime.

Roars of applause. Five minutes later, to general relief, it was Bianca's turn, and she too was warmly applauded in an impressive ball gown obviously specially commissioned, gold and white. Everyone seemed pleased that she had not tried to upstage Princess Margaret – or maybe tried and failed.

Finally, Princess Margaret made her entrance in a wonderful dress, gold and white, very regal and flanked by two ladies-in-waiting, one of them Patrick Lichfield's wife Leonora.

Now, the dinner, entertainment and dancing could begin. But, just as Colin was about to lead Princess Margaret and the rest of us into the arena, lit by flaming torches and with portable palm trees and other decorations, there was a stir. Surely not another star.

But, to a gasp of amazement and much mirth from Mick and I in particular, Oliver made a second entrance in an even more incredible outfit and flashing a huge theatrical mask.

Game, set and match.

Considering that I never commented on Mick's romance with Jerry, even though he knew that I maintained my friendship with Bryan, I thought it somewhat illogical that he should be critical of my silence when Jerry became friendly with my closest pal Robert Sangster in 1982. But up till then, we had many good times together. The key to our friendship was a mutual love of sport, particularly cricket, but Mick is also something of a *bon vivant* and found a kindred spirit. He is also better read and better educated than he lets out and I have never had a dull moment with him. He was a regular visitor for about nine years to my flat and house in London and I in turn shared drinks and meals at the oddest times with him in hotel suites all over the world.

We played cricket together in Mustique against the local team and he caught a sky-high catch off my bowling while he is himself a rather spindly but perfectly reasonable medium-paced bowler. The first time he came down to play in my annual match in Berkshire, it was rained off and we spent the whole day in the house drinking and eating. At one stage I found Mick in a side room playing the guitar and singing to my host's young daughter and her girl-friend, hardly the accepted image of the chief Rolling Stone.

The same day I elected to put on a drunken water display in the swimming-pool and Mick's hefty bodyguard and driver stood watching me making a fool of myself, far beyond the call of duty. 'Why are you here watching this idiot?' one of my friends asked him, eliciting the reply 'Mick told me to keep an eye on him. He remembers Brian Jones.' Brian Jones was the Stones' guitarist who was found drowned in a swimming-pool sometime earlier.

Mick and Jerry came to more than one of my birthday parties and he gave me the nicest pair of cuff-links that I have ever had, antique gold with little playing-cards, jack, queen, king and ace encrusted into them.

Mick preferred watching cricket to playing and he loves going to Test Matches all over the world. He also likes mingling with the players and I

214

The Aga Khan walks the course on the morning of the 1977 Derby. He was pointing out the slopes and undulations to his French jockey, Henri Samani, who was to ride Blushing Groom, the favourite. *(Daily Express)*

A photograph of the author bringing together Bryan Ferry and Bianca Jagger at the Queen's Club Pro-Am Tennis Tournament, June 1978.

The author at a party with his Aussie mate, Dennis Lillee.

At the same party, cricket fanatic Mick Jagger, being admired by top-model agent, Laraine Ashton.

John McEnroe (standing right) with his famous doubles partner, Peter Fleming (seated back), preparing to go water-skiing off the Aga Khan's yacht, Sardinia 1979.

Bryan Ferry being fitted for military trousers, prior to his forthcoming concert tour, by leading designer Anthony Price. The house was taken for a holiday fortnight in Barbados.

Part of a line-up for the author's (third from right) annual cricket match with Simon Courtauld (second from left). The others are, from left, Australian test stars David Hookes, current captain Allan Border and the legendary fast bowler Dennis Lillee, plus *Panorama* presenter Michael Cockerell.

Lieutenant Harry Benson RN pilots his Wessex helicopter during the Falklands campaign, hovering over a captured and disabled Argentinian Pucara at Goose Green airfield.

Differing reactions at a unique Barry Manilow concert at Blenheim Palace, 1983. The Duke of Marlborough (centre) applauds. So does his younger brother, Lord Charles Spencer-Churchill (left). Jane Churchill is between them, and their sister, Lady Rosemary Muir, looks faintly bored on the Duke's right. Over her shoulder, an out-of-place Lady Derby; over the Duke's shoulder, the author's wife holds her face while the author himself looks 'out of it' (left back).

The author introduces Kerry Packer (centre) to his compatriot, ex-Australian number one, John Alexander.

Tennis with two champion jockeys at Lambourn. John Francombe (left) and Steve Cauthen (second right), with local trainer Paul Cole (right).

(Below) Introducing the Aga Khan and his wife to champion American jockey, Chris McCarron, who had just ridden a winner for them at Sandown Park. *(Daily Mail)*

(Above left) Daughter Honor, fairly sure that she is enjoying her Jordanian holiday.

(Above right) Prince Ghazi, younger son of Princess Firyal of Jordan, relaxing by the pool outside Amman.

(Left) Princess Firyal of Jordan, beside the pool at her palace outside Amman.

A fascinating visit to Dubai and a non-alcoholic cocktail with host Sheikh Mohammed at his palace.

Sharing a drink with an old mate, Albert Finney, during the Barbados Pro-Am Golf Tournament, 1986.

Dining next to Diana Rigg just before making a speech at Robert Sangster's fiftieth-birthday ball.

Henry Ford II relaxing at the fabulous Roman ruins at Ephesus, during our 1986 summer yachting trip with him.

often arranged parties, particularly with the Australian players which pleased both him and them. He likes watching the matches from the players' dressing-room and balcony whether it be England, West Indies or Australia but he equally likes mixing out in the open with the fans, particularly West Indians, with whom he has a great affinity.

I took him to Lord's one day and he spent the whole day glued to his seat watching every ball to the surprise of all the other spectators in the boxes we used, who spent much of their time milling around and standing, talking at the back with drinks in hand. He is always courteous to autograph-seekers on such occasions and talks with anyone provided it is about cricket.

He became very friendly with Ian Botham and there was some talk in the press, mostly put out by Botham's publicity agent, that he would give a concert for Botham's benefit. I knew this was impossible as it costs a fortune, literally hundreds of thousands of pounds, to put on a Rolling Stones concert, even it it is in conjunction with other shows.

I went to Lord's cricket ground with Mick to sit with him in players' seats supplied by Botham when England played Pakistan in 1982. Mick very nearly became embroiled in a tricky situation. Pakistan were winning the match when Botham went in to bat for England in the second innings. Botham batted extremely well and bravely and was easily top scorer. But he received little support from his team-mates. When he was finally out, England were staring defeat in the face and apparently Botham stormed into the dressing-room, threw his bat and started abusing his team-mates. He also threw everything that came to hand. The team's physiotherapist, Bernard Thomas, knew that Mick was a friend of Ian's and also knew that he was sitting in seats provided by Botham. So he nipped down to where we were sitting and leaned over me to talk urgently to Mick. 'Ian's gone berserk in the dressing-room and none of us can do anything to calm him down. Will you come up with me? You're probably the only one he'll listen to,' he pleaded.

But Mick politely refused. 'I'm sorry, I'd like to help but it could cause more trouble.' Thomas was disappointed and looked let down but I agreed with Mick on that one. Had he gone up he could not have escaped notice, and the story would surely have got out, probably to the front pages of the newspapers. And Mick would have been blamed for causing the fracas since it had automatically been assumed for nearly twenty years that he was inevitably responsible for any row or brawl.

Mick is always frightened of being involved himself and I remember some years earlier at a night-club in Monte Carlo during Grand Prix weekend, as we were pushing our way gently through the usual seething mob to our reserved table, a drunken yob lurched into me and I thrust him aside angrily. I've never seen anyone move so quickly as Mick did to get away. Luckily nothing further came of it as I followed on but as I sat down with him at the table he leaned over and said, 'Sorry mate. I saw that and it wasn't your fault but I simply can't get involved in that sort of thing.' And he's right.

But perhaps the months I remember best of Mick were during the Rolling Stones' world tour in 1981–2. I had been in New York during my own annual round-the-world autumn trip, taking in Australia and LA *en route*, in time for his Madison Square Garden concert in November. We saw quite a bit of Mick and Jerry that week, watching some football on television together and visiting various restaurants. I remember being invited to lunch by a newspaperman friend of mine, Brian Vine. I turned up at the restaurant with my wife and we said to Brian, 'We have a friend who would love to join us if that's all right with you.' Brian agreed readily that there was no problem but his eyes were out on stalks when Mick walked into the restaurant and looked around. 'Good Lord, there's Mick Jagger,' he gasped, and was accordingly more than delighted when the singer came over and joined us. Mick was in particularly chatty mood that day and was telling us about carrying a gun with him everywhere he went, particularly after the murder of John Lennon.

When he said his good-byes, having to leave town for his next concert, I had to break the bad news to Vine, 'Sorry, but all of that was off the record.' Brian took it very well, recognizing that I had not patronized him by warning him beforehand that he must write nothing. All he asked was that he could use the introduction at the lunch, which was on him, to ring up Mick for a possible interview at a later date.

We had a pretty hectic time on that short New York visit, staying with Rick Hambro, middle of the three sons of Jocelyn Hambro, chairman of Hambros Bank. Rick was running the New York branch of the bank and lived in a very comfortable duplex apartment just off Madison Avenue near the Carlyle Hotel. We had one particularly interesting dinner-party there during which we mixed up for the first time Jerry Hall and Princess Yasmin Khan, half-sister to the Aga Khan and the daughter of Rita Hayworth, with Robert Sangster.

It was on this tour that Mick and Jerry invited me to join them on the last lap of the Rolling Stones' American tour the following month. I was delighted to accept provided that I could get away from my duties in

216

England. Needless to say, I managed to persuade both my wife and the *Daily Express*, the two possible stumbling-blocks, that this was a vital assignment and racing in England at that time of year was pretty dead anyway. So back I went to New York to stay one night with Rick again, and that evening he and Jerry and I went to a private party held in a new club. The first person I ran into was an old friend from London, Claus von Bulow, who was currently on bail following charges filed against him for the attempted murder of his wife, Sunny, allegedly by administering excessive doses of insulin which left her in an irretrievable coma. The case was something of *cause célèbre* all over the world, but particularly in New York and England, where Claus had lived for much of his life.

The prosecution case, which had been instigated to a great extent by the complaints of Sunny's two children by a previous marriage, was full of holes and I was one of many who did not believe Claus to be guilty. I had known him for many years in London, where he lived in some splendour in Belgrave Square. He was a lawyer who looked after the affairs of the late J Paul Getty, allegedly the world's richest man at the time.

Claus was a great friend of John Aspinall and was a regular visitor to the Clermont Club during the 1960s where we often lunched, dined or gambled in the same company.

Admittedly there were certain characteristics about Claus which made a few people uneasy in his presence. He was bald but very good looking, tall and very upright. He could, I suppose, look a little cruel and austere, with his thin smile. But to all of us he was just 'Clausikins' which shows how forbidding we found him. It was said that the 'von' had appeared in his family name at a somewhat recent stage and he was the victim of some cruel rumours, so ludicrous that we all laughed at them, but which did not help his case when it arose years later.

Claus was eventually acquitted after two unpleasant cases though he still had to face up to further recriminations and accusations by his stepchildren. One can understand their concern for their poor mother but she had a major alcohol problem which was relevant to her condition and much of the evidence against Claus seemed contrived and would have been in no way admissible in a British court of law. Anyway, I was well aware of his problem when I met Claus at that New York party and was careful not to mention the subject while enjoying a fifteen-minute chat mostly about the old days.

At the end, just as we were about to split and mingle with the other

217

guests, Claus leaned towards me and said in a conspiratorial voice, 'I think I should tell you that I have been in a spot of bother.' Talk about a masterly British understatement. I signified that I was aware of the bother and that it made no difference to me.

The next day after lunch Jerry and I flew down on a regular flight to Norfolk, Virginia at the expense of Mick or the Rolling Stones organization. Jerry was at her most eye-catching, wearing a full-length purple-coloured fur coat which looked very like mink and probably was. We were met at the airport by one of the entourage and driven some twenty-five miles inland to stay at a Hilton Hotel. The concerts were to take place near by at the Colosseum in Hampden.

The whole of the top floor of the Hilton was sealed off by burly security men. Mick and Jerry occupied the central suite, with me in a slightly smaller but very comfortable set-up next door and the other members of the band scattered around. Most of the time I spent in the living-room of the Jagger suite, chatting, drinking, and watching television. But that first evening, Jerry and I were immediately diverted to the stadium, arriving about an hour and a half before the concert was due to start. We were hustled back-stage through many check-points and ushered into the band's living-room adjoining their dressing-room. Mick was there to greet us and the others wandered around in various states of nervousness. They all looked very pale, not surprisingly, and Mick soon went off to be made up discuss business with the promoter, Don Graham, who was usually hovering around back-stage, and give the odd interview.

Jerry swanned around in her usual outgoing way and I quickly twigged that the best thing to do was to keep quiet and speak when spoken to.

I was also amused and rather touched when the group's chief of security, Jim Callaghan, universally known as JC, came up to me and said he was an avid reader and follower of my racing column. In fact, JC took me to everyone in sight, including the families of the members of the band, making it seem that I was almost more important and well-known than Mick and the others. I grew very fond of him and he proved a good friend later on during the tour at various other places in Europe. It also turned out that he and I had served in the same regiment, the 60th Rifles, otherwise known as the Green Jackets, I as a National Service 2nd lieutenant, he as a regular sergeant.

The excitement generated by the start of a Rolling Stones concert is intense and I was mesmerized. We had seats half at the side of the stage but mostly we wandered around back-stage, watching from the side and behind and sometimes from a pit down below the front and side of the stage. It was deafening but exhilarating particularly as I love the music and the beat. Mick could see us down there from time to time as he rushed and cavorted non-stop to all parts of the stage. There was also a horseshoe-shaped catwalk reaching far out into the auditorium round which Mick sometimes scampered as did Ronnie Wood with his guitar. The numbers which really got to the jam-packed crowd of mostly young fans were 'Jumping Jack Flash' and 'Satisfaction', two of Jagger's great theme songs. This pattern was much the same everywhere, I later discovered.

After the show, there was a party back-stage. The surroundings were not especially salubrious, rather like a small drill-hall, and the atmosphere was fairly subdued. The band took some time to cool off, shower and change, but came in one by one to join up with their families or, in Mick's case, Jerry and myself.

Later we climbed into various wagons and returned to the hotel to Mick's suite where the real party took place without many hangers-on. Basically, this was limitless booze, a lot of rather unusual food and loud music. There was no evidence of many, if any girls outside the band's entourage. At about 7 a.m. I felt ready for bed and slipped quietly to my room next door where, in my slightly inebriated state, I rang up my wife in London, Sally Aga Khan in France and may have tried to get through to Princess Margaret too!

I discovered that my friends Rick and Ron Hilton, plus Rick's pretty wife were down on the third floor in an inferior suite as Mick was occupying their usual one. I thought this very noble of them, considering they controlled the whole chain, and went down to have a drink with them. Luckily they were excited to have good tickets for the concert that night and I was able to help them with priceless back-stage passes, which they really appreciated. When it was time to leave for the concert, I enjoyed another novel experience for a fat, middle-aged racing correspondent. Mick, Jerry and I were smuggled by security men in the back lift down to the basement. At the bottom were favoured members of the hotel staff who craned to catch a glimpse of Mick as he hustled in phalanx, out of the back door towards a waiting mini-van. Mick was huddled in a huge overcoat and we rushed down a line of screaming girls, diving into the van. We sat in a row in the front with some of the other members of the band further back while others had gone in separate transport.

The girls pressed around the van, screaming their heads off and, for once, I caught Mick with a rare sense of humour failure. 'It's extraordinary, isn't it,' I commented, 'that I have this effect on young girls.' Mick growled back, missing the joke, 'You stupid ass, it's me they're screaming at.' He then grinned sheepishly when Jerry dug him in the ribs and laughed 'Got you there, didn't he?'

The pattern of the concert was similar to the previous evening though the band was in more of a party mood and slipped in an extra item or two to celebrate the end of the record-breaking US tour.

After the show, Jerry and I were on constant alert in order to be able to rush to our transport the moment Mick was ready to leave for the group's private Boeing. This was not, of course, for some time after the concert since much of the stage and lighting-kit had to be packed and rushed out to the plane. But when we were told to go, we went.

There was much fun and games aboard the jet on the way to Newark, just outside New York, and many of the glossy souvenir brochures were circulated for autographs by the band after the promoter had provided one of the those thick, silver felt-pens, ideal for signing photographs. I kept two or three of these signed souvenirs and they are useful for charity auctions. We got back to New York at some unearthly hour again and I had one drink at the old Jagger apartment before catching the Sunday morning plane back home.

My wife laughed at my story and accused me of being an overgrown schoolboy but I had appreciated and enjoyed a fascinating experience permitted to very few outsiders. And, whatever the jeers of my wife and friends, there are plenty who envy my trip and, when the Rolling Stones came to England in June, I was one of the most popular men in London, with callers on all three home telephone-lines wanting tickets for the two Wembley concerts and one at Bristol.

Tennis players are particularly keen rock fans and the Wembley concerts were at the end of the first week of Wimbledon. The two keenest players were John McEnroe and Vitas Gerulaitis, both of whom had their own contacts within the group and needed no help with tickets. But many of the others were desperate for help and Mick and his office were generous. I was able to fix up a dozen or more players each evening and they in turn made desperate efforts not to have a match on court after 6 p.m. I should think there were some funny results that year as players strove for a quick ending to their matches.

We had wonderful tickets in the front row of the Royal Box sitting with Jerry near Mick's parents and there was much comment from our envious friends around the stadium. Despite her previous jeers, my wife was only too pleased to share this regal treatment and, from time to time, we nipped down past the usual check-points to stand back-stage in a little roped-off area out of sight of most of the crowd but almost touching distance from the band.

Towards the end of the concert, Mick hustled to the back of the stage just out of view of the audience, to lie down and be revived with oxygen. The energy he expends in two hours of running, prancing and strutting is prodigious.

On the second day, I took one of my closest friends among the tennis players, John Alexander, my pro-am partner at Queen's four times in later years and then Australia's number one.

'You're sure you've got a ticket for me. A proper decent one. I'm only used to the best, you know,' he teased as we drove to Wembley. 'I think you'll find everything to your satisfaction,' I replied, dead-pan. We also had to leave a ticket for another of his player friends, Chris Lewis, the New Zealander who became a surprise finalist until overrun by McEnroe. Alexander was silenced as we reached the vast stadium with a crowd of some seventy to eighty thousand inside, passed all the security blocks with our special tickets and even went through the back-stage area where food and drink were being consumed by the semi-privileged to the holy of holies – the tuning-up cabin and the changing-rooms.

In the tuning-cabin, Keith Richards and Ronnie Wood were practising their riffs under the mesmerized glance of John McEnroe. And my friend was equally delighted when the concert started and we visited the on-stage pen to be greeted incredulously by Vitas, who thought that he was the only player to be accorded such privilege.

After this concert I rushed to my car to drive west down to Chippenham and was helped in leaving the stadium by being able to tag on to Mick's police-escorted convoy. He was making a quick getaway and changing in his hotel. So I made record time when peeling off to drive down the M4 motorway, in time for yet another concert, less spectacular, but given in a club by another great friend, Georgie Fame and his band. Fame is another sports lover and a long-time friend and we were staying down there with Andrew and Camilla Parker-Bowles at their old house, the haunted Bolyhyde Manor, where Prince Charles did much of his courting with his future bride, Lady Diana Spencer.

The object of this weekend was twofold. I always like Fame's music and had booked him for Robert Sangster's party at Newmarket for his

221

wife Susan's fortieth birthday party ten days later. So I wanted to hear Fame's up-to-date repertoire and discuss other details. The other objective was to go to the next Stones concert at Bristol, only twenty miles away, the following afternoon.

I had also promised to take Fame's step-daughter, Cosima Fry, and her husband, several other young friends and one or two older friends including champion steeplechase jockey, John Francome, and his wife, Miriam.

It was noticeable that Mick was much less nervous before this slightly less awesome audience in a provincial city and he chatted easily with all my group.

The next stop on the world tour was Nice. The band played all over the Continent and Mick rang me from Madrid before London to put a £500-pound bet for him on France in the World Cup which was being played there that year. France was unluckily and undeservedly beaten by West Germany in the semi-finals before Germany fell to Italy in the final.

Now the Stones were in the South of France and the under-manager of the hotel they were staying at in Nice was a bright young friend of mine, John Wallis, who bent over backwards to ensure smooth treatment for Jagger and ourselves when we went over to visit. We were staying at Cap d'Antibes with my wife's aunt Mary. Mick came to have dinner with us at my favourite restaurant in the old town of Antibes, 'Les Vieux Murs' on the sea-wall and promised the usual tickets for us plus three young nephews and nieces who were staying with Aunt Mary.

I had one more memorable experience at the Nice concert when I was invited to stay in the tuning-in cabin right through until the band ran on stage. It was here where Ronnie Wood and Keith Richards practised almost frenetically. Despite the casual appearance of the start of a concert, it is all carefully timed and arranged. So a road manager popped his head into the cabin at regular intervals: 15 minutes, 10 minutes, 5 minutes until there was literally a count-down and the band ran out. Experienced though they are, I believe that Mick and the Stones still endure pre-stage nerves.

This was nearly the last concert of the tour which was to end in Ireland just before the end of July. We arrived back in London from France at about the same time and we were to attend Mick's birthday party in the private room at Langan's on the Monday night before I was due to go down and stay with Bryan Ferry for Goodwood races for the rest of the week. On the Sunday, however, I began to feel ill and on

Monday, the day of the party, I felt worse. I was developing pain around the right-hand side of my body and lower chest and one or two little spots were appearing. Suddenly, about 6 p.m. I realized that I might be sickening for shingles. I rang my doctor, Johnny Gayner, who is also my regular tennis partner, and by sheer luck he was still in his surgery rather than on the tennis-court. 'Come around at once,' he commanded and I was there in five minutes. He soon confirmed my own diagnosis.

'I'm afraid you've had it,' he said dolefully, 'there's not a lot I can do for you except to help ease the pain which will get much worse very soon.'

So he gave me prescriptions for various pain-killers and some sort of paint to dab on the affected area. Then I asked the $64,000 question, 'I don't feel great but I don't want to miss Mick's party in a couple of hours time. If I dose myself up, can I go?'

Luckily he nodded. 'It's a nerve virus and not infectious,' he said, 'so it's really up to you. But I don't think you'll feel like staying up very late.' So I dosed myself up and went to the dinner and drank a lot of red wine. I enjoyed myself well enough but woke up the next morning in agony and was in bed, on and off, for four weeks.

One of my visitors when I was feeling better was Mick and from time to time we watched cricket on television and walked around for lunch to Aspinall's new club, which was then just past Harrods from my house in Hans Street off Sloane Square. So that was the ten-month period when I saw most of Mick. Earlier in the summer, too, I had helped to find him a house to rent at Finchampstead near Wokingham, and my wife and I stayed there for much of Royal Ascot.

We had an amusing day down there with David Bailey who took thousands of photographs mostly of Mick but also of Jerry and even myself around the house and walking round the local cricket pitch, which was conveniently sited near by, watching the game in progress. I also took Wimbledon doubles champion Peter Fleming, John McEnroe's partner, and when it stopped raining we all had a hit on the tennis court.

But the other musical treat for me was when Mick drove me from the house to The Who's studios at Shepperton for an all-night rehearsal. Mick drove me in an old Mercedes which he had borrowed and we were the first to arrive apart from Stu Stewart, often known as the sixth Stone, who was the group's piano and keyboard player for twenty years. It was a great shock when he died recently as he seemed imperturbable and indestructible.

223

One by one the others arrived and, without any special co-ordination, but usually led by Mick, they would burst into number after number. Apart from a couple of electricians or road-managers, I was the only other one outside the band and I sat on a packing-case drinking innumerable beers, only a matter of feet from the players. My wife subsequently accused me of being an overgrown teeny-bopper but I can honestly say that I enjoyed that night as much as anything else I have ever experienced.

The one curious point which struck me as odd was that, while Jagger, Richards, Wood, Watts and Stewart all gathered closely together, bass guitarist Bill Wyman stood or sat some way away and did not always join in. Nor did there seem much verbal communication between him and the others and this was always the case everywhere else. Even on stage he seemed remote from the others though I never saw any actual animosity between them. Mick did once tell me that Bill had chronicled every little thing that the group and its members had done since the very beginning and he was a bit worried what might come out one day.

And that was my Jagger era, lasting nearly ten years. He blamed me, quite unfairly, for participating in Jerry leaving him for a short while later that year. For when she returned to him, she looked for a scapegoat to avert the blame from herself and fingered me. How she managed to make Mick swallow this fantasy, I do not know, but she had always been fairly economical with the truth.

Soon after her return to Mick, I was staying in LA with my film producer and writer friend David Giler. We had enjoyed a late night out with plenty of cocktails when the telephone rang. A very dozy Giler took the call and buzzed through to me in my bedroom. I was even dopier but had no difficulty in recognizing Mick's voice even though he had attempted to disguise it and claimed that he was the editor of the *Daily Express*. I think he was in France which would have made it about 1 o'clock in the afternoon there but I would judge that he was not completely sober either. He ranted on for a few minutes while I played up to him; he then used a catch-phrase which could only have come via Jerry and which completely gave the show away and then rang off.

I was disappointed in him as he is more intelligent than that and, perhaps arrogantly, I believe he lost a good friend with whom he could identify. Not a grass, but a friend – something in short supply in his world.

224

More Music With Frank Sinatra

When Frank Sinatra's career took off again, after a brief lull, I was one of his greatest fans. This was the early 1950s and his album *Songs for Swinging Lovers* with orchestra and arrangements by Nelson Riddle, was my absolute favourite.

I became more aware of him as a person in the middle and late 1960s, when he would visit the Clermont during his visits to London. One of his closest friends was the Hollywood restaurateur Mike Romanoff, a little man with grey, stubby hair and an indefinable accent. He claimed Russian descent but no one believed this story and it didn't matter anyway. Romanoff lost some money, a few thousand, one night at the Clermont and was unable to pay. The next night I happened to be in the club in the main gaming-room when one of the managers whispered in Aspinall's ear that there was an urgent telephone call for him. He returned a few minutes later rather more subdued than usual and told me that the call had gone like this.

'John Aspinall. This is Frank Sinatra. You've been hassling my friend Mike for money. I don't like to hear this kind of thing. Leave my friend alone. You'll get your money in the morning.'

For once Aspers had been rendered speechless. Sure enough in the morning Sinatra arranged for the money to be sent round to the club.

A couple of summers later, I went to Deauville with my then girl-friend Sue Aylwyn and Mark Birley for a long weekend. Typically, Birley, who always does things in style, had booked the largest suite in the Normandy Hotel. On our very first evening, as we were drinking in the bar, Birley noticed the little grey-haired man sitting alone in the corner. Mark knew him of old and invited him to join us and come on to dinner. It was Mike Romanoff. Why he was alone in Deauville I do not know, but from then on he joined us for virtually every lunch and dinner, insisted on paying on more than one occasion. Not only was he good company with plenty of stories about Sinatra, but he was almost pathetically grateful for being allowed to join up with us and apart from offers of unlimited hospitality at his famous LA restaurant, Romanoff's, he also added 'Frank is coming over to do some concerts in London in the fall. I will see that you are my guests and also at his private party afterwards.'

We were delighted with his offer but were also a little sceptical since we had all heard this sort of thing before. But Mike was as good as his word and a week or two before the tour, we received four tickets for one of the concerts and an invitation to a party at Claridge's which Frank was giving in honour of Princess Alexandra. That was my first meeting with him.

Sinatra was also great friends with Danny and Natalie Schwartz, his neighbours in Rancho Mirage, Palm Springs. They were always promising us that we would get to know Frank better, but it took a while although we went to several of his concerts in London. Then one morning in March 1979, I was dozing in bed in my flat in Lowndes Street. It was 8 o'clock on Saturday and for once I was not planning to go racing, the big Cheltenham meeting having just finished. The telephone rang and it was Robert Sangster from Palm Springs. He was staying with the Schwartzes. 'Move your ass. Frank wants you to have dinner and see the show tonight.' Frank was performing at Caesar's Palace in Las Vegas. I laughed off the joke but Robert was serious. 'You can make it. Show some enterprise. Frank doesn't like it when people refuse his invitations.' I gulped my acceptance and we agreed to meet in the lobby of Caesar's Palace at 7.15 that evening. I had an eight-hour time differential in my favour, of course.

The next step was to break the news to my wife, who was snoozing beside me, and test her reaction. It was predictable. 'You stupid fool. I've never heard anything so ridiculous in my life,' she stormed. 'You are invited as well,' I countered rather lamely, knowing full well that there was no way she would go. We were due to drive down that morning to stay for a shortened weekend with Nick and Mary-Anne Paravacini down the M4 beyond Maidenhead. They were more friends of hers than mine though we were all on good terms.

I had committed myself and now I had to think of booking myself on a plane. I discovered that the first of the three planes leaving for LA that morning was the Pan Am, and discovered it was full in tourist but not

226

first class. I rang a private number for arranging emergency weekend travel available to the staff of the *Daily Express*. 'Can you book me on the Pam Am flight to LA this morning and give me an open return? First class,' I said to the man who sounded a little doubtful. 'I'll pay it back later if they want me to,' I concluded, and he agreed. It was the year that the American boy-wonder jockey, Steve Cauthen, was due to come over a few days later to ride for Robert and I had broken that story some days earlier. I planned to get an exclusive interview with him I while was in America before anyone else reached him.

Anyway Cauthen's arrival in England was accompanied by un-paralleled press ballyhoo. Only eighteen years old, he had already been champion jockey in the USA and had won the Triple Crown there on Affirmed. Sangster had signed him up but it was obvious from the time that his feet touched British soil that he would ride as first jockey for the entire Barry Hills stable.

So his first ride was at Salisbury on a very wet March day in the very first race. The meeting was televised and the camera focused on Steve from the moment he entered the paddock and then mounted and hacked to the start. Ironically, he was not riding for Sangster but for the London-based Chinese owner Keith Hsu. His mount, Marquee Universal, swept into the lead inside the final quarter mile and won amid hysterical cheering from the sodden crowd.

I am ashamed to say that I was not among them. We had gone down to stay for the weekend, not a mile from the track, with the Earl of Pembroke at his stately home, Wilton. When we saw the weather, and the traffic jam, we decided to watch the whole thing on television. We did got up to the course later on when the traffic and the rain had subsided and rescued Steve from his marathon press conference during which he fielded idiotic questions from non-racing reporters with great good humour and maturity. We took him, his father Tex, and his temporary manager and adviser, the former English jockey Jimmy Lindley, plus Barry Hills and his wife Penny, back to Wilton for tea.

Steve sat on the fender in front of a roaring fire, his legs dangling, and enjoyed a typical English winter tea. He was unphased by the splen-dours of Wilton when he was taken on a private tour by Henry and Claire Pembroke but asked sensible questions and showed surprising knowledge of the paintings and historical items there. This was the Steve that we grew to know and love. He won the Two Thousand Guineas, his first-ever English Classic, on Tap on Wood just over a month later and went on to become champion jockey in 1984, 1985 and

227

1987. But back to the Sinatra escapade.

I remembered my passport that March morning and packed a small bag but my wife still thought I was joking as we drove down the motorway towards our intended weekend retreat. When we approached London Airport, I suddenly asked her 'Have you got your passport with you?' I received another angry retort. 'Just turn left and spill me off at terminal three, please,' I requested sweetly and she was so amazed that she did as she was told. I picked up my ticket, enjoyed the rare comforts of first class, and landed at LA X airport well on schedule.

I was becoming rather hot as I had to hump my bag across to the domestic terminal to get on a one-hour flight to Las Vegas and this proved more difficult than anticipated. The first two flights were full and there were people waiting around. However, I managed to talk one of the managers into squeezing me on the 5 o'clock flight and I was in Caesar's Palace with time to spare. They looked at me as if I were barking mad when I asked for somewhere to change but was directed up to the sauna and massage suite upstairs, where I appeared with my suitcase and was able to shower and change and meet the others spot on time.

We watched the show at a table right in front of the centre stage and I was introduced to Frank's wife Barbara, very much the complete hostess, who seated us very precisely. It was the great man's usual flawless performance backed by an orchestra some thirty strong. He looked down on us from about ten feet away and, at the end, rather embarrassingly, we had to climb up on to the stage in front of the entire audience, to join Frank for drinks in his dressing-room area. There were one or two other showbiz friends there including a tiresome woman writer who monopolized more than her share of Frank's time. After a while, he led us down an underground tunnel, through the kitchens to arrive in a roped-off, specially reserved area in the casino where we sat and drank while, beyond the rope and down a step, the customers gawped at us. I remember talking quite a lot to Robert Culp, a well-known American actor who seemed to be a friend of Frank's. I gambled a bit at blackjack and what the Americans called baccarat which, in European casinos answers to the name of punto banco and is a form of chemin de fer. I won 1,500 dollars, which improved the evening still further.

At about 5 o'clock in the morning, we returned to Palm Springs in Danny's private Falcon Jet and when I was installed in my room in their house, it was 6.30 a.m. on Sunday which meant 2.30 p.m. London time

– an all-awake day of over thirty hours for me. My tennis after we woke up around midday was a little shaky but this was hardly surprising as the time change played havoc with my metabolism.

I stayed out for another two or three days, getting away with it at the office and fudged up some story which satisfied them, so much so that they stood me the cost of the ticket. I was back in time for the start of the flat-racing season that Thursday.

The longest I spent with Sinatra was during another stay not long afterwards with the Schwartzes. It was in November and I was on my way back from Australia so I was alone. I had spent a few days in LA and went to the races at Santa Anita on the Saturday before going down the road with the legendary American jockey Bill Shoemaker and his wife Cindy to their house less than a mile from the track. There was a car and driver waiting for me there by arrangement with Natalie Schwartz but I had time for a couple of drinks with Bill and Cindy whose company I always enjoy.

The telephone rang and it was Natalie. Bill took the call and handed the receiver to me, putting his hand over the speaker and whispering, with that devilish twinkle in his eye, 'Oh oh trouble.' I took the call and Natalie shrieked at me, 'You're still there. You should be on your way. Frank is giving a dinner in your honour at 8 o'clock sharp. You cannot be late. Hurry.'

'No problem,' I replied soothingly to be met with another barrage of threats. 'I think you had better go,' laughed Bill, who knew the form well. 'Sounds like you'll be eaten alive.'

So I jumped into the limousine with a friendly driver who often worked for Danny and Natalie. It was an easy two-hour journey to the house and I could see no trouble. Unfortunately in the dark, the driver lost his way when we were nearing our destination and kept driving first towards the centre of Palm Springs then the adjoining Palm Desert, getting completely lost. When we finally arrived, it was after 7.45. I was not worried as I could still make the 8 o'clock deadline but the butler greeted me with the news that I was in trouble and that I had better wash quickly and go straight on to the restaurant where the dinner was to take place. I nipped in, washed my face and hands and brushed my teeth and hair and was out again in two minutes and at the restaurant more or less on time but they were already seated, about ten of them. I was shown to the vacant spot opposite Frank and between Barbara and an elderly lady who turned out to be a backgammon enthusiast who fainted later in the evening.

Natalie looked fraught but Frank and the rest of them could not have been more relaxed and friendly and brushed aside my apologies. I was soon relaxed and tucking into the caviare that Frank had thoughtfully provided. The wine was delicious, too, and I had time to take in some of my fellow guests, none of whom was below the age of sixty. Most notable was an overweight totally bald man with a great twinkle in his eye who turned out to be Jimmy van Heusen, the great song-writer who had collaborated with Sammy Cahn in so many songs, many of them standards. Jimmy had taken his surname from the famous shirtmakers and Frank delighted in teasing him and calling him by his original Christian name which was Chester.

Natalie spent the whole evening gushing about Frank and reminding me, from time to time, how gracious it was of him to host this elegant dinner. It was gracious but I did recognize that and made the appropriate noises at intervals. Frank and I then made little speeches, the backgammon lady fainted, and we helped her out to her car where I whispered 'double six' into her unhearing ear and sent her on her way.

This was Frankfest and the next night he suggested that we three went to his house for dinner and he would cook the spaghetti himself. This is his speciality and it was indeed delicious. Once again, unnecessarily prompted by Natalie, I made the right noises, and we all got along fine, particularly Jimmy van Heusen who consumed vast quantities of Frank's spaghetti in spite of muttered warnings to hold back from a lady I took to be his wife. It was much the same group as the previous night and after dinner Frank asked me if I would like to see his latest movie, a New York detective story in his private cinema downstairs. I accepted enthusiastically and four or five of us watched the movie while Frank and Barbara and one or two others stayed upstairs drinking. When the film was over, we returned to the hallway and I made a particular point of thanking Frank for a huge mound of albums and cassettes of his brand-new triple musical package which he had given me to auction for my wife's children's charity. He was unable to sign them but promised me a stack of autographed messages to go with them next day. It was a typical Sinatra gesture based on one remark which I had made at dinner and I was in full flow of thanks when the main light went out and Frank stiffened, his face contorted with anger. I thought for one ghastly moment it was something I had said but he turned and shouted at Barbara, who may have had a cocktail or two, 'Turn that light on this instant. Do you want our guests to think we haven't paid the electricity bill?' Barbara stood defiant for a moment or two then turned the light

230

back on again and most of us shuffled as if to leave while she turned to go to bed.

Danny and Frank both motioned me to stay where I was and, when all the others, including Natalie had left, we sat at the bar while Frank totally relaxed, poured us out drinks and we talked for some hours. He also took us on a tour of his many pictures and mementoes and fascinating they were. It was the perfect, boozy all-night session and Frank made it very clear that he liked the English. He spoke glowingly of Aspinall and Birley in particular and sent messages to them. We left at around 6 a.m. which is roughly the time he normally goes to sleep due, no doubt, to the late hour he kept as an entertainer most of his life.

Next day, we had a men's lunch at the local golf and country club and Frank turned up again, and we also watched the Monday night football game from 6 till 9 p.m. on ABC and had dinner at the Schwartzs'. All in all, a memorable three days spent in great comfort during which I even managed to fit in some tennis in the mornings when Danny thoughtfully arranged for a couple of pros to partner us in a cleverly choreographed close match. Drinks were served courtside by the butler who turned out the perfect hot dog and hamburger lunch when we stayed in. Paradise, really, with a climate to match but hardly a soul under sixty. My old friend James Hanson, now Lord Hanson and the founder, with Sir Gordon White, of the fabulously successful Hanson Trust, is about the youngest householder and even he is about eight years older than me.

We all went to Sinatra's concert at the Albert Hall in seats provided by him and Danny a couple of years ago and the audience was enthralled even if the reviews were lukewarm. I thoroughly agree with Frank about the critics. Many of them are minor journalistic figures out to make a name for themselves and they get more reaction by knocking him. His voice may not be quite what it was but he still puts on a wonderful show and the audience, including cynics like me, loves it down to the last note.

Los Angeles and Hollywood

I WAS forty-three when I first visited LA in October 1978 which I did on my way to Australia. I spent my birthday there and I have been back nearly every year since.

The respective merits of New York and Los Angeles are very much a matter of taste and my wife has no doubts on the matter. She is committed to New York with the shopping, smart bars and restaurants, and a number of her friends. I suppose it is fairly characteristic of my more flamboyant tastes that, much as I enjoy New York, I infinitely prefer LA. I have many friends there, particularly in show-business, and I prefer the weather so that I always have the option of some tennis.

My host in recent years has been David Giler, best known as the co-writer and producer of *Alien* and the follow-up, *Aliens*. His partner, Walter Hill, is one of the world's finest directors. They wrote and produced *Southern Comfort* which Walter directed, but Walter's best film, in my opinion, was *48 Hours*, which launched the screen career of Eddy Murphy.

In recent years; I have always gone to LA on the direct flight from Sydney, and this always leads to a very long Sunday. There is a nineteen-hour time difference between Eastern Australia and the West Coast of the USA in November and, leaving at about 3 o'clock on Sunday afternoon in Australia the plane arrives at about 9 a.m. the same day in LA. After a few cocktails I go straight to the races at either Santa Anita or Hollywood Park at Cindy Shoemaker's table.

The other regular at the races is the trainer John Gosden, an Englishman whose father, Towser Gosden, was equally successful when training in England at Lewes in Sussex. Normally, the same evening we go on to the famous restaurant, Chasen's, where Bill Shoemaker takes

232

over as barman and distributes lethal drinks. Bill, who has ridden a world record total of nearly 9,000 winners – a record which may well stand for ever – is very much a national hero in America and in LA in particular. He is hard to miss since he is the smallest of all the jockeys which enables him to live a completely normal life as far as eating and drinking is concerned. He weighs about 100 pounds wringing wet – 7 st. 2 lb. in England – and his legs may be short but they are undoubtedly hollow since he has drunk me under the table at night-clubs the world over, including Annabel's and Tramp in London. He plays a good and stylish game of tennis though I do enjoy lobbing him – an easy shot in the circumstances which makes him very angry. His golf swing is a delight and he must have played to a lot shorter than his present 16 handicap.

We took him to my club, the famous Sunningdale, when he was in England to ride in the 1978 Derby. After lunch it was suggested that he might like to play a round on the legendary Old Course with three of the hottest handicappers there. And the standard at Sunningdale is very high indeed. My old friend Colin Ingleby-Mackenzie, a competitive 11 handicapper, volunteered to partner him but Bill was reluctant to play as he had no gear or clubs. However, we persisted and took him to the pro shop where they finally found a pair of shoes to fit him, the smallest ladies' size 3. He was lent some small ladies' clubs and his first drive went 220 yards straight down the middle. He and Colin won their match.

Bill has a highly developed sense of humour and is renowned either as a pickpocket or the reverse, planting unwelcome items in men's pockets. I went with him to South Africa on two occasions as honorary manager and speech-maker for him and another American and British champion, Steve Cauthen. After lunch one day, when there was no racing, we all went upstairs to our respective rooms for a rest. I was delayed for a few minutes and when I arrived at my room, the door was open and the maid was just pulling back the bedcover. Suddenly she let out a loud scream and jumped backwards. I took a step towards the bed and saw a scorpion on the sheet. I took one more hesitant step forward, not daring to get any closer as it looked very live indeed.

'Have you seen anyone around here when you were tidying the room?' I asked her.

'Yes,' she answered, 'a little man with grey hair came in and asked for you.'

That was it. Still gingerly I approached the scorpion and banged the bed. It leapt in the air enough to show me that it was made of rubber.

The only revenge that I was able to extract from him was that I never let on that he had fooled me. I did not mention the subject since I knew that my silence would annoy him. I only told him quite recently, some six years later, and he chuckled devilishly.

Apart from an amazing capacity for alcohol – though I should stress that he only drinks on outings and at parties – he also has amazing stamina and his marathon round on his three trips to London for the Jockeys' International America vs. Britain was phenomenal. He also showed great determination to outstay us on the occasions when he rode in the Derby. His first Derby attempt was in 1978 when Robert Sangster lured him over to ride the 33–1 outsider Hawaiian Sound, trained at Lambourn by Barry Hills. And he all but snatched the race which would have been a fairy tale. Without special riding orders, he led all the way until the last two strides when he was caught and beaten a neck in a photo-finish by Greville Starkey on Shirley Heights.

There was some criticism of Bill in the press for allowing his mount to drift out in the straight and let Shirley Heights up on the inside rail. But he explained to me later that he had allowed Hawaiian Sound to drift in order to have other horses to compete with. All the challengers came wide in the straight that year and they also let up Shirley Heights, who had in fact hung violently left from the centre and straightened and raced to the line when the rails intervened. The winner's challenge came too late for Bill and his mount to do anything about it.

One year in the evening of the British vs. American challenge at Sandown Park, it was my birthday and I invited Bill and Cindy to the party which was at the old Aspinall club off Sloane Street. All the other American jockeys had been invited to another party given by the ex-jockey and present television commentator Jimmy Lindley. Only one of the Americans, all of whom where much younger than Bill, had the stamina to go to the Lindley dinner, but Bill was first to arrive at Aspinalls and last to leave after midnight, after which he took in Annabel's and Tramp until four in the morning. Add to this the fact that he is a compulsive and discreet bill-payer almost unique among jockeys, and you can see what a remarkable man he is.

Bill's initiation into British society was a tough one during that 1978 Derby week. Robert Sangster gave a dinner-party in the private room at Les Ambassadeurs and he was drawn between Sally Aga Khan and my wife, neither of whom he had met before. But he more than succeeded and they were fascinated by him once they understood his American drawl. He does speak very quietly at times and it is one of his little tricks to talk at little more than a whisper and in complete gibberish to totally confuse the other party.

Well into his fifties now, Bill says he can't afford to give up riding since paying off two previous wives, but the truth is he is still picking off big stakes' victories including, for example, the 1986 Kentucky Derby and the 1987 Breeders' Cup Classic with a truly dashing display on Ferdinand. So why give up?

When I am in LA, the racing fraternity tends to mingle with the film professionals. One who finds this mix particularly easy is an old friend, Albert Finney, whom I have known since the late 1960s. He has played the field since being divorced from his French wife, Anouk Aimée, but his first love has always been horse-racing. His father was a bookmaker and, when he died, Albert tells of the funeral procession getting lost in the back streets of Manchester and ending up alongside the old Manchester racecourse. He wanted to put some of his money into bloodstock for tax purposes over there and he chose the stallion Seattle Slew, a phenomenal racehorse and winner of the US Triple Crown but possessor of an uncommercial pedigree. Such horses are usually a failure at stud but Albert backed his own judgement – and I for one, would have warned him off the deal – went ahead, and invested in eight breeding rights. The upshot was that Seattle Slew became for a while one of the two most important stallions in the States, and therefore the world – Northern Dancer was the other – and is still at the top of the tree.

It was another sport, American football which led to my meeting with Frank Marshall and Kathy Kennedy, the two young and incredibly successful associates of the world's most successful and brilliant film-maker, Steven Spielberg, and through them the great man himself. The whole of the Spielberg organization is built around these three who co-produce all his films.

They work incredibly hard but still have time to play. I got tickets for the Wimbledon finals for them and an actor friend about five years ago and have been their guest at all their premiers since *ET*, when Steven, despite the presence next to him of Prince Charles and the Princess of Wales was quite rightly given a hero's ovation by the packed black-tie audience. They know how to turn on the style at the parties afterwards, too, and I remember delicious dinners at the Savoy grill and Maxim's off Leicester Square. It was fascinating for an uninitiated Englishman to have dinner with the three of them at Cecconi's restaurant and hear

Spielberg expounding his views on the film world, an experience accorded to very few outsiders. They kindly offered my wife the premier rights to one of their films for her favourite charity the Invalid Children's Aid Association in 1987.

Inadvertently I was able to do them a good turn when Frank and Kathy came down to my annual cricket match five years ago, the last time that Dennis Lillee played. They got on well with the great Australian fast bowler and, some months later, Kathy had to go to court in California to give evidence on their behalf in a multi-million dollar claim for plagiarism. This is one of the hazards of their trade. One of the chief lawyers involved was wearing a tie with cricket-bats on it so Kathy, very much an all-American girl, mentioned to him that she was a personal friend of Dennis Lillee. The lawyer was flabbergasted and Kathy told me later that it did her case a lot of good, even if only to her confidence.

Other old LA friends who also live much of the time in London are James-Bond producer Cubby Broccoli and his wife Dana. They have a particularly attractive and able daughter, Barbara, who is also very involved in the business. They gave a dinner for me in the private room at Chasen's in LA four years ago and, as I was without my wife, I suggested that he might lay on a few Bond girls for me. He and Dana let me bring many of my LA friends including the Shoemakers but their end of the party consisted mainly of members of their big family. They were not going to make things easy for me, looking after my wife's interests.

During the summer of 1986, when they were looking for a successor to Roger Moore, I was anxious to find out the name of the new James Bond before it was announced as one of my bookmakers was betting on the outcome. Roger himself could not help me though we spent a week together on Vivien Duffield's wonderful fortieth-birthday cruise round Greece and Turkey, and I won a few dollars off him at backgammon. I even promised to split the proceeds with him but he was either kept out of the secret or was pledged to silence.

Cubby and Dana would not or could not give me the decisive clue either, even though I also offered them a 50–50 split, but one day in the middle of the deliberations I spotted one of my favourite actors, Sam Neill, having lunch with Barbara Broccoli in Aspinall's club. Sam looked the right man for the job to me and I backed him with my bookmaker at odds of 14–1. I was more than disappointed, therefore, when the English actor Timothy Dalton got the job and was little appeased when Cubby later told me that Sam Neill was runner-up. In fairness, my man was only really number three since the Irish actor Pierce Brosnan was offered the job first but was prevented from taking it through contractual difficulties.

Other acquaintances from LA include that great acting pair Jack Lemmon, whom I took to Sunningdale for a round of golf in September 1986 while he was in London to play in *Long Day's Journey into Night*, and racing fanatic Walter Matthau, whom I have met on the race-tracks several times though he prefers to bet on cards. He was at Newmarket in October 1986 and, no thanks to me, backed the Cambridgeshire winner Dallas at 10–1.

Larry Hagman, the star of Dallas, creates more sensation wherever he goes than almost anyone else in the film or television fields. He is based in Malibu, not far outside LA but he came over to Ireland for the Phoenix Park Champion Stakes in September 1985 and after the race we flew with Robert Sangster to stay in the Isle of Man for a couple of days. Larry and his totally nice and down-to-earth wife, Maj, loved Robert's palatial house, The Nunnery, and were taken on a scenic tour of the island in a mini-bus, causing a sensation in a little old pub by the sea where we stopped for lunch. But Larry is absolutely paranoid about cigarette smoke. Indeed any tobacco smoke. No one in our group smoked at the restaurant we went to one evening, but there was a woman puffing away in an alcove beyond us and even that worried him. When my wife sat next to him at a dinner given by Robert in the wonderful LA restaurant Le Dome in November 1986, Larry put down two little electric windmills on the table either side of him to blow away her tobacco smoke and did the same thing to Michele Phillips who was sitting on the other side of him. That must have been a nightmare evening for him. I am a non-smoker myself and sometimes get irritated by my wife's smoking habits at meal-times but the Americans seem to have almost taken no-smoking areas to an obsession in restaurants and I find myself surprisingly in sympathy with Le Dome's two charming and enlightened owners, Eddie and Michel, who when forced to create a non-smoking area put it right at the back of the restaurant in Siberia.

My Love Affair with Australia

BY the time I first went to Australia in late October 1978, I had made a whole lot of friends out there, most of them sportsmen. For no obvious reason, many of my boyhood sporting heroes had been Australians – Frank Sedgeman, Ken Rosewall, Keith Miller and Ray Lindwall and, in time, I became friends with them and many others besides. Keith Miller sat next to my mother at a lunch during the 1948 Australian cricket tour of England and he gave her his autograph for me. He was the first of them to become a close friend since he was besotted by racing and, even as a *Daily Express* cricket writer, he was more often on the racecourse than he was at the cricket ground.

'Nugget', as we called him, was very close to the jockey Scobie Breasley and rang him every morning for tips when he was in England. Scobie may have been a great rider and a wonderful judge of a horse but he did not seem to be a great tipster. I remember one day Keith ringing me to say 'Scobie has got six rides at Bath today and two of them are good things.' Inevitably the two good things lost and the other four all won. For years, Keith did not want to play cricket once he had retired and I may well have been his last ever wicket since he got me out playing for Michael Dickinson's XI against Robert Sangster's XI at Manton on 13 July 1986. Keith, well into his sixties, bowled me a slow medium-paced short ball; I tried to hit it out of the ground and came through much too fast, top edging the ball high to be caught at square-leg.

I have had the pleasure of playing tennis with many of the best Australian players some of them Wimbledon champions. Frank Sedgeman, Neale Fraser and Ken Rosewall spring to mind while latterly my four times pro-am partner at Queen's who always arranges a tennis day for me in Sydney was John Alexander, their long-time No.1. Neale

238

Fraser is another racing buff and he invited me to join him and the entire Davis Cup team for dinner at their Wimbledon house on the eve of their Davis Cup match against Great Britain in July 1986. Neale is captain of the Australian team and I was pleased to see them win the cup against Sweden in Melbourne after Christmas that year.

But it was Dennis Lillee, possibly the world's greatest-ever fast bowler, who was to become my closest pal. We met during his first tour of England but we did not do much together until the mid-1970s onwards. I also became close with the famous Chappell brothers, Ian and Greg, Rodney Marsh, the wicket-keeper, and Allan Border, Australia's most recent captain. They tended to use first my flat and then my Trevor Square house as a London base, and whenever I had my own cricket match against Simon Courtauld from 1974 onwards, there would usually be one or more of them playing for me.

Dennis was the most regular and he never missed my match when he was in England, amazing and horrifying the opposition when they saw him. Of course, he never bowled fast for me and was much keener to do well with the bat, but even off a two-pace run and bowling at quarter speed he could still make the ball fizz. In one of the matches, I told him to frighten a rather cocky friend of mine without actually doing any harm to him so Dennis walked purposefully all the way back to the boundary. Then he took one step further and relieved himself into the long grass before tearing in with a fearsome look on his face. As he reached the bowling-crease the batsman gave a yelp and retreated towards the square-leg umpire whereupon Dennis released the ball in the slowest donkey drop ever, the ball plopping on to the stumps and bowling him. Very unfairly and belatedly, the umpire called no ball.

I took him to a fair in Belgrave Square in 1975, the Belgrave Beano, when Charlotte Curzon was in attendance. His eyes lit up when he saw the coconut shy and he bought me a handful of balls. It was my turn first and I managed to knock off a coconut in my first batch and stood back with my trophy. Then Dennis took his first five balls and they all missed. 'Give me another five,' he growled. When he had missed again with these, he became frantic at the humiliation and snatched another five. By now he was flinging the balls flat out and he has a fearsome arm when he wants to. I can't remember how long it took but I know I was as relieved as he was when he finally knocked a coconut from its hoop to a great cheer from the small crowd which had gathered.

Dennis has all the charm and confidence of the best Australians but he surprised me one day in May 1981 by turning up at Kempton Park

239

races with the Aga Khan. It happened like this. We had been out late the night before and when he was not playing, Dennis could be a late sleeper. When I rang to see if he was ready to go to the races, he sounded drowsy so I told him to go back to sleep. Just in case he wanted to come late, I told him that Sally and K would be leaving from the Berkeley Hotel after 1 o'clock as they had a runner in the third race.

I rang Sally who said she would be glad to give him a lift but we both agreed that there was little chance of his making it. Some fifteen minutes before the third race I strolled to the paddock and was amazed to see Sally and K standing there with their jockey and trainer while Dennis was striding towards me with their daughter Zahrah. 'I'm taking my new girl-friend to the bookies and we're going to put a bet on her horse,' he greeted me. So I joined them on a stroll to the rails where Dennis placed £10 on the Aga's filly at 12–1 and I had a few hundred on for myself. The filly duly obliged and Dennis gave Zahrah her winnings to a bet of a pound out of his own. Sally told me later that her husband never quite got the hang of who Dennis was and viewed him with great suspicion.

His greatest betting coup, though, came on a Test Match later that season. Dennis was not really a betting man and had learnt most of his bad habits from me. The match was at Headingley, Leeds and Australia had the game sewn up. England, way behind on the first innings, were still a long way behind Australia with seven wickets down and only Ian Botham at the crease of the recognized batsmen. It was announced on television during one of the intervals that Ladbrokes were offering odds of 500–1 against England and Dennis said to his colleagues in the dressing-room. 'We've got to take that.' No one took him seriously but he went over to his mate Rodney Marsh, who reluctantly agreed to put up £5 while Dennis chipped in a tenner – 'and I wanted to make it £50 if they hadn't persuaded me not to,' he told me later. They gave the money to the team's baggage-man and he put the bet on in the Ladbroke tent though he very nearly pocketed the money as it seemed such a ridiculous wager.

Then, amidst incredible excitement from the crowd, Botham went mad and scored one of the most amazing centuries in cricket history. He didn't stop at a 100, and by the end of the innings he had helped England to a lead of 129, still barely enough in normal circumstances. But then it was the turn of Botham's friend, Bob Willis to play out of his skin and he took eight wickets to enable England to register an incredible victory.

Dennis could not wait to tell me about his amazing coup – £5,000 less tax for a tenner – and we agreed that it should be kept quiet for fear of people getting the wrong idea. There were hints about the coup in the Press but they were always denied. Then when he got back to Australia, Dennis wrote his book and told his story and the cat was out of the bag. It caused quite an outcry and the Australian authorities were not amused.

Nor would they have been amused had they known that Dennis, Allan Border and David Hookes came down to play in my cricket match in June 1983. It was a Sunday as usual and Australia had played one of their matches the day before and were due to play against India at Chelmsford the following day. They lost both matches though Dennis was considered not fully fit and was dropped from the second game so could not be blamed.

Of the others, I see most of Ian Chappell, who works as a television commentator for Channel 9 owned until recently by Kerry Packer who sold out around Christmas 1986 to Alan Bond. The most competitive of cricketers and a great Aussie skipper, Ian used to be a fanatical golfer with a single-figure handicap and ambitions to play in the Australian amateur Open. But in recent years he has switched to tennis and has become more than competent. I play with him both in England and in Sydney and it is always tough stuff. He is better than me now but we play good doubles. His game was spurred by a double defeat at my hands one morning and afternoon in 1977. That was the year that Kerry Packer was in London fighting the celebrated law case against the English cricketing authorities who were acting on behalf of cricket bodies the world over. Packer had signed up virtually all the top Australians and most of the world's best cricketers from other nations to play in his own televised competitions. It was a three-year contract and the whole thing caught the rulers of world cricket, particularly the Australians, with their pants down. Packer was around for a long time that year and we became firm friends since we have similar gambling instincts and a love of sport. Incidentally, Kerry is much misunderstood and is a kinder and more generous-hearted man than is generally realized. Even my wife has come over to him.

One July day, Packer and I challenged Ian Chappell to a tennis match. Ian was captain of Packer's Australian team. I got hold of a good American player, Claude Beer, who was world class at games like squash, real tennis and rackets. To the amazement and fury of Ian,

Kerry and I beat him and his partner comprehensively on the court in Belgrave Square. We went our separate ways for lunch with Ian scowling and demanding a return. This time we moved in the late afternoon to Queen's Club and again Kerry and I were successful, though it was much closer. 'Character,' I kept saying to Kerry and he grinned back, delighting in putting it across his own man.

Ian and Greg Chappell came over with us to stay with Robert Sangster for a weekend on the Isle of Man at about that time to see the TT races – hair-raising motor-bike events in which, every year, riders are killed both in practice and the races – and despite poor weather we packed the maximum into the two and a half days. We watched the races on the Saturday having been out late at the casino the previous night. The Isle of Man casino has two sorts of roulette table, one with a single zero, which is normal, and one with a double zero, which simply doubles the odds against the punter. I found the Chappells innocently playing on the double-zero table and quickly told them to move. Then I turned to the casino chairman, Sir Dudley Cunliffe-Owen and angrily told him it was a disgrace to let two visitors play on the double-zero table. 'You are a fat swindler,' I shouted at Dudley, an old friend of both mine and Robert's. 'It takes one to know one,' retorted Dudley, which effectively ended that conversation.

We were still annoyed with Dudley even though he gave us seats for the TT races the next day and, to teach him a lesson, and filled with plenty of alcohol, I led the Chappell brothers in relieving ourselves into the petrol tank of Dudley's car. To my fury I never heard another word about it until a second-hand report from Robert that the car had gone for a month without a refill!

That Sunday, in improving weather, Robert and I challenged the Chappell brothers to thirty-six holes of golf. They went three up on us at lunch-time and were extremely genial as we tucked into our roast beef but in the afternoon Robert and I, using our local knowledge and experience, chipped back at their lead and the Chappell language began to deteriorate while the clubs, particularly Ian's, began to fly. We squared the match at the thirty-fifth hole and the atmosphere was electric. The stakes were only a fiver each but the Aussies really cared. So it was just as well, perhaps, that both Robert and I hit our approach irons just short to the right of the last hole and they both fell into the cavern and down into the sea. The atmosphere suddenly became very relaxed.

I took Kerry Packer to the races on two occasions in 1977 and he should have won a packet both times. The first occasion was the last Saturday in September when we went to Ascot. Kerry was late picking me up from the Dorchester and I was worried that we would miss the first race since I strongly fancied a two-year-old trained by Peter Walwyn, my nap selection in the column.

'Sorry about the delay, old son,' said Kerry as I worried about the possibility of our being late, 'the Dorchester couldn't get me enough money to bet with.' All the Dorchester came up with was a measly £3,000.

We had a good run and got there in good time to bet on my selection. I advised Kerry to place £1,000 out of his wad.

'I don't operate like that, son,' responded Kerry and promptly placed the whole £3,000 at 3–1 with William Hill. The horse won and I was very relieved.

'Fine,' I said. 'Let's go up to the box and relax for the other six races and have some lunch.' Kerry was happy enough to comply but insisted on continuing to bet and by the end of the afternoon had blown the whole lot.

That was bad enough but the following Saturday at Newmarket was worse. Kerry arrived at the races after lunching there in time for the main event, the Cambridgeshire, traditionally one of the trickiest races of the season. I had long fancied a horse, Sin Timon, trained by my good friend at Newmarket, Jeremy Hindley, whom I always stayed with down there.

I had been backing Sin Timon at 33–1, 28–1 and 25–1, which was his price on the day and I had once again napped him in my column in the *Daily Express*. I took Kerry up to Leslie Spencer, who bets on the rails and he did not turn a hair when Kerry produced £2,000 and placed it on the nose of Sin Timon at 25–1.

'I must warn you Mr Packer,' laughed Leslie, 'that I won't have enough cash to pay you out here. Fifty grand is quite a lot, even for William Hill.'

'That's all right son,' replied Kerry, 'your credit is good with me.' But Leslie did not look so happy when Sin Timon came out a convincing winner and I was in seventh heaven. Kerry was pleased, too, but when we repaired to the bar for a celebration and I suggested that he really did stop this time, he said 'That's all right son, you've done your stuff, leave the rest to me.' So he started making his own bets until once again we reached the seventh race, the final event and he had given back half his winnings. This time he did ask me my views again and I told him that

243

there was a good thing in the race owned by Lord Howard de Walden but that it was very short odds. The two-year-old started at 5–4 on, Kerry put on £25,000 and the horse finished second, so he had blown back all his Sin Timon winnings.

I had one other good betting experience with Kerry which was during my first visit to Australia in November 1978. He kindly asked the Sangsters and my wife and me to dinner in his house and the talk turned to cricket. This was the year when England had sent out an only slightly weakened team to play what was virtually Australia's third XI in the official Test Matches, thanks to Packer himself for signing up most of the best players for his televised 'circus'. Kerry stated that Australia would not win a Test Match. I disagreed with him. 'Australians are always fighters,' I pointed out, 'and even the third XI will surely win one match.'

'Want a bet?' Kerry asked mischievously, his little eyes sparkling. 'I'll bet you an even 200 dollars and Robert and even 2,000.' I looked across at Robert. 'We must take this bet,' I said, and he nodded.

'That's funny, the odds have gone to 5–4. You want another 200?' asked Kerry, looking at me. I nodded.

'Good Lord,' continued Kerry, 'I think I hear 6–4. You want another 200?' I nodded again.

'Hello, I believe I hear 7–4 now. You want another 200?' I nodded once more.

Still Kerry hadn't finished goading me. 'You'll never believe this it's quite incredible but it's 2–1 now. You want another 200?' I accepted the last bet and that was it; I had a thousand dollars at an average of 6–4. Robert and I did not have to wait long and, despite our normal national bias, we were cheering on the Australians when they won the third Test though England went on to win the series as anticipated.

Among the younger Australian sportsmen, the one-time tennis doubles partners John Alexander and John Fitzgerald are two of the nicest and most amusing men I have come across in any walk of life. JA and I formed a successful partnership in the first three years at the Aspinall pro-am at Queen's on the middle Sunday of Wimbledon, reaching the final once and the semi-final twice. And we were reunited in 1987 to reach the semi-finals once more. In the final I found it hard to handle the kicking service of the tall American Brian Teacher and in one of the semi-finals, even my partner marvelled at the talent of the old-timer, my hero Ken Rosewall when he and his partner beat us in a good match and went on to win the final. Those pro-ams are tremendous fun if played in the right spirit and most of the pros get it just right. Even though there is quite a lot of money involved, most of them are very fair with the amateurs and it is the amateurs themselves who create most of the problems having too much sweepstake or betting money at stake and urging their pro-partners to try harder.

There is no prize money for the amateurs, of course, but there is nothing to stop the players taking part of the action at my auction at the supper party at Aspinall's Club the night before. When Kerry Packer won it with Wimbledon doubles champion Paul McNamee, he donated all his auction winnings to McNamee for the Australian's tennis project for under-privileged youngsters back home.

Aspinall's pro-am, which he calls a pro-gam as it is mostly gamblers he invites to play, is one of the highlights of the year. The players involved all love it and most of the top Wimbledon stars who are not actually involved look in as well. Under a huge tent put up on the hard courts behind the centre courts, Aspers dispenses the most exotic buffet-lunch anywhere in the world and the floral arrangements by his wife Sally, usually shaped like animals, are incredible.

Among those who were amazed by the whole scene in 1985 were about half the members of the Australian cricket team. No wonder they fared so badly in the subsequent Test Matches against England.

Finale

NO REGARD FOR MONEY may sound a rather flippant title for this book, but it does sum up my attitude to filthy lucre. It is an attitude that is irresponsible on occasions, and life is often a struggle as the bills pour in after a bad race-meeting. But in moments of self-doubt I am strengthened in my views – though deriving no pleasure – by the tragic example of Lester Piggott.

Here was one of Britain's greatest sportsmen, arguably the greatest-ever jockey, who ended up in prison after receiving a three-year sentence for tax offences in October 1987.

Lester had total regard for money. Stories of his tight-fistedness are legion, even if many of them are apocryphal. He made a cult of meanness and many people thought it was funny. Money was his god.

But the saddest aspect of it all was that he didn't know how to spend it. He didn't need the money he had, let alone the necessity to hoard. But he couldn't help himself.

His final demise was a chapter of needless accidents and deceptions. He couldn't bring himself to pay for the best legal advice to save himself until it was too late. He couldn't bear to level with the Inland Revenue or the Customs and Excise until he was cornered.

So society extracted the ultimate revenge and Lester was destroyed when an ounce or two of common sense and diplomacy would have saved him.

Lester and I, born only a fortnight apart in 1935, had our disagreements but I ended up very fond of him and an unqualified admirer of his riding skills.

The 'downs' in our relationship were usually caused by mischief-makers misinforming him and, in the very manner in which he avoided

246

the issue in his financial problems, he would bottle up the mischief and the slurs. However, this all happened in the past and was long forgotten and forgiven by me and, I hope, by him.

So I feel a genuine sadness as I think of Lester trying to adjust to prison life under the extra pressure of dietary problems and snooping photographers.

Despite the pleasures and privileges of the full life I have been fortunate enough to enjoy, the sadness of the kind I feel for Lester surfaces in several other areas.

The needless suicide of special friends like Mark Watney and Dominick Elwes, the horrific end of poor Gail Benson who trusted too much, and the waste of Graham Hill's life: these continually disturb me. And how will I ever forget the trauma of poor Lucan, driven by obsession to the ultimate horror?

Fresher in the memory, I sorely miss Christopher Soames and Henry Ford, both of whom died in the autumn of 1987. The measure of the characters of these two men was that, even when I did not see them for a spell, they were often in my thoughts. I associate laughter with both of them.

These are some of the sad memories. But I must admit that they only punctuate the greater quantity of happy experiences in my life. Lack of cash has been much more than compensated by the incredible good fortune of friendship.

And so life continues at a good pace, and even this year 1988, through the influence of kind and generous friends I have enjoyed trips to Barbados, Ireland, Gstaad, Oman and Dubai. All this before the end of March.

And, like all racing men, I start the new season with a mixture of optimism, anticipation and excitement.

Yes, I've been a very lucky man.

Index

Bailey, David, 223
Ballydoyle, 157, 165
Bandini, Lorenzo, 129
Barbados, 98, 172, 195
Bardsley, John, 63
Bardsley, Sally, 63
Barnes, Brian, 172
Beard, William, 78-9
Beatty, Diana (née Kirk), 92, 93, 94, 95, 96
Beatty, Earl, 92–6
Beatty, Miranda, 93
Beaverbrook, Lady, 55
Beaverbrook, Lord, 44, 55
Beer, Claude, 241
Be My Guest, 158
Belper, Lord, 57–9
Belper, Zara (later Cazalet), 57
Be Hopeful, 55
Beldale Bell, 165
Benson, Carole (née Master, *q.v.*), 46–7, 50, 52, 54, 55, 57, 58, 60, 62, 64, 73–4, 76, 81, 82, 87, 99
Benson, Carolyn (née Gerard Leigh, *q.v.*), 147, 151, 152, 153, 164, 171, 172, 201, 202, 203–4, 211, 219, 223, 224, 226, 236
Benson, Edward (CB's son), 76–7, 168
Benson, Gail (née Plugge), 117, 118–21, 247
Benson, Harry (CB's son), 54, 57, 204
Benson, Honor (CB's daughter), 154, 167, 203–4
Benson, Jonathan (CB's brother), 1, 2, 8, 20, 21, 67, 117, 205

Benson, Phyllis (CB's mother), 1–2, 7–8, 9, 24, 26–7
Benson, Stephen (CB's father), 2–6, 8, 22–3, 26, 27–8, 67–8, 208
Beresford, Lord Patrick, 134
Big Game, 55
Bigors, Tim, 162
Bindon, John, 105–6
Bingham, Lady Frances, 186
Bingham, Lord George, 177
Bird, Alex, 78
Birley, Mark, 88, 91, 139, 190, 225, 231
Birley, Lady Annabel, 91, 190, 191
Birley, Robert, 19, 27
Birley, Robin, 91, 190–1
Black, Francis, 17
Black Knight, 169
Blackwell, Blanche, 70
Blackwell, Chris, 70
Blewbury, 82
Blushing Groom, 143, 144–5, 158, 159
Bogart, Humphrey, 78
Boggon, Gordon, 21
Booth, Roy, 20
Border, Allan, 204, 239, 241
Borg, Björn, 205
Botham, Ian, 215, 240
Boussac, Marcel, 141, 142, 143
Boutin, François, 167
Bowater, Ewen, 18
Bowes-Lyon, John, 148–9
Boycott, Geoffrey, 69
Bradman, Sir Donald, 78
Bradshaw, Jon, 113
Bramall, Maj Edwin, 39
Bramwell, Anna Rose, 66

Bramwell, Michael, 66
Brand's Hatch, 123
Breasley, Scobie, 49, 238
Breeders' Cup, Aquaduct, 150;
  Los Angeles, 150, 235
Brise, Tony, 193
Broccoli, Barbara, 236
Broccoli, Cubby, 236, 237
Broccoli, Dana, 236
Brooke, Lord ('Brookie'), later
  Earl of Warwick, 80, 81–2, 87,
  90, 146
Brosnan, Pierce, 237
Brudenell-Bruce, Andrew, 169
Brudenell-Bruce, Paddy, 56
Buckley, Billy, 179–80
Buckley, Michael, 180
Bun Penny, 60
Burnett, Arthur, 60, 61
Burton, Richard, 93
Bustino, 55

Caan, James, 209
Cahn, Sammy, 230
Callas, Maria, 93
Cameron, Ian, 59
Cannes, 76, 117
Cantab, 53
Cap d'Antibes, 72, 222
Carnarvon, Earl of, 10
Carr, Terry, 16
Carvalho, Michel, 205
Cash, Pat, 204, 205
Castello, Mrs Magnus, 54
Cauthen, Steve, 227, 233
Cauthen, Tex, 227
Cawston, Derrick, 1, 2 7
Cawston, Dick, 1, 2
Cawston, Edwin, 1
Cazalet, Edward, 23, 25–6, 28,
29
Cazalet, Peter, 23, 25, 26, 28–9,
  34
Cecil, Henry, 166, 198
Cevert, François, 128, 133
Chambure, Roland de, 141, 167
Champion Hurdle, 160
Champion Stakes, 151
Chantilly, 48, 139, 140, 144, 166
  167
Chapman, Colin, 124
Chapman, Graham, 196
Chappell, Greg, 239, 242
Chappell, Ian, 169, 204, 239,
  241–2
Charles, HRH Prince, 122–3,
  135, 164, 165, 168, 201, 221,
  235
Charterhouse, 4
Cheltenham, 30, 45, 170
Chester, 38, 45, 49, 156
Christiansen, Arthur, 44–5
Churchill, Sir Winston, 13, 44,
  78, 93, 102
Cleese, Barbara (née Trentham,
  q.v.)
Cleese, John, 196, 211
Clement, Christophe, 167
Clement, Marc, 166
Clement, Miguel, 166, 194
Clement, Nicolas, 167
Clements, John, 10
Clermont Club, *passim*
Clifford-Turner, Raymond, 183
Clive, Colin, 18
Cole, Marilyn, 114
Colonist II, 102
Compton, Denis, 71
Connery, Sean, 69–70
Constantia, 41

253

Gosden, John, 232
Grace, Princess (of Monaco), 127, 130 132
Graham, Clive, 1, 41, 42–3, 44, 45, 46, 78, 85, 182, 207
Graham, Don, 218
Graham-Campbell, David, 6, 22–3, 24, 25, 27, 33
Grand National, 24, 70, 80, 81, 100, 170
Green Jackets (60th Rifles), 23, 24, 218
Grey Gauntlet, 64
Grundy, 55
Guinness, Lindy, 59

Hagman, Larry, 237
Hailwood, Mike, 128
Halifax, Peter, Lord, 168, 169
Hall, Jerry, 104–5, 195, 196, 211, 212, 214, 216, 217, 218, 219, 220, 224
Hambro, Jocelyn, 216
Hambro, Richard, 168
Hambro, Rick, 216, 217, 219
Hammond, Kay, 13
Hancock, Arthur, 162
Hanson, James, Lord, 231
Harari, Diana, 201
Harari, Philip, 201
Hardwicke Stakes, 60
Harrison, Ron, 28
Harrow School, 70
Harry Goldmine, 48
Harwood, Guy, 48
Hawaiian Sound, 162, 234
Hawkins, Chas 2
Hawkins, Jack, 41, 96
Hawkins, Phyllis (later Benson, *q.v.*)

Hawthorn, Mike, 127
Haydock Park, 38, 53
Hayes, Colin, 172
Hayworth, Rita, 137, 216
Head, Alec, 141, 167
Henry, Pat, 163
Hesketh, Alexander, 77, 197
Hesketh, Lady, 77
High Hat, 102
Hill, George Roy, 209
Hill, Bette, 124, 125, 126, 193
Hill, Graham, 115, 122–7, 128, 129, 130, 135, 189–90, 192–3, 210, 247
Hill, Walter, 232
Hill, William, 60, 100, 243
Hills, Barry, 161, 162, 167, 199, 227
Hills, Penny, 162, 227
Hilton, Ron, 219
Hindley, Jeremy, 167, 168, 197, 199, 243
Hobson, Valerie, 85
Hodge, Vicki, 105–6
Hoskyns, Percy, 97
Hot Grove, 159
Houghton, Fulke Johnson, 151
Howard, Chucker, 16
Howard de Walden, Lord, 244
Howe, Earl, 102, 106–7, 109–10, 111, 193
Hsu, Keith, 227
Hulme, Denny, 107, 133
Hunt, James, 122, 197
Hurst Park, 23, 29, 53

Idle, Eric, 196
Ingham, Staff, 54
Ingleby-Mackenzie, Colin, 15, 16–17, 48, 49, 54, 58, 67, 70,

254

Mountain, Nicky, 54
Murphy, Eddie, 232
Mustique, 102, 103–5, 195, 209, 211, 214

Nashua, 150, 165
Nassau, 115
Nasaste, Illie, 149
Neill, Sam, 236, 237
Newbury, 29, 30, 45, 64
Newman, Paul, 209–10
Newman, Robin, 28
Newmarket, 24, 26, 41, 45, 48, 66, 78, 96, 151, 152, 237, 243
Niarchos, Spiros, 115
Niarchos, Stavros, 57, 93, 115
Nicholl, Leslie, 50, 67
Nickel Coin, 24
Nicolaus Silver, 70
Nijinsky, 150
Nishapour, 143
Niven, David, 57
Norfolk, Duke of, 57
Northern Dancer, 235

Oaks Stakes, 54, 69, 161
O'Brien, David, 164
O'Brien, Jacqueline, 199
O'Brien, Phonsie, 163
O'Brien, Sue, 157
O'Brien, Vincent, 154, 157, 158, 161, 163, 164, 165–6, 199, 200
Ocho Rios, 68, 70
O'Connor, Christie jr, 172
Ogden, Richard, 62
Oh So Sharp, 160
Oldham, Gerald, 63
O'Leary, John, 172
Oman, 152
Onassis, Aristotle, 93

O'Neil, Ryan, 115
One Thousand Guineas, 54
Oppenheimer, Bridget, 164
Oppenheimer, Harry, 164
Oppenheimer, Nicky, 164
Oppenheimer, Strilly, 164
Orange Leaf, 170
Osborne, James, 91
Osborne, Lady, 88, 192
O'Sullevan, Peter, 46, 85, 100, 143, 160, 167, 207

Packer, Kerry, 169, 203, 241–2, 243–4
Paravacini, Mary-Anne, 226
Paravacini, Nick, 226
Parker-Bowles, Andrew, 221
Parker-Bowles, Camilla, 168, 221
Peacock, Andrew, 157, 170
Peacock, Caroline, 171
Peacock, Susan (later Sangster, *q.v.*)
Pearson, Michael, 111, 112
Peck, Gregory, 64
Pembroke, Earl of, 227
Pepys, Lady Marye, 21–2
Persian Lancer, 57
Peterson, Ronnie, 125
Petite Etoile, 102
Petition, 54
Petit Poussin, 55
Phil Drake, 10
Phillips, Mark, 122, 123, 134, 135
Phillips, Michele, 237
Piggott, Lester, 28, 29, 49, 55, 56, 70–1, 143, 144, 152, 158, 159, 161, 165–6, 246–7
Pigott-Brown, Sir William, 81, 82, 90, 103, 213

257

242

Sangster, Sue, 157, 171, 172, 173
Sangster, Susan (née Peacock),
149, 157, 159, 162, 164, 169–
70, 199, 222
Sangster, Vernon, 156
Santer, John, 168
Sardinia, 94, 107, 108, 137, 139,
140, 147, 150, 152, 153, 191,
194
Scalamandre, Gino, 112
Schwartz, Danny, 162–3, 164,
226, 229, 231
Schwartz, Natalie, 162, 163, 164,
226, 229, 230, 231
Scott-Malden, Christopher, 9
Seattle Slew, 235
Sefton, Earl of, 30
Sedgeman, Frank, 238
Shahrastani, 147
Shand-Kydd, Bill, 184, 185, 186,
188
Shand-Kydd, Christina, 188
Shand-Kydd, Helen, 131, 133
Shapiro, Ellie, 89
Shapiro, John, 89
Sharif, Omar, 205
Sheffield, Jane (later Stevens),
22
Shellshock, 156
Shennan, Lilah, 30
Shennan, Malcolm, 30
Shergar, 151, 152, 153
Shirley Heights, 162, 234
Shoemaker, Bill, 162, 229, 232–5
Shoemaker, Cindy, 229, 232, 234
Silk, Dennis, 71
Silverstone, 106, 123, 133
Silver Tor, 60
Simpatico, 49

Sinatra, Barbara, 227, 229, 230
Sinatra, Frank, 100, 163, 225,
228–31
Sin Timon, 243
Sir Ivor, 150
Sleeping Warrior, 28–9
Smart, Sidney, 168
Smirke, Charlie, 28
Smith, Mel, 172
Snaith, Willie, 56
Snow, Jim, 25
Snow, Philip, 25
Snowdon, Lord, 139, 213
Soames, Christopher, 101–2, 247
Soames, Mary, 101–2
Soames, Nicholas, 130, 191
Solarium, 10
Solonaway, 54
Souepi, 24–5
Speedwell, 52
Speelman, Anthony, 166, 167
Spencer, Lady Diana (later
Princess of Wales), 168, 221
Spencer, Leslie, 243
Spencer-Churchill, Jane, 168
Spielberg, Steven, 235
Starkey, Greville, 234
Statecraft, 26
Stein, Cyril, 59, 61–2
Stevens, Jane (née Sheffield,
q.v.)
Stevens, Jocelyn, 22
Stewart, Stu, 223, 224
Stiebel, Victor, 46
Stirling, Archie, 168, 172
Stolle, Fred, 206
Stolle, Ruta, 206
Stonehouse, John, 188
Stoop, Michael, 186–7